D0908653

WOMEN, THE COURTS, AND EQUALITY

Sage Yearbooks in Women's Policy Studies

—— **RECENT VOLUMES AVAILABLE IN THIS SERIES** ——

Volume 11
Sage Yearbooks in WOMEN'S POLICY STUDIES

WOMEN,
THE COURTS,
AND
EQUALITY

Edited by
LAURA L. CRITES
WINIFRED L. HEPPERLE

SAGE PUBLICATIONS
The Publishers of Professional Social Science
Newbury Park   Beverly Hills   London   New Delhi

For information address:

SAGE Publications, Inc.
2111 West Hillcrest Drive
Newbury Park, California 91320

SAGE Publications Inc.   SAGE Publications Ltd.
275 South Beverly Drive   28 Banner Street
Beverly Hills   London EC1Y 8QE
California 90212   England

SAGE PUBLICATIONS India Pvt. Ltd.
M-32 Market
Greater Kailash I
New Delhi 110 048 India

Printed in the United States of America

Library of Congress Cataloging-in-Publication Data

Main entry under title:

Women, the courts, and equality.

   (Sage yearbooks in women's policy studies; v. 11)
     1. Women—Legal status, laws, etc.—United States.
2. Sex discrimination against women—law and
Legislation—United States. 3. Courts—United States—
Officials and employees. I. Crites, Laura L.
II. Hepperle, Winifred L. III. Series.
KF390.W6W65 1986   342.73'0878'0269   86-15515
ISBN 0-8039-2811-4   347.3028780269
ISBN 0-8039-2812-2 (pbk.)

CONTENTS

FOREWORD

In a recent study conducted by the New York Task Force on Women in the Courts, it was found that women litigants, attorneys and court employees are denied equal justice, equal treatment and equal opportunity—the result of problems rooted in a web of prejudice, circumstance, privilege, custom, misinformation, and indifference. This gender bias in our courts is unacceptable.

The courts have a special obligation to reject—not reflect—society's irrational prejudices. They can do no less if they are to provide all our citizens a court system which can pride itself on the delivery of quality justice. The New York Office of Court Administration has taken steps to eliminate gender bias in our courts by the creation of a team to implement the recommendations of the Task Force report, but, in an institution such as the judiciary, which touches the lives of so many members of the public, in-house efforts are not enough. No cure for a problem of such public dimension can possibly succeed without the understanding and support of that public. Just as the Task Force report served to enlighten those concerned with the administration of our courts, so this book by Laura Crites and Winifred Hepperle should enlighten the bar, the judiciary, and the general public, thus bringing the problem of gender bias in the courts that much closer to resolution.

—Sol Wachtler
Chief Judge
New York Court of Appeals

Sixty-eight years ago Michigan legislators, joined by legislators in our sister states of Illinois and Wisconsin, became the first ratifiers of the 19th Amendment of the United States Constitution. This Amendment proscribed any denial or abridgment to the vote "on account of sex."

Like our forebears, we are still poineering in the application of equality. Many gains have been made—in the recognition of the equal but different advances women have made in the justice system; in the recognition of the different needs that women victims, witnesses, jurors, offenders, and litigants bring to the courthouse; in the innovative programs which have been developed by, for, and with the women who come to court. Much remains to be done, however. Such advances, as well as continuing examples of gender bias in the courts, are chronicled here by Laura Crites and Winifred Hepperle whom I applaud for marking the signposts and keeping us on course in our journey for equality.

In Michigan, under the leadership of the Michigan Supreme Court, we continue to seek solutions to the problem of bias in the courts. A task force on bias in the courts has been appointed to implement the court's efforts. But ultimately, reform will depend on the legal community and the public: their willingness to engage in careful self-examination and their willingness to commit to seeking solutions that will make for a justice system which demands equal justice for all.

—Dorothy Comstock Riley
Chief Justice
Michigan Supreme Court

PREFACE

Approximately ten years ago, we edited a book entitled *Women in the Court* for the National Center for State Courts. The purpose of the book was to examine the extent of judicial commitment to liberating women from a subordinate role in American society. At the time the book was published, the national Equal Rights Amendment was moving toward becoming the law of the land, state ERAs had been passed in several states, and the "radical" phase of the women's movement appeared to have given way to a social consensus that women did indeed have legitimate grievances. It was a time of active enforcement of EEO laws and during the administration of a president who was firmly committed to equal rights for women. The period could be characterized by a sense of optimism, moderated by an understanding that the ultimate success in achieving the goals of the women's movement was still not assured. Our belief at that time was that the role of the courts could be pivotal in determining whether the progress made by women would be solidified or would ultimately fade away as had been the case during other periods of short-lived social progress for women.

The conclusion of the book was that significant evidence existed that judges remained influenced by traditional beliefs regarding the role and nature of women and that these beliefs were affecting their decisions regarding women.

We have undertaken a second book addressing the same subject for several reasons. First, we continue to believe that the courts play a crucial role in the progress and ultimate success of the women's movement. Second, for a variety of reasons, the first book was not widely distributed and thus the conclusions and analysis reached only a limited number of people. Finally, we felt that significant events had taken place in the last ten years that might provide a different assessment.

The last decade has witnessed what appear to be substantial achievements on behalf of women in our society. A greater proportion of women are employed than in any other peacetime period in our history, and are employed in a greater variety of occupations as a result of the equal employment opportunity and affirmative action laws. Feminist-supported legislation designed to improve the rights, opportunities, and treatment of women has passed in a variety of areas, including spouse abuse, no-fault divorce, and rape victim testimony. And, finally, there is a greater level of consciousness regarding the nature and extent of the victimization of women and of the extent of discrimination that has been part of the female experience in our country.

Recent years have also witnessed setbacks for the women's movement, among which was the defeat of the Equal Rights Amendment. Progress toward equal rights for women has been negatively affected by increased conservatism as witnessed by the growing strength of the religious right, the fight over abortion, and reduced emphasis on enforcement of equal employment opportunity and affirmative action laws. And a large group of women have experienced a serious decline in economic health. This includes a rise in the percentage of female-headed households below the poverty line, reduced support for social welfare programs—which dispro-portionately affect women—and a wage disparity (women's wages are 64% of male wages) that has not narrowed in the last fifty years.

The purpose of this book is to take the pulse of the courts—have judges and those working in the court system kept in step with the progressive commitment to equal rights for women, or is there reason to believe that a reversion is taking place, in this all-important institution, to the limited, traditional view of women advocated by an increasingly vocal minority.

We would like to acknowledge several people for their help in the preparation of this book, not the least of whom are the contributing authors. As many women have moved beyond active involvement in promoting a recognition of the needs and condition of women in our society to focus on their own personal issues, a group of women continues to commit themselves to assuring that the next generation of women will have the same freedom of choice and life options that we currently experience. The authors represented in this volume constitute such a group. We want to express our appreciation to them not only for their diligence and commitment in contributing to this volume but also for their personal and professional dedication to the next generation of women and men.

As these authors have touched the lives of many women and men there are individuals who have touched our lives through their support, encouragement, and role modeling. We appreciate the opportunity to acknowledge their influence publicly. Laura Crites has drawn particular strength and encouragement from the lives and examples of four people—Betsy Crites and Joseph Moran, whose deep professional and personal commitment to creating a just and peaceful world have made the world better for me and for countless others; Laura Hardy Crites, whose lifelong dedication to instilling in generations of students a commitment to justice has guided me in the use of education as the medium for my own efforts; and Timothy Keck, who provides me with a daily reminder of the goodness, gentleness, and fairness possible in the opposite sex.

Winifred (Wendy) Hepperle also takes this opportunity to acknowledge the professional and personal rewards and continuing influence resulting from her work with the California Supreme Court under Chief Justice Donald R. Wright, during her service as the court's public information attorney.

> —*Laura L. Crites*
> —*Winifred L. Hepperle*

I

WOMEN'S RIGHTS AND
THE SUPREME COURT

The Supreme Court has played an important role in determining the route and progress of the women's rights movement. The major strides made by women over the last decade in establishing their legal right to equality have been frequently a result of Supreme Court decisions. During this time, women and men have challenged traditional laws in a wide variety of areas, including employment and pay equity, reproductive freedom, educational equality, sex bias in insurance benefits, gender bias in selection of jurors, and age of majority. Although the Burger Court has taken on these issues and through them substantially advanced the position of women in our society, the record of the Court on sex discrimination has been far from firm. Analysis of Supreme Court decisions in 1977 showed the following:

- The Supreme Court was unwilling to subject sex discrimination to the same strict scrutiny standard applied to instances of race discrimination.

- The Supreme Court showed decreasing support for women's rights issues. At the beginning of the Court's examination of these issues, six justices exhibited profeminist voting records. By 1977 only four justices were predictably profeminist.

- Analysis of the decisions and opinions indicated that the Supreme Court justices were deciding cases on the basis of their personal value systems rather than by the application of neutral legal principles.

- The Supreme Court was walking a fine line between constitutional interpretation (the judicial role) and constitutional enactment (the legislative role).

There was reason to believe that further progress would be suspended until the outcome of the vote on the Equal Rights Amendment.

In Part I, Deborah Rhode examines the record of the Supreme Court on sex discrimination cases, focusing in particular on progress, if any, made by the justices in overcoming personal attachment to sex-role stereotypes. Her analysis includes such issues as the justices' ability to move beyond a focus on gender differences to an understanding of gender disadvantages and the perspective from which the Court has understood gender differences. Certainly the Court's willingness in *Geduldig v. Aiello* to exclude pregnancy-related conditions from disability insurance coverage while including prostate-related conditions suggests the dominance of a male perspective. It is difficult to imagine an all-female Supreme Court arriving at the same decision.

In the final analysis, the Supreme-Court justices have apparently been unable or unwilling to expand the focus of their decisions beyond gender differences to incorporate a recognition of the underlying causes of social and economic disadvantages women experience. Until they are able to do so, the role of the Court in achieving further progress in overcoming these disadvantages will likely be marginal.

1

JUSTICE, GENDER, AND
THE JUSTICES

Deborah Rhode

For the last two centuries, gender has shaped both the legal and cultural landscapes of American life. However, it is only during the last two and a half decades that gender discrimination has given rise to legal remedies. American law has evolved within a context in which the sexes have been more often separate than equal, and much nineteenth- and early twentieth-century jurisprudence served largely to reinforce that social structure. During the last quarter century, the reemergence of a feminist movement has helped prompt a fundamental rethinking of discrimination doctrine. Yet, while contemporary legal ideology has played an important part in reshaping sexual roles, it has failed to confront their underlying premises adequately. By focusing on gender differences rather than on gender disadvantages, the courts have too often misperceived the problem and misconstrued the solution.

DOMESTICITY AS DESTINY

Throughout this nation's history, sex has been of critical significance in defining social norms. For the most part, men have dominated the public and women the private sphere, and legal doctrine has both reflected and reinforced that cultural pattern. Under early common law doctrines of marital unity, husband and wife were one, and, as a practical matter, the one was the husband. Until the latter part of the nineteenth century, married women lacked the capacity to enter contracts, to engage in licensed occupations, to hold, inherit, or dispose of property, and to participate in political activities (see *United States v. Yazell,* 382 U.S. 341, 361 [1966], Black, J., dissenting; Blackstone, 1756/1982: 442-445; Kanowitz, 1970: 35-37; Berkin and Norton, 1979).

Given the limitations of available research, the extent to which these formal disabilities in fact constrained female opportunities is difficult to assess. Equitable principles governing trust agreements and "feme sole trader" status did make it possible for some women to protect their financial assets or to pursue various vocations (see Beard, 1946: 155-156; Basch, 1982: 30-35; Salmon, 1983; Jensen, 1979; Chused, 1983). However, it was not until legislative enactment of married women's property acts during the latter half of the nineteenth century that wives gained any independent legal status or contractual capacity (see Basch, 1973: 186; Rabkin, 1975: 683; Speth, 1982: 69-70). And even after those reforms, late nineteenth- and early twentieth-century jurisprudence defined sexual roles that were more separate than equal.

Resistance to female participation in public pursuits, particularly paid labor, reflected a broad array of ideological and economic concerns. To many constituencies, any encouragement of women's emancipation could not help but breed domestic discord, drive down male wages, coarsen female sensibilities, and invite those best equipped for motherhood to refuse its "sacred call" (Collins, 1912: 27, 30; see also Kraditor, 1971: 12-37; Sinclair, 1965: 323; Owen, 1912; Stanton et al., 1881: 629-630; Kessler-Harris, 1979: 348). The clearest jurisprudential reflection of such concerns occurred as the American bar contemplated women's intrusion in its own profession. Although women had occasionally served in the capacity of attorney during the colonial era, the formalization of minimum licensing standards in the late eighteenth and early nineteenth centuries made females and felons equally unwelcome (see Bittenbender, 1981; Dexter, 1972: 139-175, 196; Kerber, 1980: 149-153; Drinker, 1961: 461; Rhode, 1985: 491-497). By the close of the Civil War, however, a trickle of would-be practitioners began challenging their exclusion and the resulting legal opinions remain of interest as cultural texts. What is perhaps most striking is the utter unself-consciousness with which an exclusively male judiciary interpreted statutes adopted by exclusively male legislatures to determine issues of male exclusivity.

The most celebrated case involved Myra Bradwell's unsuccessful 1873 petition to the U.S. Supreme Court. Speaking for himself and two colleagues, Justice Bradley revived the cult of domesticity and infused it with constitutional as well as spiritual significance:

> The natural and proper timidity and delicacy which belongs to the female sex evidently unfits it for many of the occupations of civil life. . . . The constitution of the family organization, which is founded in the divine ordinance as well as in the nature of things . . . is repugnant to the idea of a woman adopting a distinct and independent career from that of her husband.

That Mrs. Bradwell, apparently unaware of the Creator's mandates, had already launched a successful independent career as a publisher and editor of a legal newspaper was a matter the Court politely overlooked. Similarly, that other female applicants to the bar might not be married was of no importance; after all, they should be married. Single women were

> exceptions to the general rule. The paramount destiny and mission of women are to fulfil the noble and benign offices of wife and mother. This is the law of the Creator. And the rules of civil society must be adapted to the general constitution of things, and cannot be based upon exceptional cases [*Bradwell v. State,* 83 U.S. 130, 137 (1872), Bradley, J., concurring; for a discussion of Bradwell's career, see Scott, 1984: 323-330].

Although the precise method of divine communication was never elaborated, it was apparently accessible to many other nineteenth-century jurists. Courts in Pennsylvania, Wisconsin, and the District of Columbia were all able to discern "unwritten laws" that destined women's nature for nurture.[1] Womanhood's "gentle graces . . . its tender susceptibility, its purity, its delicacy, its emotional impulses, its subordination of hard reason to sympathetic feeling" were particularly ill suited for the "forensic strife" and "nastiness which finds its way into courts of justice."[2]

Yet what remained unclear was why woman's gentle graces and reproductive responsibilities should bar her from the more prestigious professions but not from certain more taxing or indelicate work such as nursing, domestic service, or field labor. Moreover, as urbanization and industrialization reduced the economic centrality of the home, and a growth in educational opportunities and feminist sentiments widened women's vocational interests, certain legal barriers began to weaken. By the close of the century, the "natural law" that had initially decreed woman's exclusion from the professions was increasingly reinterpreted to recognize her inherent right to gain a livelihood.[3]

It was, however, a restricted right. Despite the erosion of formal legal restrictions, discrimination by employers and educational institutions persisted throughout much of the twentieth century. Administrators of major graduate, business, and professional schools excluded women out of concern for their distracting influence or cognitive infirmities. Since employers' salary, promotion, and placement practices reflected similar prejudices, the limitations of job opportunities for female graduates remained a deterrent to professional training and the cycle of discrimination perpetuated itself (Harris, 1978; Walsh, 1977: 186, 224; Barnes, 1970: 283; LaZarou, 1978; Woody, 1929/1974: vol. 1, 454; vol. 2, 151, 153).

At the lower reaches of the occupational hierarchy, women's maternal mission continued to be a major obstacle to equal opportunity. During the latter part of the eighteenth and early nineteenth centuries, state legislatures began passing protective labor statutes that restricted working hours and conditions, guaranteed minimum wages, or excluded women from certain jobs. In a celebrated 1908 decision, *Mueller v. Oregon*, the Supreme Court gave such legislation what became a somewhat mixed blessing. The majority upheld restrictions on women's working hours, while adhering to a precedent that disallowed comparable restrictions for men. Having in view not only woman's health but also the "strength and vigor" of her offspring, the Court was willing to sustain legislation that would protect her "from the greed as well as the passion of men" (*Mueller v. Oregon,* 208 U.S. 412, 422 [1908]).

Although approximately 80% of the female work force at the time was single, this maternal mission ideology dominated protective labor decisions for the next half century. It was "known to all men," the Supreme Court confidently announced in a subsequent case in 1910, that "while a man can work for more than ten hours a day without injury to himself, a woman, especially when the burdens of motherhood are upon her, cannot" (*Ritchie & Co. v. Wayman,* 244 Ill. 509 [1910]). Curiously oblivious to such universal male knowledge were the legislators who declined to extend hourly restrictions to some of the most grueling domestic and agricultural occupations, as well as the husbands who declined to share the major household tasks that prolonged wives' working days.

What was "known to all men" was also often uninformed by any inquiry into what was desired by most women. As far as courts and counsel were concerned, female workers' preferences were beside the point. The nineteenth-century notions of domestic destiny reflected in *Bradwell* reemerged in the early twentieth century in new Darwinian form. Limitations on night work, wage rates, or choice of occupations were necessary irrespective of the preferences of "ignorant women . . . who could scarcely be expected to realize the dangers not only to their own health but to that of the next generation" (summary of facts of knowledge submitted on behalf of the people, *People v. Charles Schweinler Press*; quoted in Baer, 1978: 84).

In fact, as most contemporary scholarship suggests, the problems giving rise to protective labor legislation were attributable less to women's ignorance than their lack of alternatives. And the solution endorsed by courts and legislators often perpetuated the inequalities to which it was addressed. By making women more expensive and less available for night or overtime shifts, sex-based restrictions increased female unemployment, limited women's occupational choices, and further depressed their bargaining leverage. Throughout the first half of the twentieth century, women were "protected" out of many of the most desirable occupations (Baer, 1978; Kessler-Harris, 1972: 194-211; Baker, 1969: 90; Foner, 1979: 94-96; U.S. Women's Bureau, 1928: 53). That is not, of course, to deny the substantial benefits that many women workers experienced under protective statutes. Nor is it to minimize the inequalities that made special solicitude for women workers seem defensible. Female employees faced competitive disadvantages in the public sphere and bore special burdens in the private sphere. Most women were crowded into low-paying nonunionized jobs, and assumed substantial household obligations in addition to the 12- and 14-hour working days common in unregulated industries (see Baker, 1969: 207; Becker, 1981: 222). Nonetheless, by linking statutory protections to the sex of the worker rather than the nature of the work, courts ultimately reinforced the subordination that made protection necessary.

Moreover, the rationale underlying such legislation often spilled over into other contexts in which such protection was far less defensible. As late as 1961, the Supreme Court was still invoking woman's domestic destiny as a justification for her automatic exemption from jury service. Despite a certain measure of "enlightened emancipation," women remained at "the center of home and family life," and their private duties trumped public responsibilities (*Hoyt v. Florida,* 368 U.S. 57, 61-62 [1961]). The irony, however, was that courts talked most reverently of woman's custody over the home when restricting her activities outside it. When her custody was in fact at issue, the rhetoric suddenly shifted. Throughout the nineteenth and early twentieth centuries, men generally enjoyed exclusive power to manage marital property, determine domicile, and dictate their households' standard of living (see Kanowitz, 1970; Johnston and Knapp, 1971: 675; and statutes cited in Note, 1950). Although women did receive certain preferences including, for example, spousal support, such rights were unenforceable in the context of ongoing marriages; the manner in which heads of households provided, or failed to provide, for their families was not a "fit subject for judicial scrutiny" (*McGuire v. McGuire,* 157 Neb. 226, 59 N. W.2d 336 [1953]; *Miller v. Miller,* 78 Iowa 177, 182 [1889]; Kanowitz, 1970; Johnston and Knapp, 1971; statutes cited in Note, 1950).

Until the mid-1960s, women's subordinate status in both the public and the private sphere remained largely immune from legal challenge. For over a century, the Supreme Court declined to invoke the equal protection guarantees of the post-Civil War amendments to provide equal protection for women. Even after gender classifications became subject to more searching scrutiny, some vestiges of the separate spheres ideology lingered on.

THE EVOLUTION OF DISCRIMINATION DOCTRINE

The reemergence of a feminist movement in the 1960s drew into question certain central tenets of legal ideology. The proliferation of statutory mandates and state constitutional provisions against sex discrimination were both a catalyst and consequence of changing attitudes toward the status of women. Against this new legal and cultural backdrop, courts began reassessing what standards should be applicable to sex-based discrimination, what forms of differential treatment should count as discrimination, and what significance should attach to schemes that purported to benefit rather than burden women. On the whole, this doctrinal development has reflected substantial progress toward gender equality. Yet the unevenness of development has also suggested limitations in conventional approaches to discrimination law.

American equal protection analysis has evolved largely within an Aristotelian framework, which mandates similar treatment for those similarly situated (Tussman and tenBroek, 1949: 341; Gunther, 1972). Under this approach, gender discrimination does not pose constitutional difficulties if the sexes are dissimilar in some sense related to regulatory objectives. Not only has this approach failed to generate coherent definitions of difference, it has obscured the relationship between cultural and biological constructions of social roles. Gender distinctions have been both over- and undervalued. In some cases, courts have allowed biology to determine destiny; in others, they have failed to appreciate the significance of woman's special circumstances in constraining her social opportunities. Too often the focus has been on gender difference, too infrequently on gender disadvantages.

A critical threshold question facing the courts has been the appropriate standard for assessing sex-based discrimination. By the midtwentieth century, equal protection analysis had crystallized into a two-tiered scheme of review. The lower level of scrutiny, applicable for general economic regulation, required only that the distinctions at issue be rationally related to a legitimate state purpose. For cases involving "fundamental interests" (such as speech or voting) or "suspect" classifications (race, alienage, or national origin), the reviewing court engaged in "strict scrutiny," and required that states establish a "compelling" interest that could not be more narrowly achieved. Since gender distinctions traditionally had triggered the more relaxed standard, women's rights groups in the 1970s directed much of their effort toward doctrinal or constitutional changes in that framework.

One opportunity to press for such modifications arose in 1971, when the Supreme Court first held that a gender classification violated equal protection guarantees. Speaking for a unanimous Court, Chief Justice Burger declared in *Reed v. Reed* that an Idaho statute preferring males as estate administrators failed to bear a fair and substantial relationship to the legislative purpose. Ironically, this landmark decision was directed at a statute no longer in force, and the Court's analysis was not particularly instructive about the fate of other gender classifications. Indeed, the Chief Justice's opinion offered no analysis of the appropriate standard of review. Nor did the decision explain what was constitutionally inadequate about the asserted justification for the statute; that is, that men would be more likely to have business experience, and a sex-based preference was therefore a rational means of minimizing costs and controversies in estate administration (*Reed v. Reed,* 404 U.S. 71[1971]).

Similar problems plagued the Court's subsequent grapplings with gender standards. In *Frontiero v. Richardson* and *Craig v. Boren* (1976) the justices divided over the appropriate level of review, but a majority finally settled on a new intermediate framework; sex-based classifications had to be substantially related to an important governmental objective. *Frontiero* involved a federal scheme that allowed male but not female members of the armed forces automatically to claim their spouses as dependents for purposes of gaining housing and medical benefits. *Craig* concerned an Oklahoma statute prohibiting the sale of beer to males under age 21 and females under 18. In decisions that signaled a heightened sensitivity to gender discrimination, the Court struck down both regulations (*Frontiero v. Richardson,* 411 U.S. 677 [1973]; *Craig v. Boren,* 429 U.S. 190 [1976]). Somewhat less encouraging was the majority's failure to provide an adequate account of what was harmful about gender classifications in general or the federal and Oklahoma provisions in particular. Nor were the harms self-evident. To many observers, most of the women directly affected by the regulatory schemes did not appear disadvantaged; servicemen's wives did not have to prove dependency and female drinkers could purchase beer at an earlier age than their male counterparts. Equally problematic was the absence in both *Frontiero* and *Craig* of any coherent justification for the newly articulated intermediate standard of review.

Many of the courts' and commentators' difficulties in supplying such a justification has stemmed from a weddedness to prior equal protection paradigms and a preoccupation with the form in which they are cast. All too often, the focus of debate has been whether sex discrimination is sufficiently similar to race discrimination to warrant the same level of strict scrutiny. On that point, a majority of the Supreme Court has appeared to share Justice Powell's view that "the perception of racial classifications as inherently odious stems from a lengthy and tragic history that gender based classifications do not share (*Regents of the University of California v. Bakke,* 438 U.S. 265, 311-315; opinion of Justice Powell). It has also often been argued that since women are not a discrete and insular minority, they can adequately assert their interests through majoritarian political processes. On that view, heightened protection by a nonmajoritarian branch of government is unnecessary (Ely, 1980; see *United States v. Carolene Products,* 304 U.S. 144 [1938]).

Yet, as critics have often noted, such arguments undervalue key continuities between different forms of discrimination. Both sex and race are identifiable, immutable, and involuntary attributes that generally bear "no relation to ability to perform or contribute to society" (*Frontiero v. Richardson,* 411 U.S. 677, 686 [1978]). Both have served historically to deprive individuals of fundamental civil rights, and have exposed them to systematic deprivations and brutalities. Numerical majorities can assume—and in American culture have assumed—the functional characteristics of minorities. Women, no less than racial or ethnic groups, have suffered subordinate treatment on the basis of ascribed attributes and have internalized the social values that perpetuate such subordination. And, as a practical matter, it is women's "non-discrete and insular status," their lack of segregation and self-identification as a group, that has disempowered them in the political process (Chafe, 1981: 76-78; Ackerman, 1985: 713; Hacker, 1951-52: 60; Hochschild, 1974; Wirth, 1952).

Yet to underscore the parallels between racial and sexual subordination is not to endorse the kind of unqualified analogy drawn by a minority of justices in *Frontiero*, or by other courts and commentators in similar contexts (*Frontiero v. Richardson*, 411 U.S. 677 [1978]; *Sail'er, Inc. v. Kirby*, 5 Cal. 3rd 1, 485 P.2d 529, 95 Cal. Rptr. 329 [1971]). Women as a group have not been segregated and stigmatized in the same way as blacks. Most females have lived on terms of intimacy with members of the dominant group, and have enjoyed economic and social privileges traditionally denied to minorities. Racial discrimination has, on the whole, been intended to degrade and disempower. Sex-based distinctions, by contrast, have reflected a more complicated set of motives, including the kind of paternalism enshrined in *Muller* and the seemingly benign assumptions about female drinking patterns reflected in *Craig*.

Nor does it follow, as critics of intermediate scrutiny have frequently assumed, that altering the Court's formal standard would alter its substantive decisions. Although one of the primary rationales advanced for a federal Equal Rights Amendment has been that it would subject sex-based classifications to the strictest level of scrutiny, a decade's experience with comparable state provisions reveals no systematic relationships among results, rationales, and standards of review (Note, 1982: 1324; Rouse, 1978: 1282, 1308; Kurtz, 1977: 101).[4] It is, of course, true that scrutiny of racial classifications generally has been "strict in form and fatal in fact"; except in affirmative action contexts, almost no racial discrimination has passed muster (Gunther, 1972: 8). But those results indicate an attitude that is reflected in, rather than compelled by, the formal level of review. It is the perspective from which courts have understood gender differences, rather than the precise standard those differences must satisfy, that has impeded progressive change. What is needed, then, is less focus on women's and minorities' respective place in an oppression sweepstakes and more attention to the continuities and discontinuities in various patterns of discrimination.

Essential to that analysis is a clearer appreciation of the harms that flow even from largely accurate or ostensibly benign sexual stereotypes.

The fundamental problem in *Craig* was not the issue on which the majority decision appeared to turn: the absence of sufficient statistical relationships among sex, alcohol purchases, and traffic safety. Nor were the difficulties in *Frontiero* and *Reed* attributable to incorrect generalizations about sex and dependency. The problem rather, was that legal legitimation of such stereotypes tends to reinforce the inequalities they reflect. To proceed on assumptions that women are less likely than men to engage in public affairs or to have independent sources of support lends credibility to roles that are separate but scarcely equal. Even the more favorable stereotypes present in *Craig*—that women mature earlier and are less likely to drink and drive—reinforce a cultural message that does not necessarily redound to women's advantage. The potency of that message was, ironically enough, underscored by the male plaintiff-appellant's brief in *Craig*. In some detail it described the insult that Oklahoma's statute visited on a hypothesized combat-eligible male artillery lieutenant ("with all the power and responsibility that entails") who was forced to idle his jeep while his 18-year-old date, a non-combat-eligible WAC clerk-typist, purchased a six-pack for him (reply brief for the appellants, *Craig v. Boren,* 190, p. 13, n. 6).

More direct evidence of how stereotypes about sexual maturation work to women's disadvantage has also been readily available. Indeed, it was conspicuous in a case that had reached the Court in the preceding term. The 1973 case of *Stanton v. Stanton* involved a Utah statute that specified 21 as the age of majority for males and 18 as the age for females (*Stanton v. Stanton,* 421 U.S. 7 [1975]). As applied, the statute would have terminated a father's obligations to support a daughter three years earlier than it would have ended such obligations for a son. Plaintiffs argued, and the Court agreed, that the statute reflected self-perpetuating assumptions that males required extended support and education since they were destined for the 'marketplace and the world of ideas," while females, who tended to mature and marry earlier, needed less assistance. What was missing in *Craig* and *Frontiero* was some comparable recognition that gender distinctions concerning drinking and dependency, although more subtle in implication and mixed in consequences than distinctions concerning parental support, nevertheless contributed to the same ideological preconceptions.

Similar inadequacies characterized other early Supreme Court holdings on ostensibly benign discrimination. For example, a 1974 decision, *Kahn v. Shevin*, upheld a Florida property tax scheme that granted an exemption (worth approximately $15) to widows but not to widowers. In the majority's view, such differential treatment bore a substantial relation to the state's interest in compensating women for past economic discrimination and in mitigating the financial difficulties disproportionately faced by older single women (*Kahn v. Shevin*, 416 U.S. 351 [1974]). Again, in 1978 in *Schlesinger v. Ballard*, the Court upheld, on compensatory grounds, a system that subjected female naval officers to a less stringent up-or-out promotion system than their male colleagues (*Schlesinger v. Ballard*, 419 U.S. 498 [1978]).

What was troubling about both cases was less what was said than what was unsaid. A threshold difficulty in Kahn was the majority's unsupported and presumably unsupportable assumption that the Florida legislators who authorized the widow's exemption in 1885 were motivated by a desire to redress sex-based discrimination. Even if one accepts that compensatory justification, Florida's flat grant of $15 to all widows irrespective of their financial circumstances was, as the dissent noted, a highly overinclusive and underfunded response to the feminization of poverty among the elderly. *Schlesinger* was equally problematic for other reasons. In effect, the Court's decision left unchallenged the underlying discrimination against women that made a longer promotion period appropriate; that is, their exclusion from combat-eligible positions and the weight accorded that exclusion in allocating advancement opportunities. Yet legitimating the inadequate compensatory aspects of a structurally inequitable system comes at a cost; it deflects attention from more fundamental reform while perpetuating assumptions that women need special preferences in order to attain comparable positions.

Also absent from these decisions was any exploration of the costs that gender stereotypes impose on men as well as women. Again, the Court's attachment to prior paradigms, built on theories of discrete and insular minorities, has impeded satisfactory analysis of the way traditional sexual roles have constrained male aspirations and opportunities. That is not to imply indifference to men's grievances. An overview of the first decade and a half of Supreme Court gender discrimination decisions reveals that males have been more successful than females both in gaining access to the Court and in obtaining favorable results (Kay, 1985: 39, 67-72). Among the most important decisions have been those granting men eligibility for alimony and social security benefits and access to an all-female nursing school. As those cases acknowledge, benign and invidious discrimination are often neither readily distinguishable nor dichotomous categories. Preferences for female nursing school applicants, for example, perpetuate assumptions about nursing as a women's profession that have served historically to devalue its status and depress its wages.[5] While the evolution of discrimination doctrine has witnessed increasing sensitivity to the costs of gender stereotyping, that development has remained incomplete in both its analytic and its practical dimensions. Such limitations have become particularly apparent in contexts that do not appear to present women as "similarly situated" to men.

DEFINITIONS OF DIFFERENCES

Since traditional jurisprudential frameworks have required similar treatment for those who are similar and different treatment for those who are different, a central issue is what counts as a relevant difference. That issue becomes particularly problematic in cases involving gender, where biological capacities and cultural constraints are deeply interrelated. Attempts to sort out those relationships have yielded a set of chaotic characterizations in both statutory and constitutional contexts.

Some of the clearest jurisprudential difficulties began in litigation under Title VII of the 1964 Civil Rights Act (42 U.S.C Sec. 2000). In relevant part, the statute prohibits sex-based discrimination in employment practices, but provides a defense for "bona fide occupational qualifications"(BFOQs). The first Title VII case to come before the U.S. Supreme Court concerned the scope of that defense, and did little to clarify the legal issues presented. *Phillips v. Martin Marietta Corporation* involved a policy that barred job applications from women but not men with preschool children. A divided court of appeals had sustained the policy on the theory that Congress could not have been so irrational as to bar "consideration of the differences between the normal relationships of working fathers and working mothers to their preschool age children and to require that an employer treat the two alike in the administration of its gender hiring policies." In a brief *per curiam* opinion, the Supreme Court reversed. Although finding that the employer's policy constituted sex discrimination within the meaning of the statute, the Court remanded for two determinations: whether conflicting family obligations were "demonstrably more relevant to job performance for a woman than a man" and, if so, whether that would constitute a BFOQ defense for the employer's policy (*Phillips v. Martin Marietta Corporation,* 411 F.2d 1, 3-4 [5th Cir 1969]; reversed and remanded, 400 U.S. 542 [1971] [per curiam]).

Although a substantial improvement over the court of appeals opinion, this summary disposition raised troubling issues. In particular, it implied a possible legal justification for self-perpetuating sex stereotypes about parental roles and obligations. To deny women responsible job opportunities because of disproportionate domestic responsibilities could not help but encourage couples to replicate that pattern. By wedding itself to a theoretical framework that asked only if the sexes' different circumstances were, under current social practices, relevant to their differential treatment, the Court was blinded to more fundamental questions concerning the legitimacy of that treatment and the cultural norms underlying it. Should any individuals be subject to categorical deprivations based on their parental roles, particularly if such deprivations serve to reinforce an unequal division of domestic responsibilities?

Similar difficulties arose in the next major BFOQ case to reach the Court. At issue in *Dothard v. Rawlinson* were Alabama prison regulations that prevented women from serving as guards in positions requiring close physical contact with inmates. The Court began its analysis by suggesting that Congress intended the BFOQ to be "an extremely narrow exception" to general prohibitions on job discrimination, and that in the "usual case" whether a job was too dangerous was for each individual woman to determine for herself. However, the majority went on to conclude that Alabama's restrictions were justified by "substantial" expert testimony indicating that women would pose a "substantial" security problem because of their special susceptibility to sexual assault.

The factual basis for that testimony, however, was somewhat less substantial. It consisted largely of the Alabama prison commissioner's ruminations about male superiority and two prior disturbances involving women, neither of whom were guards. Never did the state explain why *sexual* assaults, as opposed to assaults in general, posed a particular threat to prison safety, an omission particularly notable given studies suggesting that women are generally more successful than men at defusing violent situations. Nor did the Court explain its refusal to credit equally "substantial" evidence indicating that properly trained female guards had not presented security risks in any Alabama institution or in other state maximum security prisons (*Dothard v. Rawlinson,* 433 U.S. 321 [1977]; see Horne, 1980).

Dothard's conflicting signals—its rhetoric limiting BFOQs and its rationale affirming them—complicated the evolution not only of Title VII defenses, but also of equal protection law. One positive development has been the refusal to view sex-based protective labor legislation as a defense to discrimination charges; individual job applicants must have an opportunity to demonstrate their ability to perform the tasks at issue.[6] More disturbing has been the reliance on *Dothard* to justify gender preferences in a variety of unrelated cases, including everything from disparities in criminal sentencing statutes to bans on male nurses (but not male doctors) for female nursing home patients (*Fessel v. Masonic Home of Delaware, Inc.,* 447 F. Supp. 1346 [D.Del. 1978], aff'd mem., 591 F.2d 1334 [3rd Cir. 1979]; see also sources cited in Powers, 1980: 1281, 1294). That sex but not race has constituted a permissible occupational qualification suggests a limitation both in prevailing commitments to eradicating gender discrimination and understandings of its origins. If, for example, a state were to argue that prison administrators feared greater risks of disturbances if white prisoners had black rather than white guards, or that elderly white nursing home patients objected to physical contact with black nurses, that presumably would not provide a legal justification for racially based hiring. In such circumstances, we are more prepared to pay the costs of color- than gender-blindness.

Those different degrees of commitment may, in part, stem from a failure to identify the full countervailing costs of gender consciousness in employment decisions. No matter how "bona fide," sex-based hiring generally perpetuates the occupational stereotypes and segregation that contribute to women's subordinate labor force status. Challenging those stereotypes requires challenging the legal ideologies that sustain them, and further legislative or judicial curtailment of the BFOQ defense would be a useful step in that direction.

A related area where comparable curtailments would be desirable involves women and the military. Female participation in the armed forces has been constrained by both cultural expectations and legal restrictions. Until the early 1970s, women constituted less than 1% of American military personnel, and were confined largely to health care and administrative occupations. While their participation grew significantly over the next decade and a half, such increases occurred largely without judicial intervention (Binken and Bach, 1977: 1, 15). The Supreme Court's first decision on point left unchallenged the same stereotypes about female frailty and male aggression reflected in *Dothard.* The 1981 case of *Rostker v. Goldberg* involved a male plaintiff's challenge to the 1976 compulsory draft registration system that excluded women. Once again, the similarly situated paradigm obscured analysis. Speaking for the majority, Justice Rhenquist reasoned that the purpose of the registration system was to prepare for a draft of combat-eligible troops. Since women were not similarly situated as to combat eligibility, Congress was free to exclude them from registration (*Rostker v. Goldberg,* 453 U.S. 57, 78-79 [1981]).

There were a number of difficulties with this line of analysis, not the least of which was its patent disregard of prior precedents and legislative history. Under the conventional test for gender classifications, it was hard to see how women's exemption served substantial governmental interests that could not be more narrowly achieved. Even assuming the legitimacy of women's exclusion from combat, the legitimacy of their exclusion from registration did not follow. According to government estimates, about one-third of those drafted during a national mobilization would not need combat skills. The registration system at issue included non-combat-eligible males, and uncontroverted Defense Department studies suggested that some 80,000 women draftees could be used without administrative difficulties in a total draft of 650,000 (*Rostker v. Goldberg,* 453 U.S. at 97, 100-101; Marshall, J., dissenting).

Moreover, by analyzing the case purely in terms of asserted registration needs, the Court sidestepped the more fundamental values at issue. Much of the congressional opposition to female registration reflected precisely the kind of sex-role assumptions that the Court had come increasingly to disapprove in other contexts: that women's responsibility was primarily in the private, and men's in the public, sphere. Legislative debates concerning registration reflected an extended array of gender stereotypes about male bonding, female domesticity, chivalrous instincts, and biological incapacities (see U.S. Senate, 1980: 126; testimony summarized in Estrich and Kerr, 1984: 98; William Westmoreland, quoted in Ruddick, 1984: 3; Lipman-Blumen, 1984: 192). Yet the evidence available about female performance in combat, simulated combat, and related police, prison, and military contexts has afforded little support for these gender generalizations. Millions of women here and abroad have served with distinction in such positions, and serious problems of incapacity have yet to be demonstrated. Technological advances have made physical strength unnecessary for many combat-related tasks, and gender-neutral guidelines have shown their effectiveness in matching individual capacities with job requirements (see evidence discussed in Binken and Bach, 1977: 13, 50, 81-91, 123-127, 134-137; Goodman, 1979: 243; Kornblum, 1984: 351; Rogan, 1981: 258).

What was missing in *Rostker,* as in the Court's earlier decisions concerning benign discrimination and standards of review, was sensitivity to the full costs of sex-role stereotypes. In military contexts, gender generalizations have served to limit women's access to desirable jobs, opportunities for promotion, eligibility for veteran's benefits, and chances to capitalize on combat experience in subsequent private and political positions (see Binken and Bach, 1977: 35-37; Mall, 1985; Goodman, 1979: 257-264; Kornblum, 1984: 369-396; Stiehm, 1981: 299). That is not to deny the tangible benefits of exemption from compelled military service. Nor is it to discount the views of many feminists who believe that female participants would have relatively little to be gained by inclusion in a system so dominated by male values and male decision makers. But it is difficult for women to attain true equality of respect and treatment as citizens while exempt from one of citizenship's central responsibilities. The stereotypes that perpetuate such exemptions cannot readily be contained. Assumptions about women's physical incapacities and maternal responsibilities inevitably spill over to other areas of social life and reinforce expectations about gender roles and hierarchies. The issue in *Rostker* was more fundamental than the Court's analysis acknowledged. And the result of its decision was to legitimate assumptions for which both men and women have paid a heavy price.

One final area in which judicial definitions of difference have proved equally problematic concerns pregnancy. During the mid-1970s, the Supreme Court reached the somewhat novel conclusion that discrimination on the basis of pregnancy did not "involve gender as such." According to a majority of justices, employer benefit plans that provided coverage for virtually all medical disabilities except pregnancy did not violate constitutional or statutory guarantees, since there was "no risk from which men were protected and women were not." Rather, employers were entitled to treat childbirth-related disabilities as involving "additional risks" and "unique characteristics," and to distinguish between "pregnant women and non-pregnant persons" in granting medical benefits (*Geduldig v. Aillo,* 417 U.S. 484, 496-97, no. 20[1974]; *General Electric Co. v. Gilbert,* 429 U.S. 125, 135-36 [1976]). At no point did the Court explain what made pregnancy more "unique" than the male reproductive conditions entitled to coverage (e.g., prostatectomies and vasectomies).

In any event, to characterize pregnancy as a "unique" risk both assumes what should be at issue and makes that assumption from a male reference point. Men's physiology sets the standard, against which women's claims appear only "additional." The notion that distinctions based on pregnancy are not distinctions based on "gender as such" obscures the most basic physical, cultural, and historical meanings of reproduction and the disadvantages that have flowed from it. Approximately 85% of female employees can expect to become pregnant at some point in their working lives, and employer maternity policies have been notably inadequate (Kamerman et al., 1983: 1-25; Mangione and de Mandilovitch, 1973: 32; Williams, 1984-85: 325). The traditional assumption has been that pregnant workers are provisional workers who would (or should) not return to their jobs for substantial periods after childbirth. That attitude, in turn, has discouraged development of public and private assistance that might enable women to become less provisional. By focusing on gender differences rather than on gender disadvantages, the Court's approach exacerbated both women's economic inequality and the stereotypes underlying it.

Recognition of that fact helped prompt the 1978 Pregnancy Discrimination Act (42 U.S.C. Sec. 2000e[k] [1982]), which amended Title VII to require that women "affected by childbirth and related condition . . . be treated the same as other persons not so affected but similar in their ability or inability to work." While that act has had enormous positive influence on maternity policies, it has by no means solved the problems of reconciling women's family and market roles. In effect, the statute simply prevents employers from singling out pregnant workers for special disadvantages. It does not affirmatively require or encourage provision of disability leaves, job security, flexible schedules, or child-care arrangements that would enable parents to accommodate work and family obligations.

The inadequacies of existing law grew increasingly apparent during the mid-1980s, when litigation involving maternity leaves brought the issue again before the Supreme Court. *California Savings and Loan Association v. Guerra* concerned challenges to a California statute that required employers to provide job-protected leaves for pregnant women but not for other temporarily disabled employees. A divided Court upheld the legislation. Speaking for the majority, Justice Marshall rejected claims that the statute was inconsistent with federal Pregnancy Discrimination Act provisions requiring pregnancy to be treated "the same" as other disabilities. To hold otherwise, the Court reasoned, would be inconsistent with the legislative history and purpose of the Act, which sought to guarantee women's right to " 'participate fully and equally in the workforce. . .' " (___ U.S. ___ [1987], [quoting 123 Cong. Rec. 29658] [1977]).

To women's rights advocates, the *California Federal* decision was not an unmixed blessing. Despite urging by the National Organization for Women, the majority declined to require that employers comply with the language and purpose of both state and federal statutes, by granting job-protected leaves for all disabled workers. Yet, as the NOW amicus brief noted, the interpretation that the Court ultimately adopted makes pregnant workers more expensive and risks replicating the experience of sex-based protective labor legislation earlier in the century. All too often, such legislation "protected" women out of the jobs most desirable to male competitors. Moreover, to require that leaves be available only for mothers is to reinforce, both in fact and appearance, an unequal allocation of parental responsibilities. Without a broader range of legal guarantees, women cannot hope to realize opportunities for truly "full and equal" participation in the work force.

A comparable point can be made about other legislative and doctrinal developments. Contemporary equal protection frameworks have, to be sure, made an enormous contribution in raising the costs and consciousness of gender discrimination. But its underlying causes have too often remained unchallenged and its consequences too indirectly addressed. In many contexts, the legacy of separate spheres ideology lingers on. Women continue to assume disproportionate obligations in the home that amplify their difficulties in the workplace (see studies cited in Freedman, 1983: 913, 914 n. 4). Sex stereotypes and inflexible job structures contribute to women's concentration in low-status, low-paying employment sectors. After two decades of experience with statutes requiring equal pay and employment opportunities, the economic position of women workers relative to men has only marginally improved, and the problem of women in poverty has worsened.[7] Reported incidents of violence against women have increased, and assistance to the needy has decreased.[8] Far too often, these issues have remained beyond the boundaries of traditional gender jurisprudence.

What that suggests is the need both to rethink our legal paradigms and to recognize their limitations. The animating concern must extend beyond formal parity between the sexes to the quality of life for both sexes. Judicial and legislative strategies must focus not simply on access to, but alteration of, existing social institutions. Greater emphasis must be placed on a broad range of issues, including occupational segregation, workplace priorities, governmental assistance, and family structures. That these concerns have not been central to the judicial agenda suggests limitations not only in our legal institutions but also in our social vision. Without a fundamental reordering of cultural values, women cannot hope to secure true equality in employment opportunities, economic security, and social status. In that reconstructive enterprise, the law can play a modest but more effective role.

NOTES

1. *In re* Kilgore, 17 Phila. 192, 193 (1884); In the Matter of Goodell, 39 Wis. 232, 244 (1875); *Lockwood v. United States,* 9 Ct. Cl. 346, 348, 355 (1873).

2. In the Matter of Goodell, 39 Wis. 232, 244 (1875).

3. *In re* Petition of Leach, 134 Ind. 665 (1893); *People v. Ritchie,* 155 Ill. 98, 40 N.E. 454 (1895).

4. For examples of cases reaching contrary results despite similar issues and similar standards, compare *A. v. X.Y.Z.,* 641 P.2d 1222 (Wyo.), cert. den., U.S. 1021 (1982) (upholding discrimination against putative father) with *R.McG. and C.W. v. J.W. and W.W.,* 615 P2.d 666 (1980) (protecting rights of putative father); *People v. Salinas,* 551 P.2d 703 (Colo. 1976); *Archer and Johnson v. Mayes,* 194 S.E.2d 707 (Va. 1973); *MacLean v. First Northwest Industries of America,* 635 P.2d 683.

5. See, for example, *Orr v. Orr,* 440 U.S. 268 (1979); *Califano v. Goldfarb,* 430 U.S. 199 (1977); *Weinberger v. Wiesenfeld,* 420 U.S. 636 (1975); *Hogan v. Mississippi University for Women,* 458 U.S. 718 (1982).

6. *Rosenfeld v. Southern Pacific Company,* 444 F.2d 1219 (9th Cir. 1971); *Bowe v. Colgate Palmolive Co.,* 416 F.2d 711 (7th Cir. 1969); EEOC Guidelines on Discrimination Because of Sex, 29 C.F.R. Sec. 1604.

7. Women typically earn about 64 cents for every dollar earned by men, and this ratio has not significantly improved since enactment of equal pay legislation (see Treiman and Hartmann, 1981: 13-43; Hartmann, 1984: 4; Hartmann et al., 1985). For statistics concerning women in poverty, see U.S. House of Representatives (1983) and U.S. Department of Commerce (1983: 1-5).

8. For statistics on rape, see U.S. Federal Bureau of Investigation (1984: 14); reported rapes increased 50% between 1975 and 1984. For statistics on domestic violence, see U.S. Department of Justice (1980), Polk (1985: 191), Lerman (1984: 61, 67), and Fromson (1977:135). For discussion of the decline in welfare assistance, see, for example, Bowden and Palmer (1984: 177, 179-200).

REFERENCES

Ackerman, Bruce (1985) "Beyond Carolene Products." Harvard Law Review 98 (February).

Baer, Judith A. (1978) The Chains of Protection. Westport, CT: Greenwood.

Baker, Elizabeth (1969) Protective Labor Legislation (rev. ed.). New York: AMS.

Barnes, Janette (1970) "Women and entrance to the legal profession." Journal of Legal Education 23.

Basch, Norma (1982) In the Eyes of the Law. Ithaca, NY: Cornell University Press.

Beard, Mary R. (1946) Women as a Force in History: A Study in Traditions and Realities. New York: Macmillan.

Becker, Susan D. (1981) The Origins of the Equal Rights Amendment: American Feminism Between the Wars. Westport, CT: Greenwood.

Berkin, Carol and Mary Norton (1979) "Equality or submission: feme covert status in early Pennsylvania," in Women of America. Boston: Houghton Mifflin.

Binken, Martin and Shirley J. Bach (1977) Women and the Military. Washington, DC: Brookings Institution.

Bittenbender, Ada M. (1891) "Women in law," pp. 200-221 in Annie Nathan Meyer (ed.) Woman's Work in America. New York: Henry Holt.

Blackstone, William (1982) Commentaries on the Laws of England (15th ed.). Oxfordshire: Professional Books. (Original work published 1756)

Bowden, D. Lee and John Palmer (1984) "Social policy: challenging the welfare state," in John Palmer and Isabell Sawhill, The Reagan Record. Cambridge, MA: Bollinger.

Chafe, William (1981) Women and Equality: Changing Patterns in American Culture. New York: Oxford University Press.

Chused, Richard (1983) "Married women's property law 1800-1850." Georgetown Law Journal 71 (June).

Collins, Franklin W. (1912) Statement in Woman Suffrage (hearings before the Senate Committee on Woman Suffrage, Senate Document No. 601, 62d Congress, 2d session), pp. 27, 30. Washington, DC: Government Printing Office.

Dexter, Elisabeth (1972) Career Women of America. Clifton, NJ: A. M. Kelley.

Drinker, Sophie (1961) "Women attorneys of colonial times." Maryland Historical Society Bulletin 56 (December).

Ely, John Hart (1980) Democracy and Distrust. Cambridge, MA: Harvard University Press.

Estrich, Susan and Virginia Kerr (1984) "Sexual justice," in Norman Dorsen (ed.) The Rights of Groups.

Foner, Philip S. (1979) Women and the American Labor Union Movement, Vol. 2. New York: Free Press.

Freedman, Ann E. (1983). "Sex equality, sex differences, and the Supreme Court." Yale Law Journal 92.

Friedman, Lawrence (1984) A History of American Law. New York: Norton.

Fromson, Terry L. (1977) "The case for legal remedies for abused women." New York University Review of Law and Social Change 6.

Goodman, Jill Laurie (1979) "Women, war and equality: an examination of sex discrimination in the military." Women's Rights Law Reporter 5.

Gunther, Gerald (1972) "Foreword: in search of evolving doctrine on a changing court: a model for a newer equal protection." Harvard Law Review 86.

Hacker, Helen Mayes (1951-52) "Women as a minority group." Social Forces 60.

Harris, Barbara J. (1978) Beyond Her Sphere: Women and the Professions in American History. Westport, CT: Greenwood.

Hartmann, Heidi (1984) Statement in Women in the Work Force: Pay Equity (hearings before Joint Economic Committee, 98th Congress, 2d session). Washington, DC: Government Printing Office.

Hartmann, Heidi I., Patricia A. Roos, and Donald J. Treiman (1985) "An agenda for basic research on comparable worth," in Heidi I. Hartmann (ed.) Comparable Worth: New Directions for Research. Washington, DC: National Academy Press.

Hochschild, Arlie (1974) "Making it: marginalities and obstacles to minority consciousness," in Ruth B. Kundsin (ed.) Women and Success: The Anatomy of Achievement. New York: William Morrow.

Horne, Peter (1980) Women in Law Enforcement (2nd ed.). Springfield, IL: Charles C Thomas.

Jensen, Elizabeth (1979) "The equity jurisdiction and married women's property in ante-bellum America: a revisionist view." International Journal of Women's Studies 2 (March-April).

Johnston, John D., Jr., and Charles L. Knapp (1971) "Sex discrimination by law: a study in judicial perspective." New York University Law Review 46.

Kamerman, Sheila, Alfred J. Kahn, and Paul Kingston (1983) Maternity Policies and Working Women. New York: Columbia University Press.

Kanowitz, Leo (1970) Women and the Law. Albuquerque: University of New Mexico Press.

Kay, Herma Hill (1985) "Models of equality." University of Illinois Law Review.

Kerber, Linda (1980) Women of the Republic: Intellect and Ideology in Revolutionary America. Chapel Hill: University of North Carolina Press.

Kessler-Harris, Alice (1972) Out to Work. New York: Oxford University Press.

Kessler-Harris, Alice (1979) "Where are the organized women workers?" in Nancy Cott and Elizabeth Pleck (eds.) A Heritage of Her Own. New York: Simon & Schuster.

Kornblum, Lisa (1984) "Women warriors in a man's world: the combat exclusion." Law and Inequality: A Journal of Theory and Practices 2.

Kraditor, Aileen (1971) The Ideas of the Woman Suffrage Movement, 1890-1920. New York: Norton.

Kurtz, Paul (1977) "The state equal rights amendments and their impact on domestic relations law." Family Law Quarterly 11.

LaZarou, Kathleen (1978) "Fettered Portias: obstacles facing nineteenth century women lawyers." Women Lawyers Journal 64 (Winter): 21-30.

Lerman, Lisa (1984) "A model state act: remedies for domestic abuse." Harvard Journal on Legislation 21.

Lipman-Blumen, Jean (1984) Gender Roles and Power. Englewood Cliffs, NJ: Prentice-Hall.

Mall, Janice (1985) "Military as a ticket to the mainstream." Los Angeles Times (September 15): Pt. VI, 8.

Mangione, Quinn and Baldi de Mandilovitch (1973) "Evaluating working conditions in America." Monthly Labor Review 96 (November).

Note (1950) "Sex, discrimination and the Constitution." Stanford Law Review 2.

Note (1982) "The interpretation of state constitutional rights." Harvard Law Review 95.

Owen, Harold (1912) Women Adrift: A Statement of the Case Against Suffragism. New York: E. P. Dutton.

Polk, Kenneth (1985) "Rape reform and criminal justice processing." Crime & Delinquency 31, 2.

Powers, Katheryn (1980) "The shifting parameters of affirmative action: pragmatic paternalism in sex-based employment discrimination cases." Wayne State Law Review.

Rabkin, Peggy (1975) "The origins of law reform: the social significance of the 19th century codification movement and its contribution to the passage of the early married women's property acts." Buffalo Law Journal 24.

Rhode, Deborah (1985) "Moral character as a professional credential." Yale Law Journal 94 (January).

Rogan, Helen (1981) Mixed Company: Women in the Modern Army. New York: Putnam.

Rouse, Driscoll (1978) "Through a glass darkly: a look at state equal rights amendments." Suffolk University Law Review.

Ruddick, Sara (1984) "Women in the military." Report from the Center for Philosophy and Public Policy 4 (College Park, MD).

Salmon, Marilynn (1983) "The legal status of women in early America: a reappraisal." Law & History Review 1 (Spring): 129-151.

Scott, Anne F. (1984) Making the Invisible Woman Visible. Champaign: University of Illinois Press.

Sinclair, Andrew (1965) The Better Half: The Emancipation of the American Woman. New York: Harper & Row.

Speth, Linda E. (1982) "The married women's property acts, 1839-1865: reform, reaction, or revolution," in D. Kelly Weisberg (ed.) Women and the Law: A Social and Historical Perspective, Vol. 2. Camridge, MA: Schenkman.

Stanton, Elizabeth Cady, Susan B. Anthony, and Matilda Joslyn Gage [eds.] (1881) History of Woman Suffrage, Vol. 1. Rochester, NY.

Stiehm, Judith (1981) Bring Me Men and Women: Mandated Change at the U.S. Air Force Academy. Berkeley: University of California Press.

Treiman, Donald and Heidi Hartmann [eds.] (1981) Women, Work, and Wages: Equal Pay for Jobs of Equal Value. Washington, DC: National Academy Press.

Tussman, Joseph and Jacobus tenBroek (1949) "The equal protection of the laws." California Law Review 37.

U.S. Department of Commerce, Bureau of the Census (1983) Money Income and Poverty Status of Families and Persons in the United States: 1982, Current Population Reports, Consumer Income. Series P-60, No. 140 (July). Washington, DC: Government Printing Office.

U.S. Department of Justice, Bureau of Justice Statistics (1980) Intimate Victims: A Study of Violence Among Friends and Relatives. Washington, DC: Government Printing Office.

U.S. Federal Bureau of Investigation (1984) Uniform Crime Reports: Crime in the U.S. Washington, DC: Government Printing Office.

U.S. House of Representatives (1983) Background Material on Poverty (House report no. 15, 98-15, 98th Congress, 1st session). Washington, DC: Government Printing Office.

U.S. Senate (1980) Report of the Subcommittee on Manpower and Personnel of the Senate Armed Services Committee. 126 Congressional Record 13880; 126 Congressional Record S6530-50. Washington, DC: Government Printing Office.

U.S. Women's Bureau (1928) The Effects of Labor Legislation on the Employment Opportunities of Women (bulletin no. 65). Washington, DC: Government Printing Office.

Walsh, Mary Roth (1977) Doctors Wanted—No Women Need Apply: Sexual Barriers in the Medical Profession, 1835-1920. New Haven, CT: Yale University Press.

Williams, Wendy Webster (1984-85) "Equality's riddle: pregnancy and the equal treatment/special treatment debate." New York University of Journal of Law and Social Change 13.

Wirth, Louis (1952) "The problems of minority groups," in Ralph Linton (ed.) The Science of Man in the World Crisis. New York: Columbia University Press.

Woody, Thomas (1974) A History of Women's Education in the United States (2 vols.). New York: Octagon. (Original work published 1929)

II

WOMEN AS VICTIMS, LITIGANTS, AND OFFENDERS

Major changes have taken place during the last decade that may have influenced the courts' treatment of female victims, litigants and offenders. Perhaps of most significance is the fact that women are appearing in court in greater numbers than ever before. While once a largely male domain addressing conflicts between, and the behavior of, males, women are now frequent visitors to the courtroom as offenders, victims, and litigants. For example, between 1974 and 1984, the arrest rate for women and girls increased by 203% (FBI, 1984). While women constitute only 17% of total arrests, they are no longer only occasional defendants in the criminal court.

Women are also appearing in court as rape victims in greater numbers. The crime of rape is increasing faster than any other serious crime. Between 1975 and 1984, incidences of reported rapes increased 50% (FBI, 1984). It is uncertain to what extent this is due to increased rapes or to greater willingness by women to report their victimization. Some studies show that no more than 10% of rape victims report the crime to police. Others suggest the figure is as high as one in three (Nelson, 1978). Regardless, the result is that more cases of rape are reaching the courtroom.

The same is true for child sexual assault. Greater social sensitivity to this crime as well as national publicity focusing on notorious examples such as the McMartin Pre-school case have increased the likelihood that child sexual assault cases will be reported to the criminal justice system. Although boys are frequently victims, sexual assault of children continues to affect girls disproportionately.

Another crime that finds women the victims in large numbers is spouse abuse. Once a crime that was hidden behind closed doors, wife abuse has now come out into the open. Some studies estimate that one in three women will be victims of violence at the hands of their mates (Walker, 1984). Wife abuse is probably the most common form of violence in the United States today. Growing social awareness, social services designed to support and assist the victim, and new legislation mandating criminal justice system response have all encouraged battered wives to report their victimization. Ten years ago, police were refusing to arrest the abusers, and prosecutors were refusing to prosecute those they did arrest. Today, the emphasis is on treating spouse abuse as a crime. Propelled by law suits brought by battered women as well as by legislation, police departments are now implementing arrest policies. Prosecutor offices are establishing "no drop" policies for spouse abuse cases. And women are bringing their own cases to court through requests for restraining orders. In Hawaii, such requests have increased from approximately 300 in 1983 to nearly 1400 in 1986. It is no longer the rare case of wife abuse that reaches the courts.

The final area in which women are appearing in courts in greater numbers than before is as divorce litigants. "In 1940 there was one divorce for every six marriages, while, in 1980, there was one for every two marriages" (*Monthly Labor Review*, 1983). It is estimated today that two out of every three new marriages will end in divorce (Hewlett, 1986). Thus women are now actively involved in seeking justice and fairness at the hands of the court.

A second area of change over the last decade is the increased understanding we have regarding the effect of victimization on the lives of women. The "rape trauma syndrome" first surfaced in the psychiatric community in 1974 (Burgess and Holmstrom, 1974). We also now have the "battered woman syndrome" (Walker, 1984) and the "battered child syndrome" or "child abuse accommodation syndrome." Their value in the courts is to aid jurors in understanding the often confusing behavior of victims. Use of expert witnesses in describing these syndromes in court has not always been openly received, however. For example, seven state supreme courts have ruled on the rape trauma syndrome with three ruling in favor of it and four ruling against it.

In addition to information on the effects of victimization on women, we also know more than before about the effects of divorce on the woman and her children. Lenore Weitzman's important book *The Divorce Revolution* documents the economic impact of divorce on women, showing high numbers of them plummeting into poverty.

A third area in which apparent change has taken place in the last decade is in social awareness and sensitivity to the victimization of women and children. Rape, wife abuse, and child sexual assault are not new crimes. Their history is centuries old. But in the last ten years, they have surfaced and have been embraced as issues that warrant public concern.

We now have stark evidence regarding the reality of women's lives. According to the articles in this section, women have nearly a 50% chance of being a victim of rape or attempted rape. More than one in three girls will experience some incident of incestuous or extrafamilial sexual abuse by the age of 18. One in three women will be victims of violence in their own homes at the hands of their mate, and women who leave that mate will typically experience a 74% drop in income, sending them and their children below the poverty level. Much of this expanded awareness and public concern is due to the women's movement and accompanying changes in social attitudes regarding the rights and treatment of women.

A final area of change responds to all of the areas addressed above. Increased numbers of women as offenders, victims, and litigants, combined with greater knowledge and social concern regarding the reality of their lives, have been influential in the passage of legislation designed to improve the treatment they receive in the criminal justice system in general and in the court in particular. Such legislation has addressed the traditional tendency to treat the rape victim as the offender, the battered wife as property of her husband, the incest victim as seducing her abuser, and the female offender as someone in need of paternalistic and long-term protection by the criminal justice system.

The potential within this legislation for assuring women fair and just treatment in the court is profound.

Given the changes that have taken place, what treatment can women now expect in the court system? As more women's lives are being affected by judicial decisions, can they expect fairness and an understanding free of sex-role bias when they enter the courtroom. The authors set out to answer this question. Crites examines the judicial record in responding not only to battered wives and their abusers but also to legislation that has been passed to protect women from abuse. Spencer looks at the implementation in the courtroom of legislation designed to reduce the second victimization of women and child victims of sexual assault that typically occurs during trial. Weitzman documents the effect of no-fault divorce legislation on the lives of women and their children. And Chesney-Lind analyzes the outcome for girls of legislation regarding status offenses and reviews research examining paternalistic treatment of women offenders. The authors seek to look within the mind of the court to determine how legislative implementation is affected by continuing attachment to traditional beliefs regarding the role and nature of women. Their conclusions have important implications for future efforts in assuring fair and equitable treatment of women in the courts.

REFERENCES

Burgess, Ann W. and Lyndia L. Holmstrom (1974) "The rape trauma syndrome." American Journal of Psychiatry (September).

FBI (1984) Uniform Crime Reports. Washington, DC: Government Printing Office.

Hewlett, Leslie (1986) A Lesser Life: The Myth of Women's Liberation in America. New York: William Morrow.

Monthly Labor Review (1983) December.

Nelson, James F. (1978) "Alternative measures of crime: a comparison of the Uniform Crime Report and the National Crime Surveys in 26 American cities." Presented at the annual meeting of the American Society of Criminology, Dallas, November.

Walker, Lenore (1984) The Battered Woman Syndrome. New York: Springer.

2

WIFE ABUSE:
THE JUDICIAL RECORD

Laura L. Crites

Traditional judicial response to wife abuse has mirrored that found in society at large. Abuse within the family was considered a private matter and it was viewed as unseemly to bring to the public eye the chastisement of a wife by her husband (Martin, 1976). Both the judiciary and society were guided, in part, by the traditional, religiously directed belief that the husband was the head of the household, responsible for internal discipline. It was, therefore, not only his right, but his responsibility, to punish transgressions on the part of his wife and children. During the Middle Ages, church fathers exhorted men to "beat their wives and wives to kiss the rod that beat them" (Davis, 1973: 25). The first book of church law, the Decretum, written in 1148, required that "a man must castigate his wife and beat her for her correction, for the Lord must punish his own"—man being the Lord's agent for authority (Davidson, 1977: 12).

The theological basis for this assumption that wives should be under the control and authority of their husbands, and that women were appropriate objects of abuse, was the belief that women, in the form of Eve, had introduced sin into the world, thus precipitating the fall of the human race.

Secular law reflected this religious belief, allowing, under early British Common Law, a husband to beat his wife with "a rod no thicker than his thumb" (Davidson, 1977: 18). Wife abuse was permitted by law in the United States until the late nineteenth-century. In 1874, North Carolina rescinded its law permitting wife abuse but refused the wife the right to prosecute if her husband did assault her. The reasoning was that if no permanent damage has been inflicted nor malice nor dangerous violence shown by the husband, it is better to draw the curtain, shut out the public gaze, and leave the parties to forgive and forget (Davidson, 1977: 19).

Thus the prevailing view throughout Western history supported by religious and secular law has been that women, because of their inherent nature, were to be controlled by their husbands and that physical force was a legitimate means of asserting that control. Further, the husband was the legitimate and legal head of the household, representing the family to the outside world and guarding its privacy from intrusion.

Significant changes have taken place in the United States during the last decade in our attitude and response to wife abuse. Although battered wives were once at the mercy of their husbands or reliant only on their own resources in escaping, shelters are now available to women and their children throughout the country—in rural as well as urban areas. Only a few years ago, the phenomenon of wife abuse was little known or recognized. Though a part of the lives of hundreds of thousands of women, wife abuse was a well-kept secret and surfaced only under crisis conditions. Today, the phenomenon is well known and has been identified by the FBI as probably the most frequently occurring crime in the United States today. It has been featured in newspaper and magazine articles as well as being the subject of special television documentaries and dramas. This social concern over wife abuse has also been translated into legislation in almost every state, recognizing the right of women to be free from abuse by their husbands and lovers and, in many instances, providing special legal remedies in the form of temporary restraining orders or protective orders for women (Lerman, 1980). In short, wife abuse has become a recognized public concern of significant proportion.

Many factors have influenced this rise in public interest. Breines and Gordon suggest several reasons including the growing concern during the last two decades over the so-called crisis in the family of which family violence was seen as symptomatic. The tendency toward permissive parenting that was popular during the post-World War II period also may have influenced a general social intolerance of violent coercion within the family. The women's movement is credited for forcing into the public eye those problems related to women that were previously considered personal. A special focus of the women's movement was the role and treatment of the woman in the family because the family structure was seen as the prototype for the domination of women. And, finally, Breines and Gordon point to the 1960s and 1970s as a period of self-exposure, ushering in the demise of an older etiquette of modesty. A characteristic was the increased acceptability of what they call "a confessional mode," which saw individuals publicly sharing the once-private aspects of their lives (Breines and Gordon, 1983: 400-401).

Other influences affecting our attitude toward family violence include a recent concern over the rights and treatment of victims of crimes as evidenced by the 1983 President's Task Force Report on Victims of Crimes. Following on its heels was the 1984 Attorney General's Task Force on Family Violence, which calls for a "legal response to family violence (which is) guided primarily by the nature of the abusive act, not the relationship between the victim and the abuser" (Attorney General, 1984: 4). It argues for the deterrent effects of punishment and details a recommended criminal justice system response that conveys, at each step of the process, the message that "beating one's wife or children is a crime" (Attorney General, 1984: 5).

Certainly, the women's rights movement has had a major impact on not only the open recognition of the problem of wife abuse, but also on changes in the social and systemic response to this crime. Supporters of the movement have lauded the plethora of state laws protecting battered women as symbolic of progress that the movement has promoted for women in general and abused women in particular. Indeed, much of the effort of the early women's movement was directed toward legislative changes as the primary vehicle for assuring and solidifying the rights of women. Underlying this effort appeared to be the assumption that, of the two routes to assuring legal equality for women—through legislative enactment or judicial decision making—the former would appear to be the more stable and less vulnerable to individual biases and whims. This confidence in the legislative process failed to take into consideration, however, the possibility that individuals or groups responsible for carrying out the law would simply refuse to do so.

Such realization dawned first with examination of the police record in enforcing criminal assault laws as they applied to family violence. Police have been not only particular targets of criticism in their seeming insensitivity to family violence (Martin, 1976; Roy, 1977), but they also have been the objects of empirical research to determine the most effective police response to stopping it (Sherman and Berk, 1984). As a result, mandatory police training has been instituted at the state and local level (Lerman, 1980) and special police family violence training manuals have been published (Loving, 1980; IACP, 1976).

Such critical scrutiny, however, has left the judiciary largely untouched. A review of the judicial record in the early 1970s chronicled the inadequacy of the criminal courts in responding to family violence and concluded that such violence between partners should not be referred to criminal courts (Parnas, 1970, 1973). A more recent study of the criminal court response to domestic violence legislation examined the failings of what the researchers considered to be the key actors—the victim, the batterer, and the prosecutor—though ignoring entirely the role of the judge, even though the authors specifically targeted the ineffectual sentences of those men who were convicted of wife abuse (Quarm and Schwartz, 1983). Another study of the utilization of Ohio's Domestic Violence Act briefly addressed judicial reluctance to issue temporary restraining orders on the grounds that such measures constitute inappropriate adjudication of "household disputes." Nevertheless, the author reserved her critical analysis for the police and prosecutors (Grim, 1983).

Two studies do target the judicial record for critical review, however. Marcus examines not only the judicial record in refusing to treat wife abuse as a crime, but also challenges the constitutionality of this response (Marcus, 1981). The U.S. Commission on Civil Rights also addresses the court response in its comprehensive study of battered women and the administration of justice (U.S. Commission, 1982).

It is particularly important that judges no longer be exempt from analysis and criticism in their response to spouse abuse. Whereas judges once saw only an estimated one out of 100 cases of spouse abuse, they are now seeing increasing numbers as domestic violence legislation begins to be utilized by victims as well as police and prosecutors. For example, the number of victims requesting temporary restraining orders from the Honolulu Family Court increased from approximately 300 in 1983 to nearly 1400 victims in 1986.

As the number of cases reaching the courtroom grows, judges and judicial proceedings will become critical in the effort to stop family violence. This article examines both the judicial record in response to spouse abuse and the commitment of the judiciary in fulfilling both the letter and intent of legislation designed to protect battered women.

Though the changes cited earlier suggest that society is no longer willing to permit the unlicensed abuse of women by their husbands, there is disturbing evidence that judges have yet to abandon the historical view of wife abuse.

While some judges are concerned about wife abuse and use their authority to assure that the rights of the abused are enforced, there appears to be a substantial residual group of judges who are unready and unwilling to implement new legislation protecting battered women or to respond to growing social pressure that assault on a wife or lover within the home is no less assault than is the same behavior on the street against a stranger.

The judicial pattern of response to wife abuse reveals an apparent unwillingness to see wife abuse as a crime and a tendency to side with the husband in "domestic disputes." Through their actions, they continue to decriminalize wife abuse and de facto grant a class-based exemption from prosecution for domestic assailants.

The judicial record will be examined through a pattern of judicial sentences of convicted wife abusers, judicial response to protective order legislation, and statements of judges.

PROTECTIVE ORDER LEGISLATION

Perhaps of most significance in assessing the judicial record on wife abuse is the response of the judiciary to protective order legislation because such legislation was often viewed by those promoting its passage as a major achievement in providing a victim with enforceable legal rights to be free from abuse.

A picture of the judicial pattern in responding to such legislation is formed from review of surveys of judges in New Hampshire, Ohio, Pennsylvania, and New York and from interviews with those working on behalf of battered women in Colorado, Kentucky, and Hawaii.

A survey of judicial attitudes in New Hampshire found some judges openly hostile to that state's Protection of Persons From Domestic Violence law, which provided for protective orders for abused women. One shelter filed a formal complaint against a judge for refusing to sign restraining orders (New Hampshire, 1980: 6).

A review of courts in Ohio found many judges and, in one case, an entire court, refusing to issue civil protection orders. (By contrast, the Lucas County, Ohio, judges and professional court staff not only cooperate fully with the intent and letter of the law but have also developed a domestic violence kit to aid women in filing their own petitions for a protection order without the expense of an attorney) (Grim, 1983: 721).

A review of judges in Pennsylvania found general resistance and often hostility by judges to honoring the state's Protection From Abuse Act. Further, Court of Common Pleas judges in that state were found instructing weekend district justices under their authority not to sign protective order petitions. One former police captain expressed his frustration:

Not being a lawyer, I don't know how to go about getting judges to obey the law, but I know a number of them that don't ... I listened to a district justice here say that the judge was her boss and he had said she shouldn't use the Protection From Abuse Act. Her boss, it seems to me, is the people who elected her to office, and I don't think any other elected or appointed official has a right to tell her that she cannot use the law. The law specifically provides for her to take action on the weekend. She has [the tool] and her judge won't let her use it [U.S. Commission, 1982: 40].

In a New York family court, judges have avoided condemning the violence of the husbands by issuing "mutual orders of protection" ordering both parties to refrain from harming each other. One specific case of judicial reluctance to issue a protective order in that court involved a woman who had been beaten frequently for 18 years. The judge refused to grant her an order of protection even though the husband admitted the beatings, ordering instead that both parties go for counseling, this, even though the wife protested that they had unsuccessfully tried counseling (U.S. Commission, 1982: 49).

Several shelter directors and attorneys in rural Colorado have simply accepted that judges in their counties will not sign protective orders and that Colorado's law providing for such orders will only have meaning when the judges have been replaced over time (Price, 1985). A rural courts consultant writes from Kentucky,

the court won't issue protective orders unless I force them to. Since I'm here only intermittently and this project is really about other things, that's no help to the women in danger. The court also believes that women should have to pay $60 to file a request for a protective order. I can just see it now. A woman is running out of the house to escape her violent husband. She stops. Runs back and says "Say honey, could I have $60 to file a protective order request?" [Fahnestock, 1985].

SENTENCES

Judges have also indicated their reluctance to view wife abuse as a crime and their tendency to side with the husband through the sentences given convicted wife abusers. According to the U.S. Civil Rights Commission Report, "when abusers are convicted, judges seldom impose sanctions commensurate with the seriousness of the offenses or comparable with sanctions for similar violence against strangers" (U.S. Commission, 1982: 59). This is particularly significant given that normally only the worst cases of wife abuse reach the courtroom for trial.

A review of 20 cases in the Denver District Court involving the most severe injuries to the battered women showed that the most common sentence given was a $25 fine. Injuries included cuts on the women's face, brain damage, attempted strangulation, abuse of a pregnant victim's stomach, and destruction of eyes, ears, and limbs (U.S. Commission, 1982: 45).

A similar review of 98 successful prosecutions of batterers in Seattle in a two-month period in 1979 found that only 16% received a jail sentence (City of Seattle, 1979: 6). The seriousness of the injuries appeared to have no impact on the sentence of battering men. In one New York case, a man who had cut his wife's face received a sentence of unsupervised probation (U.S. Commission, 1982: 45).

In an Ohio county court known for harsh sentences, 64% of those who were found guilty of battering their wives served no time at all in jail. Less than 10% were sentenced to alternative programs such as counseling or drug therapy, and 27% served no days either in jail or on probation. Less than half of those found guilty were fined and only 12% received a fine of more than $100 for physically assaulting their wives. The most common sentence was probation but victims were rarely informed that further assault would constitute a violation of probation (Quarm and Schwartz, 1983: 207).

Honolulu Family Court judges are, in general, very supportive of women's efforts to obtain temporary restraining orders against their abusers. They readily approve the orders and send abusive men to a six-month judiciary-funded counseling program. It is a different story, however, for judges presiding over the criminal calendar. A five-month study was done, from January to June 1987, to determine the impact of a new mandatory arrest policy implemented by the Honolulu Police Department in late December 1986. The researcher found a dramatic increase in both arrests and prosecutions in domestic violence cases, reflecting not only the new policy but also an increase in the seriousness with which these cases were viewed. The judges, however, refused to share this concern. In spite of a law which requires that the guilty defendant *must* serve 48 hours in jail and *should be* ordered into counseling, only one of the 111 defendants who pled or were found guilty was sent to jail and eight ordered into counseling (Folis, 1987).

Individual cases provide further illustration of the pattern of sentences for abusive, even homicidal, husbands. In a much publicized Denver case in 1984, a judge sentenced a man to two years on work release for fatally shooting his wife five times in the face. The "extraordinary mitigating circumstances" cited by the judge for sentencing to less than the minimum required by law was that the wife had engaged in the "highly provoking acts" of leaving her husband without warning, being loving and caring up to the morning she left, and obtaining a restraining order and proceeding with a separation from her husband without telling him where she was. This case also provides an example of judicial identification with the husband. In his sentencing statement, the judge cited the above "highly provoking acts (as having) affected the Defendant sufficiently so that it excited an irresistible passion *as it would in any reasonable person under the circumstances*" (emphasis added). It should be noted here that this judicial interpretation of the violence conflicted with expert testimony of a psychologist who testified that the defendant was not "having any irresistible impulse" at the time of the killing (*People v. District Court of the City and County of Denver*, Supreme Court State of Colo No 835A284, brief of amicus curiae [Colorado Coalition for] Justice for Abused Women at 15-16, citing sentencing statement of trial court judge. Have since dropped "Colorado for" segment of name).

Another example of inadequate sentencing was the Kansas judge who suspended the fine of a convicted abuser and ordered him to go out and buy his wife a box of candy (Jones, 1981: 48). A Phoenix shelter director tells of an abuser who had severely assaulted, kicked in the head, and robbed his wife. The man was released on his own recognizance although he had prior assault charges and the victim was put in jail for protective custody (U.S. Commission, 1982: 42).

While judges seem unwilling to view wife abuse as a serious crime, they appear to exercise little leniency toward women who kill their husbands in self-defense or after years of abuse (Marcus, 1981: 1727; Brown, 1985; Lindsey, 1978).

In a study of 42 women from 15 states who were charged with killing their husbands (all of whom had a documented history of physical abuse at their husband's hands), 9 were acquitted, 11 received probation or a suspended sentence, and 20, or 61%, of those convicted received jail terms of from six months to 50 years. These women, according to the psychologist who studied them, felt "hopelessly trapped in a desperate situation, in which staying meant the possibility of being killed, but attempting to leave also carried with it the threat of reprisal or death" (Brown, 1985: 20).

In 1977, approximately 40% of the women in the Women's Correctional Center in Chicago who were serving time for murder or manslaughter were there for killing their abusers (Lindsey, 1978: 67).

Judges are not unmindful of the apparent double standard applied to wife abuse cases. In testimony before the U.S. Commission on Civil Rights, several Connecticut judges admitted that they "treated assault in the home differently from assault in the street" (p. 45). One judge testified that he thought the treatment of wives and girlfriends should be upgraded. He admitted that domestic assault had been "minimized sometimes, and I think that those women should be accorded the same rights that a strange woman gets when she is struck out in the streets" (p. 45).

REASONS FOR JUDICIAL RESPONSE

Why have battered women not been accorded those same rights? A dominant reason appears to be judicial attachment to the historical view of wife abuse and sexist beliefs that supported it (Marcus, 1981; U.S. Commission, 1982; Crites, 1985). Rather than in criminal cases addressing the issue as the state versus the accused and their judicial role as enforcing civil or criminal laws, many judges show a strong tendency to see such violence as simply a conflict between lovers or spouses. In interpreting it thus, they set aside their judicial objectivity and take sides based on beliefs that appear to be heavily influenced by sex-role stereotypes and the traditional roles of men and women in our society. Many judges appear to be unwilling to undermine the dominant role of the husband in the marital relationship and equalize the power distribution by bringing the weight of the bench against the abuser. Instead, they show a strong tendency both to side with and to identify with the husband in what might be seen as the continuing "battle of the sexes." Evidence is drawn first from the nature of judicial objections to protective order legislation.

HUSBAND'S SUPERIOR RIGHTS

A primary objection of judges to temporary orders of protection is that they are seen as violating the due process rights of the husband and are, therefore, unconstitutional. They see the husband's right to due process as superior to the wife's right to protection from assault. This judicial stance regarding wife abuse is especially enlightening in view of the fact that temporary restraining orders have long been available to corporations and in other areas of civil disputes without concern for or challenge to their constitutionality.

Judges have also objected to ex parte protective orders that exclude the husband from his home temporarily without hearing his side. In the words of one Pennsylvania judge:

> For any individual as a judge, to issue an order based on somebody's affidavit excluding that individual from his home, this is a very, very drastic situation because I think the individual excluded from the home also has constitutional rights that have to be protected, so that I am not favorable to granting exclusionary orders except under very drastic circumstances and I don't know that I've ever signed one [U.S. Commission, 1982: 50].

Such anxiety over banning a husband from his home on the basis of violence against his wife suggests, at the least, a greater legal concern for his right to access to his property than her right to be free from violent assault. It also suggests that these judges are still bound by the traditional social view that a man's home is his castle and that what goes on therein is not the affair of the courts. A Pennsylvania attorney argued this point when she said:

> Many times when they say "I don't think this act is constitutional and I'm not going to enforce it" . . . they are not enforcing it because they don't believe men should be out of their homes for abusing their wives because it goes on in every family, and I have been told that by more judges than I care to tell you [U.S. Commission, 1982: 51-52].

Ex parte protective order legislation has been upheld as constitutional in both Missouri and Pennsylvania. The appeals court in Missouri weighed the due process rights of the respondent and the safety rights of the victim and ruled that sufficient procedural safeguards existed in requiring petitioners to show "an immediate and present danger of abuse" before an order may be issued. The court also gave more weight to the safety rights of the victim, citing a governmental interest in preventing domestic violence.

PRIVACY

Judges have also expressed an unwillingness to open the doors of the court to domestic violence cases on the basis of a desire to maintain family privacy. Illustrative is the comment of a judge presiding over the case of a high-salaried executive who had been brought before the bench for wife abuse. Though the offender had broken three bones in his wife's face and had a history of wife abuse, the judge negotiated an informal settlement behind closed doors. He explained, "This is the best way of handling this type of situation. This is a family matter. They can settle this without airing a lot of dirty linen" (Davidson, 1977: 12).

In taking this perspective on wife abuse, in view of the fact that the wife is seeking legal intervention, the antithesis of privacy, the judge is essentially supporting the view that (1) the husband is the head of the household and can claim the right of privacy for all its members regardless of their wishes; and (2) that, in view of the husband and wife's competing interests, the husband's right to privacy is superior to his wife's right to forego privacy and request protection (Marcus, 1981: 1660).

KEEPING FAMILIES INTACT

Many judges feel reluctant to treat wife abuse as a crime out of a desire to keep the family intact and to avoid working a financial hardship on the family (U.S. Commission, 1982; Crane et al., 1985). Both views operate to the benefit of the abusive husband and apparently fail to consider the condition and wishes of the victim. It is the violence that is, in fact, destroying her and the family. Further, in bringing a case to court, the battered wife has evidently chosen physical safety over financial security. It is also the case that criminal offenders such as burglars are unable to argue financial hardship on their families as a basis for immunity from prosecution.

It is ironic that, given this desire to keep the family intact, a woman who does drop charges against her husband is often punished by the judiciary. Her case is frequently treated less seriously when she returns after further abuse. Judges have charged her with "crying wolf" and no longer deserving of the court's attention. One justice of the peace has made his policy clear that if a woman drops charges he will not accept another complaint from her for six months. A New Hampshire judge gave instruction to a police officer in the courtroom that "if she comes in and makes a complaint to you about her husband anymore, I don't want you to take it" (U.S. Commission, 1982: 48), giving license to her husband to do what he wants to his wife. One woman complained that the judge appeared to be more critical of her for not taking action against her husband before than for her husband's violence. In her words, the judge's attitude was "if you never tried to get help before, then I will not try to help you now" (U.S. Commission, 1982: 49). She was punished for years of sacrifice to keep the family together and was treated as the offending party for having played the role of patient wife and dutiful mother.

Such judicial bias against women who drop charges also ignores the reasons women do so—chief of which, according to one prosecutor, is fear. Over a one-year period, over 50% of the women who came in to drop charges in Santa Barbara, California, were accompanied by their abusers and were responding to threats of further abuse unless charges were dropped (Lerman, 1981: 2).

More enlightened prosecutors and judges have begun refusing the wife's request to drop charges or to amend the conditions of or withdraw a restraining order. Further, wives who refuse to testify as a victim will be subpoenaed as a witness. The intent of this approach is to communicate clearly to the abuser that his abuse is a violation of the law and the case is thus in the hands of the court. By doing so, it greatly reduces the pressure that an abuser can bring to bear on his victim in the belief that she can stop the court process. When the victim is responsible for filing a complaint, pressing charges, and testifying as the victim, the appearance to the abuser is that he is in trouble because of her not because of his behavior. Consequently, he will frequently exert his considerable power to have her withdraw the case. This "new" approach lifts from the victim the burden of stopping the violence and brings to bear the force and power of the justice system.

JUSTIFICATION FOR ABUSE

Many judges appear to have difficulty viewing cases of wife abuse as an action of state versus the offender and examining the merits of the case on the basis of criminal evidence. Instead, they often seem to see it as a case of the wife versus the husband, a personal relationship in which relationship dynamics and the wife's behavior play a dominant role.

A New York state family court judge attempted to defend this view in a letter to the editor of a local paper:

> Those who want to throw all these conflicts (crimes in the family) into the criminal court ask why should charges of disorderly conduct, harassment, or assault between family members—usually the husband the aggressor and the wife the victim—be treated any differently from a crime committed by a stranger?

> The answer begins with the fact that the men in many of these cases have no criminal records or histories of aggression against anyone except the complainant. The question of how to prevent further offenses and to protect the victim therefore differs greatly from the prevention and protection problem in cases of criminals who attack strangers. The motive lies in the personal relationship; it is not robbery [Armstrong, 1982: 5].

What relationship factors, then, appear to make assault on one's wife less a crime than assault on a stranger. A dominant factor appears to be what is viewed by the court as the wife's contribution to her own victimization—what did she do to deserve the abuse. In order to measure misbehavior/deviancy that would appear to have justified abuse, one must have a standard of appropriate behavior. For women, that standard requires that they be "chaste, gentle, gracious, ingenuous, good, clean, kind, virtuous, non-controversial and above reproach" (Stanko, 1985; Fox, 1977: 805). Society is less sympathetic to a woman's difficulty in living up to this standard than it is with a husband's attempts to maintain self-control in the face of her violations. Much of our social humor focuses on the man's efforts to maintain control as he is bombarded with the effects of a nagging, spendthrift, demanding wife. Thus when he does lose his temper, he is often seen as the victim.

An unfaithful, promiscuous wife is perhaps the most frequently offered justification by the abusing husband for his violence and may receive considerable weight in court. It should be noted that extreme irrational jealousy is one of the most common characteristics of abusing husbands. Many women are locked in their homes by husbands who fear they will stray sexually, are followed to and from work, are beaten when another man's eyes linger too long on her, and are constantly scrutinized for evidence of unfaithful behavior.

Even so, judges may be particularly open to charges that the woman was sexually unfaithful. In the words of a judge presiding over the case of a man who had killed his girlfriend for suspected sexual activity with another man:

> Those who engage in sexual relationships should realize that sex is one of the deepest and most powerful of human emotions and if you're playing with sex, you're playing with fire. And it might be that the conventions which surround sex, which some people think are old hat, are there to prevent people if possible from burning themselves [Stanko, 1985: 87].

Another judge counseled a woman who had been attacked by her husband while giving three male friends a ride home: "Running about in cars in the early hours of the morning with other men in the car is likely to attract the kind of response it did on this occasion" (Stanko, 1985: 95).

A judge's religious view of women may also influence his response to a perceived inadequacy in her wifely performance. An Ohio judge ordered a woman, appearing in court to testify regarding her husband's attacks, to study the Bible, attend the local fundamentalist church, and try harder to be a good wife. He then dismissed the charges against her husband and told the wife that he did not want to see her in court again (Jensen, 1977-1978: 585).

In short, a primary reason that judges continue to de facto decriminalize wife abuse appears to be the continued belief that a husband's rights and needs supersede his wife's and that a wife either asked for or deserved the abuse. According to Lynn Gold-Biken, who has conducted education efforts for judges in Pennsylvania, a significant obstacle to implementing that state's Protection From Abuse Act is "the innate prejudice that is brought by the bench to their role as judges—the attitudes that women like to be beaten, the attitudes that we will not put a man out of his house for this because it goes on in every family" (U.S. Commission, 1982: 57).

OTHER REASONS

In addition to stereotypic views of the male/female relationship, judges may also be effected by a lack of awareness of both the seriousness of the crime and the complex psychosocial dynamics of wife abuse. Little effort has been made, however, to educate them. During the National Judicial College's comprehensive training effort to inform judges of the needs of victims and witnesses, the problem of domestic abuse was rarely addressed. Little training has taken place on the state level either. The nationwide state training calendar of the National Association of Judicial Educators for 1985-1986 showed only four training programs for judges on wife abuse throughout the country. A training session on this subject at a 1985 conference for judges from six western states, however, found them to be extremely responsive to information on the nature of wife abuse as well as their role in stopping it (Crites, 1985b).

CONCLUSION

Though many judges are sensitive to the complex issues of wife abuse and are responding appropriately, a large group of judges are influenced, if not controlled, by their traditional, sexist beliefs. As a result, many women who turn to the courts for protection from abuse by their husbands, former husbands, or lovers are not only not afforded that protection but are left even more vulnerable to abuse for having tried. A man who feels justified in assaulting his wife or lover may become even more violent when she attempts to confront and stop his abuse through use of civil or criminal remedies, especially if those within the justice system appear to support him by refusing to apply sanctions.

Achieving judicial commitment to upholding laws against wife abuse will undoubtedly require a multidimensional approach. Certainly a major effort should be conducted to educate judges. Such training should not only address the nature, extent, and seriousness of the crime but also the conscious or unconscious prejudices that judges may bring to these cases.

Appeals should be filed in cases where the decision flies in the face of reason and unbiased judgment. The Denver court judge referred to earlier was removed from hearing domestic violence cases and the sentence changed to reflect the seriousness of the crime as a result of an appeal and public outcry.

Those working on behalf of battered women should not feel hesitance in publicizing cases in which judges refuse to uphold the letter and intent of the law. Efforts should be made to remove the judge from the bench if the abuse of his authority continues.

Momentum to change the justice system response to wife abuse is gaining. Successful suits against police departments are forcing changes in departmental policies regarding arrest of the abuser. Public awareness of the nature and extent of the problem is supporting women in recognizing that they are not alone and that they have a right to be free from abuse. State legislation is now in place in most states that recognizes the needs of the victims. Judges should not be permitted to continue decriminalizing wife abuse based on their personal prejudices and belief systems.

REFERENCES

Armstrong, L. (1982). The Home Front: Notes from the Family War Zone. New York: McGraw-Hill.

Attorney General (1984) Task Force on Family Violence Final Report. Washington, DC: Government Printing Office.

Breines, W. and Linda Gordon (1983) "The new scholarship on family violence." Signs (Spring): 490-531.

Brown, Angela (1985) "Assault and homicide at home: when battered women murder in self defense," in M. J. Sakes and L. Saxe (eds.) Advances in Applied Social Psychology, Vol. 3. Hillsdale, NJ: Lawrence Erlbaum Associates.

Crane, S. W., P. Pahl, J. Young, J. Shenk, J. Mort-O'Brein, K. Kertson, and R. Ryan (1985) "The Washington state domestic violence act: an evaluation Project Part II." Response (Fall): 9-13.

Crites, Laura (1985a) "A judicial guide to understanding wife abuse." Judges Journal 24, 3 (Summer).

Crites, Laura (1985b) Training session conducted for Montana State Supreme Court at Western Regional Judicial Conference.

Davidson, Terry (1977) "Wifebeating: a recurring phenomenon throughout history," pp. 2-24 in Maria Roy (ed.) Battered Women. New York: Van Nostrand.

Davis, Elizabeth G. (1973) The First Sex. Baltimore: Penguin.

Fahnestock, Katie (1985) Personal communication (10/29).

Folis, Ed (1987) Unpublished research paper.

Fox, Green L. (1977) "Nice girl: social control of women through a value construct." Sign 2, 4: 805-817.

Grim, Nancy E. (1983) "Domestic relations: legal responses to wife beating theory and practice in Ohio." Akron Law Review 16 (Spring): 705-745.

International Association of Chiefs of Police (1976) Police Training Keys #245 and #246. Gaithersberg, MD.

Jensen, L. (1977-1978) "Battered women and the law." Victimology 2: 585-589.

Jones, Ann (1981) Women Who Kill. New York: Fawcett Columbine.

Lerman, Lisa (1980) "State legislation on domestic violence." Response 2, 12 (August/September).

Lerman, Lisa (1981) "Criminal prosecution of wife beaters." Response (January/February).

Lindsey, K. (1978) "When battered women strike back: murder in self defense." Viva (September): 58-59, 66-74.

Loving, Nancy (1980) Responding to Spouse Abuse and Wife Beating: A Guide for Police. Washington, DC: Police Executive Forum.

Marcus, Maria L. (1981) "Conjugal violence: the law of force and the force of law." California Law Review 69: 1657-1733.

Martin, Del (1976) Battered Wives. New York: Pocket Books

New Hampshire Advisory Committee to the U.S. Commission on Civil Rights (1980) Domestic Violence Reform: One Year Later.

Parnas, L. (1970) "Judicial response to intra-family violence." Minnesota Law Review 54: 585.

Parnas, L. (1973) "Prosecutorial and judicial handling of family violence." Criminal Law Bulletin 9: 733, 747-748.

Price, Alice (1985) Personal communication with San Luis Valley, CO, attorney who represents battered women (5/24).

Quarm, Daisy and Martin D. Schwartz (1983) "Legal reform and the criminal court: the case of domestic violence." N. Kentucky Law Review (Spring): 199-225

Roy, Maria [ed.] (1977) Battered Women. New York: Van Nostrand Reinhold.

Sherman, Lawrence and Richard Berk (1984) "The Minneapolis domestic violence experiment." Police Foundation Reports (April).

Stanko, Betsy (1985) Intimate Intrusions: Women's Experience of Male Violence. London: Routledge & Kegan Paul.

Steinmetz, Robert L. (1982) "Ex parte ruled constitutional." Journal of Family Law 21 (November): 163-167.

U.S. Commission on Civil Rights (1982) Under the Rule of Thumb: Battered Women and the Administration of Justice. Washington, DC: Government Printing Office.

3

SEXUAL ASSAULT:
THE SECOND VICTIMIZATION

Cassie C. Spencer

Women live in an environment of violence. It occurs in the form of "street hassling" and noxious male comments about a woman's body; it occurs with exhibitionism; it occurs with wife battering, incest, and rape (Leidig, 1981). Even though numerous studies have indicated an underreporting of these violent acts, the available numbers regarding their occurrence are staggering. In a randomly selected sample of 930 women, 44% reported at least one experience of completed or attempted rape (Russell, 1984). Based on data from the same survey, it was estimated that there is at least a 46% chance that a woman will become a victim of rape or attempted rape sometime during her life (Russell, 1984). Rape statistics have been rising since 1933 (except for a brief interlude during the 1940s), and the rate of increase for incidents of rape is greater than other crimes of violence (Bowker, 1978, 1981).

Children are also vulnerable. In fact, Russell's research indicated that 38% of the women respondents had at least one experience of incestuous and/or extrafamilial sexual abuse before they reached the age of 18 (1984). Judith Herman (1981) cites numerous other surveys and personal accounts that indicate sexual abuse to be a problem of potentially monumental proportions (Kinsey et al., 1953; Landis, 1956; Gagnon, 1965; Finkelhor, 1979; Maisch, 1972; Lukianowicz, 1972; Meiselman, 1978; Justice and Justice, 1979; Angelou, 1970; Butler, 1978; Brady, 1979).

These percentages are frightening, but the impact becomes even more alarming when compared with the low numbers of these crimes that are reported. Russell's survey (1984) found that only 9.5% of rape cases, 6%

of extrafamilial child sexual abuse cases, and 2% of incestuous child sexual abuse cases are made known to police. It has been speculated that one of the reasons for this underreporting may be the treatment these victims receive within the legal system (Karmen, 1982; Robin, 1977). For instance, a rape victim's past sexual relationships historically have been fair game for defense attorneys to reveal in the courtroom as proof that the woman's testimony was questionable and that in reality she consented to the violent act. Many cases of child sexual abuse have been dismissed because children were not "competent" to testify, or they had been badgered and confused on the witness stand until the jury no longer perceived them as credible. Young girls also have been charged in court with being exceptionally seductive, thereby diminishing the adult males' responsibility for having sexually molested them.

However, the women's movement has raised the public consciousness and, as a result, there has been a recent trend in many states to make changes in legislation and courtroom procedures to address these issues. Forty states now have "rape shield" laws that bar evidence of a woman's sexual history from the court proceedings (*Oakland Tribune*, 1985). In an effort to curb child sexual abuse, 47 states have introduced or passed legislation that alters traditional legal procedures, including the allowance of videotaped testimony and the abolishment of requirements to prove children "competent" to testify (*Wall Street Journal*, 1985).

But will these efforts make a difference in decreasing the second victimization that occurs in the courtroom? This chapter will address this question by reviewing the attitudes regarding women, children, and sexual assault, studies of legislative reform, and their impact in the judicial arena.

ATTITUDES

Myths and stereotypes about women have persisted since the beginning of time. Two in particular seem to dominate cases of rape: woman as "virtue" and woman as the "lying temptress."

The misogynist image of the woman as the "lying temptress" in Western culture can be traced to the story of Adam and Eve in the Garden of Eden (Tong, 1984). Eve seduced Adam, destroyed his innocence, and was punished by having to bear children in pain. Augustine, the Bishop of Hippo, expanded upon this story and concluded that woman's one role in life was procreation, that pleasure in sex was sinful, and that the hope for woman was in resurrection where her body then will be minus reproductive organs (Tong, 1984). Echoing these "teachings," religious leaders through the ages "claimed that because of her sexual being and reproductive function, woman was less rational and less spiritual than man; that is, less able to distinguish between truth and falsity" (Tong, 1984).

This image of the woman as a liar has tainted rape laws and produced stringent rules of evidence and requirements for proof (Tong, 1984; Robin, 1977). It also has influenced the minds of jurors. A woman perceived as "virtuous" on the witness stand can have more hope that the rapist will be convicted. Barbara F. Reskin, a professor of sociology at the University of Michigan, conducted an investigation of jurors' attitudes and discovered they were more likely to treat a case of rape as serious if the woman appeared "chaste" (*Oakland Tribune*, 1985). However, if a woman is perceived as the "seductress," chances of a conviction are slim. Existing data shows that conviction rates for rape are lower than for other felonies (Bulkley, 1981; Lloyd, 1981). It would appear that jury attitudes more often favor the defendant and not the victim (Tong, 1984; Robin, 1977; Brownmiller, 1975; Bailey and Rothblatt, 1985).

Rape is the only crime where the victim must prove nonconsent. This requirement also is grounded in the myth that women lie and make false reports. This attitude was most explicitly expressed by the cautionary instructions given to jurors that were based on words of Sir Matthew Hale, Lord Justice of the King's Bench, in the seventeenth century. He said that a rape accusation is "easily to be made and hard to be proved, and harder to be defended by the party accused, tho' never so innocent." Although these instructions have been abolished in most states, the beliefs still are perpetuated by the fear that men will be wrongly condemned and become victims of women's unjust accusations. In actuality, the data indicate that false reports of sexual assault are no more frequent than false reports of other crimes (Buckley, 1981; Lloyd, 1981).

Other dogmatic presumptions that have convicted women of "consenting" to the rape have been the Freudian theory regarding women, namely, that they are masochistic by nature, so they welcome rape to satisfy their self-destructive needs; that women in general have personality problems, are hysterical, and thus have no credibility; and that previous sexual relationships (particularly if they are viewed as nontraditional) are tantamount to nymphomania. In essence, women are lying when they cry "rape." These beliefs are summed up in the quote from a judge, "No woman can be raped against her will" (Marsh et al., 1982: 62).

The child victim of sexual abuse fares no better. She also is accused of "seducing" the perpetrator. An example is found in a quote from the popular book, *Lolita*, when the protagonist proclaims, "I had thought that months, perhaps years, would elapse before I dared to reveal myself to Dolores Haze, but by six she was wide awake, and by six fifteen we were technically lovers. I am going to tell you something very strange; it was she who seduced me" (Nabokov, 1966: 122-123). In addition, children, even more than women, are feared as liars, the meaning of which is softened with the argument that children are prone to fantasize, are easily persuaded and misled, and, therefore, cannot be credible witnesses.

All of the above attitudes represent the underlying problem of blaming the victim for the sexual assault (Leidig, 1981). It is important to understand why this occurs, because the basis for this phenomenon affects the effectiveness of legislative and courtroom procedural reforms.

BLAMING THE VICTIM

There are several reasons why rape victims may be blamed for contributing to or causing their own victimization. First is the influence of the "just world hypothesis" that affects our reaction to all victims. This hypothesis stems from our need to live in a world that we see as predictable. Thus we want to believe that fairness forbids that nasty things happens to nice people. The victim either wasn't nice or the victim precipitated the nastiness (see Kushner, 1981).

Another reason is that the sexual victimization of women is often seen in the courtroom through the male perspective. "A woman's behavior is not portrayed from a woman's point of view but from an understanding of women's behavior from a man's point of view" (Stanko, 1985: 92). Because of different socialization of men and women, visiting a man's apartment, accepting a ride home from a party, going out for drinks and dinner with a man, when viewed through the male lens, may be seen as a woman's invitation to sexual relations. "Women's sexuality is seen as underscoring women's relationships to men; any 'occasional' release of male aggression towards women and their sexuality can be portrayed as 'natural' behavior" (Stanko, 1985: 92).

Comments from judges underscore the influence of the male perspective on their view of rape victims. Examples include the Connecticut judge who dismissed charges against a man involved in a gang rape because of temporary impotence with the comment, "You can't blame someone for trying. This man tried and failed" (*Ladies Home Journal*, 1983: 145).

Finally, it is argued that blaming the rape victim permits the continuation of a social structure that controls and subordinates women (Leidig, 1981; Klein, 1981; Karmen, 1982; Marsh et al., 1982).

> Sexual harassment, wife-beating, and rape are all crimes in which male offenders try to exert control over female victims. But victim-blaming (has the effect of) depoliticizing and personalizing acts that are inherently connected to the distribution of power and legitimacy of authority, and thereby obscures the sources and consequences of crimes against women [Karmen, 1982: 193].

In other words, rather than strive for attitudinal changes that would effectively stop the violence or threats of violence against women and children, and ensure economical, political, and psychological equality, blame is placed on the victim, and the sexual assault is either dismissed as never happening or as the victim having caused it. The woman/child is lying, the woman/child seduced the perpetrator, or the woman is promiscuous and, therefore, must have consented.

LEGISLATIVE REFORM—RAPE

The focus of rape reform law varies from state to state but, in general, has addressed these issues: redefining rape, establishing "degree" of rape, changing resistance and consent standards, barring evidence of previous sexual history, implementing tougher penalties, rewriting language so that it is "neuter," and deleting requirements for corroborating evidence. Many of these changes have taken place only within the past decade after years of archaic statutes.

It is no coincidence that this ameliorative mood followed on the heels of the women's liberation movement. Presumably, with these revisions, women have gained more power to obtain justice for their victimization. But have they? And if so, to what extent? The authors of the study of Michigan's rape reform laws imply that legislative changes are not enough and state that "criminal justice"—in particular the judicial process—is a system in which the behavior of participants is influenced more by informal norms and expectations than by external forces" (Marsh et al., 1982: 5). For example, in 22 states, rapists now can be sentenced with life imprisonment, and, in Mississippi, rape is punishable by death (*Oakland Tribune*, 1984). Yet one study clearly revealed that the willingness to prosecute and sentence a rapist is still determined by judgments of a woman's character:

> While some of the public attitude data support a "get tough" law-and-order approach to rape, judgements on specific rape situations suggest that this view applies only to "real rapes" and that there is a strong public defensiveness against innocent men being trapped in rape charges by vindictive or disreputable women [Williams and Holmes, 1981: 177].

A "real rape" has been distinguished from a nonrape for police officers by classifications of "unprecipitated" (good) and "precipitated" (bad) rapes (Tong, 1984). The "good" rape has all the elements prosecutors like to take into court: strong evidence of nonconsent such as victim injuries, the presence of a weapon, breaking and entering, and stranger-on-stranger rape. The "bad" rape is the acquaintance rape, the rape with no evidence of resistance, the rape of a prostitute. These distinctions reflect the societal and legal expectations for women to be chaste aud resist an attack to the utmost to "defend her treasure" (Brownmiller, 1975: 433). The fact seems to remain that substantive change is still dependent on public attitudes and society's distribution of power. This theory will be explored in more depth by examining the impact of major reforms that have focused on legal requirements that seem to have originated from the myths of women as liars and seductresses.

CORROBORATION

In the past, strict corroboration rules made it nearly impossible to obtain a conviction. For example, in New York, 2415 rape complaints eventually led to only 18 convictions. For this reason, most states now have either abandoned or modified the requirements (Tong, 1984; Robin, 1977). Yet eliminating the corroboration rule is one thing; obtaining convictions without it is another.

> When a jury has only the word of the complainant against the defendant that a rape even occurred, the jury will experience considerable discomfort. That is, in a judicial system that systematically favors defendants, juries are going to have difficulty with uncorroborated rape cases [Tong, 1984: 105].

In fact, Bailey and Rothblatt (1985) cite numerous court decisions requiring corroborative evidence for conviction (*State v. Fisher* [1973] 190 Neb742, 212 NW2d 568; *United States v. Wiley*, 492 F2d 547 [D.C. Cir. 10/12/73]; *People v. Tucker*, 363 NYS2d 180 [NY 1975]; *People v. Rodriguez* (1978) 58 Ill App3d 775, 16 Ill Dec. 187, 374 NE2d 1063; *State v. Phillips* [1979, Mo App] 585 SW2d 517; *People v. Raker* [1979] 75 Ill App3d 975, 31 Ill Dec. 650, 394 NE2d 852).

NONCONSENT AND SEXUAL HISTORY AS EVIDENCE

Regardless of statutes that have dropped the resistance requirement as proof of nonconsent and curtailed the allowance of sexual history as evidence, the basic question still rests on whether the sexual act occurred between two consenting adults. Interpretation of "nonconsent" in the initial rape laws meant the victim had to resist to the utmost in order to prove she did not want the sexual encounter.

> In a leading decision on the meaning of "utmost resistance", the Wisconsin Supreme Court said the phrase requires "the most vehement exercise of every physical means or faculty within the woman's power to resist the penetration of her person, and this must be shown to persist until the offense is consummated," and it overturned the rapist's conviction in that case because the victim, facing a larger and stronger combatant, had simply tried to escape. The court ruled that "resistance is opposing force to force, not retreating from force" [Robin, 1977].

In some cases, these resistances resulted in death. "Rape has been the *only* violent crime requiring proof of resistance by the victim" (Marsh et al., 1982: 21). Mary Ann Largen, policy analyst for the Center for Women Policy Studies in Washington, has been interviewing numerous judges and lawyers on the need for rape law reform. According to her research, the majority of states still retain the consent issue as a major element in the revised laws, although it has been modified to become the "relative resistive standard" (Largen, 1985). This means the woman no longer has to fight until the point of death or serious injury to prove nonconsent, but she still has to show some resistance whether it be screaming, bruising, or the like. For example, "one defense attorney recounted a case under the new law in which he requested the judge to instruct the jury that consent was implied because the victim did not scream when she was attacked. The judge granted the request" (Marsh et al., 1982: 59).

Ms. Largen analyzed three rape reform models. In Florida, force and consent continue to be key elements for the defense. In Georgia, as in most southern states, resistance is still required, and "reform" statutes reflect the old law mentality. In other words, a woman cannot do anything, or neglect to do anything, that would be construed as "asking for it." Michigan exemplified the most innovative change by turning the element of proof from the prosecution to the defendant. Rather than victim resistance, "the statute regards evidence of coercion used by the actor, not of the victim's unwillingness, as tantamount to non-consent" (Marsh et al., 1982: 23).

Court decisions regarding this issue range from the Indiana Supreme Court statement that "there is no requirement that a woman scream or physically resist when by such an act she may very well anger or frustrate her assailant and thereby endanger her life further" (Bailey and Rothblatt, 1985; *Spaulding v. State* [1978, Ind] 373 NE2d 165), to the overturned conviction of rape in a Hawaii Appellate Court because the element of resistance required by statute was not established beyond a reasonable doubt (Bailey and Rothblatt, 1985; *State v. Lama* [1981, Hawaii App] 624 P2d 1374).

In yet another case, a Manhattan judge ruled that "conquest by con job" was seduction and not rape (e.g., the man used deception and impersonation rather than physical force; the woman did not actively resist or struggle). The judge's concluding statement in the decision: "Bachelors and other men on the make, fear not. It is still not illegal to feed a girl a line" (Robin, 1977).

One of the tactics used to prove victim consent was, and often still is, an in-depth examination by the defense of the woman's previous sexual life-style. The argument, validated by jurors' verdicts of "not guilty" for the defendant, is that if the woman is perceived as "promiscuous" or labeled a prostitute, she automatically is suspect and guilty of consent (Tong, 1984). The passage of "rape shield laws" would appear, on the surface, to eliminate this information from court proceedings. However, as with all laws, there are exceptions. In *People v. Mandel* ([1978, 2d Dept] 61 App. Div. 563, 403 NYS 2d 63), the court acknowledged the statute making past sexual conduct inadmissible in sex offense cases. However, it referenced the exception to this legislation that such evidence may be admissible if it is relevant. Thus evidence that the complainant had engaged in sexual intercourse with men other than the defendants should have been allowed.

Other exceptions include a complainant's reputation for unchastity (*McElveen v. State* [1982, Fla AppDl] 415 So 2d 746); previous sexual conduct and actions similar to those displayed with the defendant (*Winfield v. Commonwealth* [1983, 225 Va 211, 301 SE2d 15]); complainant's prior sexual acts with men other than the defendant when the physical condition of the complainant is relied upon as corroboration evidence (*State v. Murphy* [1976] 134 Vt 106, 353 A2d 346); and prior consent by the complainant to sexual intercourse with the defendant (*United States v. Kasto* [1978, CA8SD] 584 F2d 268, cert. den. 440 UX 930, 59L Ed2d 486, 995 Ct. 1267).

Additional reasons for the admission of previous sexual conduct have been when the woman had a psychiatric history, a criminal record, a history of making rape reports, or a history of prostitution. With these allowances, there seems to be no recognition that regardless of previous sexual history and behaviors, even one experience can be rape if the woman does not want the sexual encounter.

Much of the admission of sexual history is based upon the judge's discretion; he can order an "in camera" hearing to determine the appropriateness of including this information in the trial proceedings. The following quote from a judge (who vowed he always ruled out such evidence) silences a victim's chances for justice as effectively as the pounding of a gavel: "What does sex past have to do with a case unless she's a prostitute? Or if she's out hitch-hiking with a short skirt and no bra, she asked for it and I'll admit [that evidence]. That isn't past sexual history information and therefore it's not restricted" (Marsh et al., 1982: 61).

The authors of the Michigan study of rape law reform state that "the occasional but continuing improper use of sexual history evidence would seem to reflect biases that are pervasive despite the legislative attempt to hamper judicial discretion" (Marsh et al., 1982: 61). Judges' attitudes do influence their decisions. One study of 38 Philadelphia judges who try rape cases revealed that their personal attitude toward the victim would affect their interpretation of the evidence (Bohmer, 1974).

Despite Michigan's rape shield law, which did reduce the importance of sexual history, three-fourths of the defense attorneys said they sought this information, and many were able to introduce it as evidence (Marsh et al., 1982). Once it is revealed, even if omitted from consideration by a sustained objection from the prosecution, the damage to the victim is done. A study into jurors' decisions regarding rape found that behaviors most likely to prejudice the jury against the rape victim included perceived promiscuity, keeping late hours, going alone into bars, use of birth control pills, giving birth to an illegitimate child, or having the same address as a boyfriend (*Oakland Tribune*, 1984).

One breakthrough for women in proving nonconsent has been the recognition by the American Psychological Association in 1980 of the "rape trauma syndrome" as a legitimate disorder. One of the first studies of this syndrome was published in 1977 by Ann Wolbert Burgess and Lynda Lytle Holmstrom, who described the manifestations in two phases. The first is the acute phase of tremendous disorganization. The woman exhibits a wide range of emotions from shock to fear, anxiety, and anger. Primary feelings are fear of violence and death. Another reaction is to blame herself for the rape. She also experiences somatic reactions such as gastrointestinal pains, actual physical trauma like bruising and soreness, and skeletal muscle tension. The second phase is a more long-term process. Part of it involves reorganizing her life with motor activity such as changing residence or telephone number. Nightmares are present as are numerous phobias resulting from the trauma (e.g., fear of being alone, sexual fears, fear of people behind them). With this recognition and legitimacy, it is argued that a display of these symptoms in a woman who reports rape should be admitted as evidence that sexual victimization has occurred.

Use of this diagnosis in the courtroom as proof of nonconsent has been controversial. It has been upheld in Kansas, Montana, and Arizona and denied in Minnesota, Missouri, and Oregon (*Oakland Tribune*, 1985). Arguments for its use emphasize that it is a real psychological occurrence to rape victims and thus assists the credibility of the woman. Opponents contend that the symptoms are common, and could be related to other stresses besides rape. Yet the hope is that once allowed as testimony, the conviction rate will increase. As it stands now, jurors still appear reluctant to condemn the male victim as a rapist unless the woman puts up a horrendous fight and her trauma is very physical and very visible. Judges also continue to be influenced by the presence or absence of physical injuries. One judge stated that unless there was extensive physical trauma, a hostile vagina will not admit a penis (Robin, 1977).

MARITAL RAPE

The traditional definition of rape is "*illicit* carnal knowledge of a female by force and against her will (Black, 1968, emphasis added). This implies that in a legal marriage, no rape can occur because the offender is not "illicit." The source of this comes from a statement by Sir Matthew

Hale that a husband cannot be guilty of rape because of the consent and contract between a husband and wife and the consequent "wifely duty" to engage in sex when the husband so desires and demands (Tong, 1984). The reasons devised to support this edict have been that it prevents wives from making false complaints; rape laws are designed to protect women from evil strangers, not husbands; if women can charge husbands with rape, it will prevent their reconciliation; there would be insurmountable proof problems; and the state should not intervene in the sanctity of marriage (Tong, 1984; Morris, 1981).

Changes are being made, but it is a tedious process. In 43 states, women cannot charge their husbands with rape (Morris, 1981). Some decisions support the marital exemption rule (*People v. Kubasiak* [1980] 98 Mich. App529, 296 NW2d 298); others reject it. In *State v. Smith* ([1981] 85 NJ 193, 426 A2d 38), a man can be convicted of the rape of a woman despite legal marriage where the act was accompanied by violence and the couple had been living separately, though not legally separated, for six years (Bailey and Rothblatt, 1985).

As a rule, however, states are beginning to question the rightness of the marital exception rule. "Many authorities are increasingly convinced that what makes rape wrong is not that it takes place outside the marital chamber, but simply that it is a blatant instance of *nonconsensual* sexual intercourse" (Tong, 1984: 960).

In summary, though it has not proven to be a panacea, rape reform legislation is nonetheless essential for the ultimate goal of justice. The study of Michigan's reform laws (Marsh et al., 1982) did show an increase in convictions and a lessening of the victim's trauma. However, it indicated also (as did the other studies cited) that the woman's character and credibility still remain the central focus. Depending on each state's legislation, judges still can and are admitting sexual history as evidence. The burden of proof regarding consent still lies with the victim. Old attitudes remain to influence jurors' and judges' decisions. Woman are still at risk for "date rape" and "acquaintance rape," and beliefs persist that rape is easily charged and needs to be rigorously investigated to protect males from false accusations. It seems clear that other strategies aside from revised statutes are critically important. "If rape emanates from our social system and its race and sex-based inequality, the problem will not be substantially alleviated without radical social change, and ultimately a more egalitarian social system must be the goal of the anti-rape movement" (Williams and Holmes, 1981: 171).

LEGISLATIVE REFORM—
CHILD SEXUAL ASSAULT

Recently, public outcry against child sexual abuse has escalated to unprecedented proportions. This rage has been channeled into two primary avenues to confront and end the atrocity: development and implementation of numerous prevention programs and legislative reform. Prevention programs seem to be beneficial in that they arm the child with both knowledge of potential dangers and limited measures to escape harm. It must be noted, however, that no study to date has measured the effectiveness of these efforts nor the possible damage to a child who says "no" to a perpetrator who is physically abusive as well. Additionally, the question must be asked as to why the responsibility for prevention of a violent act against children has been placed on the child? Why has not the focus instead been on stopping the perpetrator before the act can be initiated? It must be noted that 97% of the perpetrators of child sexual assault are men and 75% of the victims are girls (Rogers and Thomas, 1984). Again, the answer seems to lie in the maintenance of men's power over women and children. To stop the perpetrator effectively, as with rape, social equality is essential. "Real changes will only occur when 'primary prevention' is instituted—e.g. the reduction or elimination of sexism" (Leidig, 1981: 205).

Legislative reform in child sexual assault has assumed two primary objectives: increase the chances for conviction as well as the penalties for the crime and reduce the legal traumatization to the child. The first objective includes such revisions as incorporating tougher penalties and reporting requirements, abolishing age requirements as a qualification to be a competent witness, and abolishing requirements for corroborative evidence. The second objective is addressed by allowing videotaped testimony and providing exceptions to the hearsay rule.

Many of these changes have been a step in the right direction, but a more in-depth look reveals that the overt goals are tainted and slowed by the attitudes and power control discussed at the beginning of this chapter.

Perpetrators of child sexual abuse, in the majority of states, can be prosecuted under both criminal child sex offense statutes and incest statutes. The primary difference between the two is that many states limit the act of incest only to sexual intercourse; thus to prosecute sexual assault such as fondling or fellatio, charges also must be filed under the criminal child sexual offense provisions. Both are often invoked for purposes of plea-bargaining. Moreover, most incest statutes do not mention victim age requirements, while criminal child sex offense statutes limit the victim's age to anywhere from 11 to 17 (Kocen and Bulkley, 1981). There has been growing debate whether or not to repeal incest laws (Bulkley, 1981). Some arguments in favor of repeal are that the incest laws are redundant, provide lower penalties, and create more difficult proof problems (Wulken and Bulkley, 1981). Opponents argue that the incest statutes provide protection for some age groups (predominantly those 16 to 18) that are not included in many criminal statutes. While both sides have some validity, it would seem that what is needed is a statute that covers *all* the concerns (e.g., age definition of child sexual abuse, penalties, and so on). However, in outlining some problems that seem especially reflective of attitudinal bias, the following discussion will focus on the criminal child sex offense statutes.

Some of the major trends in the revision of laws include clearly defining sexual acts (as opposed to just labeling it "carnal knowledge"), instituting levels of penalties based on the age of the victim, and protecting children from family members as well as strangers (Kocen and Bulkley, 1981). These are improvements over previous legislation, and age-old attitudes are fading. But they are still present. For example, although adolescents now are provided some protection where they were not before, the analysis revealed that 34 states reduce the penalty for child sexual abuse as the victim grows older. In some states, maximum penalties were only 1 to 1.5 years for victimization of an adolescent. This seems to reflect the attitude that women "ask for it." As the girl child approaches womanhood, it could be deduced that there is a corollary increase in the belief that "she wanted it. " Consequently, the perpetrator is not as guilty and should not be punished as harshly.

A major reform has been the trend to eliminate the requirement of corroborative evidence in child sexual abuse cases. As discussed in *Child Sexual Abuse and the Law* (Bulkley, 1981), corroboration is a necessity either because it is required by statute or is needed to dispel myths surrounding child sexual victimization, or both. These myths consist of the fears that complainants frequently make false reports, that the judge or jury will automatically be sympathetic toward the woman or child and prejudiced against the accused, and that children are susceptible to overt or covert influences and prone to fantasize.

The findings of this report regarding the legal requirements for corroboration are as follows. Three jurisdictions mandate corroborative evidence for prosecution in *all* cases of child sexual assault. Three states require it for only some offenses (e.g., statutory rape in Georgia and sexual assault against adolescents in Mississippi and Ohio). In Texas, corroborative evidence must be introduced if the crime is reported six months after the event. Idaho requires corroboration when the "complainant's reputation for veracity and chastity has been impeached," and Illinois requires it if the child's testimony is not clear and convincing. None of the other states requires corroboration, but in 11 states, it is judicially mandated if the child's testimony is inherently improbable or has been impeached.

Thus approximately 30 states do not require corroborative evidence for prosecution of child sexual abuse cases. The conclusion of the Bulkley report was that "the corroboration rule as a legal requirement is a rule whose time has passed" (Lloyd, 1981: 114). In practice, however, because of ingrained attitudes regarding children in general and their credibility in particular, chances of conviction may be slim if not impossible without it. In fact, the second most cited reason for not prosecuting intrafamily offenders was a lack of corroborative evidence; the first was incompetency of the child witness (Wulken and Bulkley, 1983: 3). A recent example of this was uncovered in the *Report on Scott County Investigations* (Humphrey, 1985), where a county attorney dismissed charges against 21 citizens accused of child sexual abuse. Although there was "no doubt that a number of children in Scott County were victims of sexual abuse" (Humphrey, 1985: 17), one of the compelling reasons for the dismissals was the lack of corroborative evidence, particularly as it was in conjunction with impeached credibility of the children.

Even if corroborative evidence is sought, it is elusive. Eyewitness testimony is usually nonexistent. Medical evidence is often scarce either because the sexual abuse took the form of something other than intercourse or the report was delayed for days, months, or sometimes years due to the psychological dynamics surrounding its occurrence. Behavioral indicators may have the most promise for use as corroborative evidence; however, the defense can, and often does, introduce doubt in the minds of judges and jurors. For instance, psychosomatic complaints are attributed to other stresses aside from sexual abuse. Play or behavior that includes sexual components inappropriate to the child's development level is termed "seductive" and "promiscuous." Suggestions to use expert testimony linking a child's testimony and other evidence to the "child sexual abuse syndrome" encounters due process problems relating to its use in criminal prosecution.

The end result seems to be the child's word against the defendant's. In this type of battle, in most cases, the child will lose.

Twenty-three states now have abolished requirements that children be shown competent in order to testify (*USA Today*, 1985). Nevertheless, even though the belief persists of their incompetency, recent research has introduced convincing evidence to repudiate this position. Gail S. Goodman and Vicki Helgeson (1986) report the following findings. Although children recalled less than adults, what they did recall was just as accurate. In fact, adults tended to make more errors than children. One of the biggest hesitancies in admitting children's testimony has been the firm conviction that children are open to suggestive comments and, therefore, will easily go along with statements that are untrue. But in Goodman's research, when leading questions were asked about the central event as opposed to peripheral events, children were as resistive to being misled as adults.

Time and again, though, children's competency and credibility are challenged. Part of this stems from a protective or defensive strategy to deny that the sexual molestation occurred. If it did not occur, the perpetrator cannot be held responsible.

This persistent belief that the child may be an incompetent witness may be perpetuated by legal tactics that are used with children. Goodman and Helgeson state that "while children can be accurate witnesses if handled properly, the adversary system is often harsh in its dealings with children" (1986). The harshness is evident in a variety of practices. One is repetitive interviews of the child regarding the molestation. It is argued that the numerous actors involved (e.g., police, social workers, doctors, district attorneys) need this information firsthand for effective prosecution. Yet, requiring the child to repeat the events again and again borders on abusiveness and might confuse the child. Consequently, there is a trend to reduce the number of interviews for the child, but one study revealed that only one-third of the jurisdictions have procedures for joint interviews (Wulken and Bulkley, 1983).

Other traumas are encountered when the child must testify in court. As with any case involving adults, the defense has the right to cross-examine the child. The major goal of this procedure is to discredit the witness.

> Attorneys may attempt to confuse the child by the use of double negatives, "big" words, and difficult sentence constructions.... A defense

attorney's accusatory manner may intimidate the child. Furthermore, the attorney may undermine the child's confidence by asking about peripheral detail or about the specific order of events that occurred many months or years ago [Goodman and Helgeson, 1985].

The cross-examination can sometimes last for days. In the well-publicized McMartin Pre-school case in California, one child was cross-examined by seven different attorneys for 16 days (*Oakland Tribune*, 1985c).

Many child advocates have passed or have attempted to pass legislation to prevent this type of psychological harm to the child victim. Some of these changes have been to replace the child's physical presence in the courtroom with a videotaped testimony; to take the child's testimony outside the presence of the jury or public (one-third of the jurisdictions have procedures for this); or to be lenient in granting hearsay exceptions. For example, while hearsay exceptions have been allowed for some time (such as the "excited utterance" rule), many jurisdictions also are considering a "residual" exception (Goodman and Helgeson, 1986). With this, a judge may consider any statement by a child to be credible, no matter the time that has elapsed, and may permit an adult to testify about the child's utterance rather than requiring the child to testify. Some believe that this hearsay exception is one of the most effective changes that can be made in protecting children from the courtroom trauma (Steinhauser, 1986).

While these changes are innovative and have the child's best interests at heart, they may not withstand the legal tests of court decisions. Many critics of these legislative revisions claim that they violate the Fourteenth Amendment right to due process, the Sixth Amendment right to confront a witness, and the First Amendment right for the public to attend criminal trials. In the situation regarding the use of a videotaped deposition, it would seem that the defendant's Sixth Amendment rights would not be jeopardized. According to the U.S. Supreme Court decision in *California v. Green* (399 U.S. 149 [1970]), three principles underlying the right to confrontation were identified: the need to subject the witness to the oath, the usefulness of cross-examination in sorting out the truth, and the need for the jury to observe the witness' demeanor in order for the jury to evaluate his or her veracity (Bulkley, 1981). All of these principles seemingly would be upheld through the videotaped deposition. This can be arranged one of two ways. In the first, the child would be examined and cross-examined with the defendant being physically present. The intention of this tactic is to prevent the child from testifying in a stressful and overwhelming courtroom environment. In the second method, the child is examined and cross-examined, but the defendant would *not* be within the child's sight. Instead, the defendant would view the proceedings behind a two-way mirror or on a monitor and be able to halt the testimony with a buzzer in order to confer with counsel. The additional advantage to this would eliminate the necessity for the child to face the perpetrator. Problems arise with both these strategies, however. Many courts are not yet equipped to tape testimony with the use of two-way mirrors or monitors. In addition, the ability of a jury to encounter the child face-to-face may be extremely valuable for eliciting sympathy and thus hopefully a conviction (Steinhauser, 1986). Finally, if courts were to begin using two-way mirrors for this process, this practice may not hold up to constitutional challenge. Based on an appellate decision in *United States v. Benfield* (593 F2d 815 [8th Cir., 1979]), the right to confrontation may require a *face-to-face meeting*. In this case, a kidnap victim was extremely traumatized and subsequently hospitalized on a psychiatric ward as a result of the crime. Her testimony was videotaped, but the defendant was forced to observe behind a two-way mirror. The appellate court held that the defendant's right to confrontation had been violated. "A videotaped deposition supplies an environment substantially comparable to a trial, but where the defendant was not permitted to be an active participant in the video deposition, this procedural substitute is constitutionally infirm" (Melton, 1981: 189).

To diminish some of the stress that occurs from repeating embarrassing or traumatic events in front of a large audience of strangers, some legislation has been passed to limit the number of persons present in trials involving a child witness. However, two constitutional issues come into play: the right of the defendant to a public trial and the right of the public to know about criminal trials. There have been several rulings regarding these rights and the constitutionality of closed trials during testimony of child sex offense victims (*State ex. rel. Oregonian Publishing Co. v. Diez, Or.*, 613 F. 2d 23 [1980]; *R.L.R. v. State*, 487 F.2d 27 [Alaska 1971]; *Richmond Newspapers, Inc., v. Virginia*, 448 U.S., 100 S. Ct. 2814, 2840 [1980]; *Gannett v. De Pasquale*, 443 U.S. 368, 388 n. 19 [1979]; *State v. Sinclair*, No. 21375 [S. Ct. S.C. Jan. 13, 1981]; and *Globe Newspaper Co. v. Superior Court*, 101 S. Ct. 259 [1980]). The general conclusion of these rulings is that "while these issues are certainly not settled, there seems to be ample reason to doubt the constitutionality of attempts to alter standard criminal procedure in order to protect child victims" (Melton, 1981: 194).

In summary, there have been numerous attempts to protect children from traumatic courtroom events that stem from a system designed primarily for adults. Some have been successful while most have had little or no impact. Statutes have been revised to eliminate the age requirement for competency, but children are still deemed suspect. Most jurisdictions do not require corroborative evidence but, without it, chances for a conviction are slim to nonexistent. Use of a videotaped deposition is constitutionally questioned and, in most cases, would still not prevent the child from having to face the perpetrator when testifying against him. Although some judges may be successful in clearing the courtroom when the child testifies, this action is subject to appellate challenge. The one bright light is the hearsay exception; perhaps the child will never have to take the witness stand. In most cases, however, this will only be done if there is sound corroborative evidence (e.g., medical indications of physical assault) to support the hearsay testimony. Yet, as indicated earlier, this type of corroborative evidence, particularly in intrafamilial sexual abuse cases, is usually scarce.

What can be done then to lessen the emotional shock and wounds children may experience in the legal arena? Some suggestions have focused on increased power for the judge. In other words, it may be beneficial to give judges specific statutory authority to protect children from abusive and intimidating tactics, limit the length of cross-examination, allow frequent rests, permit a supportive adult nearby, and allocate money to remodel courtrooms to make them less intimidating (Girdner, 1985). If these changes are enacted, the question remains as to their constitutionality. And if they are ruled constitutional, the question must be asked will judges utilize them and adhere to their intent? It is hoped that the answer will be yes.

REFERENCES

Angelou, Maya (1970) I Know Why the Caged Bird Sings. New York: Random House.
Bailey, F. Lee and Henry B. Rothblatt (1985) Crimes of Violence: Rape and Other Sex Crimes Cumulative Supplement. Rochester: Lawyers Cooperative Publishing Co.
Black, H. C. (1966) Black's Law Dictionary. St. Paul: West.
Bohmer, Carol (1974) "Judicial attitudes toward rape victims." Judicature (February): 303-307.
Bowker, L. (1978) Women, Crime and the Criminal Justice System. Lexington, MA: Lexington Books.

Bowker, L. (1981) Women and Crime in America. New York: Macmillan.

Brady, Katherine (1979) Father's Days. New York: Seaview.

Brownmiller, Susan (1975) Against Our Will. New York: Simon & Schuster.

Bulkley, Josephine [ed.] (1981) Child Sexual Abuse and the Law. A Report. Washington, DC: American Bar Association National Legal Resource Center for Child Advocacy and Protection.

Bulkley, Josephine [ed.] (1983) Innovations in the Prosecution of Child Sexual Abuse Cases. A Report. Washington, DC: American Bar Association National Legal Resource Center for Child Advocacy and Protection.

Burgess, A. W. and L. L. Holmstrom (1977) "Rape trauma syndrome," pp. 315-328 in D. Chappell et al. (eds.) Forcible Rape: The Crime, the Victim, and the Offender. New York: Columbia University Press.

Butler, Sandra (1978) Conspiracy of Silence: The Trauma of Incest. San Francisco: New Glide.

Finkelhor, David (1979) Sexually Victimized Children. New York: Free Press.

Gagnon, John (1965) "Female child victims of sex offenses." Social Problems 13: 176-192.

Goodman, G. S. and V. Helgeson (1986) "Children as witnesses. What do they remember?" (unpublished)

Gridner, B. (1981) "Out of the mouths of babes." California Lawyer (June).

Herman, Judith L. (1981). Father/Daughter Incest. Cambridge, MA: Harvard University Press.

Humphrey, Hubert, III [Minnesota Attorney General] (1985) Report on Scott County Investigations. Scott County, Minnesota.

Justice, Blair and Rita Justice. (1979) The Broken Taboo. New York: Human Sciences Press.

Karmen, Andrew (1982) "Women victims of crime—Introduction," pp. 185-201 in The Criminal Justice System. New York: Clark Boardman.

Kinsey, Alfred C., Wardell B. Pomeroy, Clyde E. Martin, and Paul H. Gebhard (1953) Sexual Behavior in the Human Female. Philadelphia: Saunders.

Klein, Dorie (1981) "Violence against women: some considerations regarding its causes and its elimination." Crime and Delinquency (January): 64-80.

Kocen, Lynne and Josephine Bulkley (1981) "Analysis of criminal child sex offenses statutes," pp. 1-20 in Josephine Bulkley (ed.) Child Sexual Abuse and the Law. A Report. Washington, DC: American Bar Association National Legal Resource Center for Child Advocacy and Protection.

Kushner, Harold (1981) When Bad Things Happen to Good People. New York: Avon.

Ladies Home Journal (1983) "Why rape has become more violent, more sadistic." (September): 143-147.

Landis, Judson (1956) "Experiences of 500 children with adult sexual deviance." Psychiatric Quarterly (Supp.) 30: 91-109.

Largen, Mary Ann (1985) Personal communication (December).

Leidig, Marjorie W. (1981) "Violence against women: a feminist psychological analysis," pp. 190-205 in S. Cox (ed.) Female Psychology: The Emerging Self. New York: St. Martin's.

Lloyd, David (1981) "The corroboration of sexual victimization of children," pp. 103-124 in Josephine Bulkley (ed.) Child Sexual Abuse and the Law. A Report. Washington, DC: American Bar Association National Legal Resource Center for Child Advocacy and Protection.

Lukianowicz, Narcyz (1972) "Incest." British Journal of Psychiatry 120: 201-212.

Maisch, Herbert (1972) Incest. New York: Stein & Day.

Marsh, G., A. Geist, and N. Gaplan (1982) Rape and the Limits of Law Reform. Boston: Auburn House.

Meiselman, Karin (1978) Incest. San Francisco: Jossey-Bass.

Melton, Gary (1981) "Procedural reforms to protect child victims and witnesses in sex offense proceedings," pp. 184-198 in Josephine Bulkley (ed.) Child Sexual Abuse and the Law. A Report. Washington, DC: American Bar Association National Legal Resource Center for Child Advocacy and Protection.

Morris, Jeannie (1981) "The marital rape exemption." Loyola Law Review 27: 597.

Nabokov, Vladimir (1966) Lolita. New York: Berkley Medallion.

Oakland Tribune (1984) "Old attitudes, laws on rape undergo change." (May 6).

Oakland Tribune (1985a) "Rape victim lifestyle sways jurors decisions. (June 23).

Oakland Tribune (1985b) "Courts wary of rape trauma syndrome." (September 8).

Oakland Tribune (1985c) "A 'botched' MacMartin Pre-School case many conclude." (June 16).

Robin, Gerald D. (1977) "Forcible rape: institutionalized sexism in the criminal justice system." Crime and Delinquency (April): 136-153.

Rogers, C. M. and J. M. Thomas (1984) "Sexual victimization of children in the U.S.A.: patterns and trends." Clinical Proceedings CHNMC 40 (May/June and July/August).

Russell, D.E.H. (1984) Sexual Exploitation: Rape, Child Sexual Abuse and Workplace Harassment. Newbury Park, CA: Sage.

Ryan, W. (1976) Blaming the Victim. New York: Vintage.

Stanko, Elizabeth A. (1985) Intimate Intrusions: Women's Experience of Male Violence. Boston: Routledge & Kegan Paul.

Steinhauser, Karen [Deputy District Attorney in the Domestic Violence Unit, Denver, Colorado] (1986) Personal interview (January).

Tong, Rosemarie (1984) Women, Sex and the Law. Totowa, NJ: Rowman & Allanheld.

USA Today (1985) "Fears, fantasy come to play in courtroom." (January 29).

Williams, J. E. and D. A. Holmes (1981) The Second Assault: Rape and Public Attitudes. Westport, CT: Greenwood.

Wood, Pamela (1977) "The victim in a forcible rape case: a feminist view." American Criminal Law Review (Winter).

Wulken, Donna and Josephine Bulkley (1981) "Analysis of Incest Statutes," pp. 52-66 in Josephine Bulkley (ed.) Child Sexual Abuse and the Law. A Report. Washington, DC: American Bar Association National Legal Resource Center for Child Advocacy and Protection.

4

JUDICIAL PERCEPTIONS AND PERCEPTIONS OF JUDGES: THE DIVORCE LAW REVOLUTION IN PRACTICE

Lenore J. Weitzman

In 1970, California launched a legal revolution by instituting the first no-fault divorce law in the United States. The new law not only changed the rules for divorce, it also changed the rules for dividing property and awarding support.

Before 1970, every state required fault-based grounds, such as adultery or mental cruelty, for divorce. When California eliminated the need for grounds, it permitted divorce at either party's request. All that was needed was one spouse's claim that "irreconcilable differences" had caused the breakdown of the marriage.

This seemingly simple move pioneered sweeping reforms that quickly spread to other states. While not all states adopted the California model (and totally abolished fault), by 1988 every state had adopted some form of no-fault divorce law.

Although these laws were designed to create more equity, they have had unintended consequences: they have created substantial inequalities between divorced men and women and have led to the impoverishment of many divorced women and their children.

This chapter has two aims. First, it describes the social and economic consequences of the legal changes in the rules for divorce (including the new standards for dividing property and awarding support). Second, it examines how judges interpret and apply the new legal rules and explores the impact of their decisions on divorced men, women, and children.

The data reported below were collected as part of a ten-year study of the social and economic effects of California's no-fault divorce reforms. The research involved the analysis of statistically random samples of 2500 court dockets and in-depth face-to-face interviews with over 400 attorneys, judges, and divorced men and women (see generally Weitzman, *The Divorce Revolution*, 1985, especially pp. 403-412).

THE UNINTENDED CONSEQUENCES

When I began my research, I shared the reformers' optimism and assumed that only good could come from an end to the vilification and sham testimony of the old fault-based system of divorce. How much better, I thought, to end a marriage in a nonadversarial fashion that sought to reduce the acrimony and hostility. And how much better to encourage parents to fashion fair and equitable financial arrangements for themselves and their children.

Equally important, the new law promised equality for men and women. Here, finally, was a law that recognized wives as equals in the marital partnership. California was the first state to guarantee wives an equal share—a mandatory 50% of the property accumulated during the marriage.

When, in the early days of my research, I began to confront cases of upper-middle-class women who had been married for 20 to 30 years, and who were being cut off with only a few years of alimony and hardly any property, who were being forced to move so their homes could be sold, and who with little or no job experience and minimal court-ordered support, were headed for near-poverty, I assumed that they were the exceptions—the women who had incompetent lawyers or the wrong judge.

Similarly, when I first confronted cases of young mothers who were awarded so little child support that it was not enough money to cover the cost of day care, and who then told me that the child support order "wasn't worth the piece of paper it was written on" because they couldn't collect the support the court had ordered, I again thought that these women were the exceptions. Perhaps they hadn't fought hard enough to press for their legal entitlement to adequate support for their children.

But as the systematic data from the court dockets became computer printouts with statistically significant results, it became clear that these women were not the exceptions. The data revealed a disquieting pattern, —a pattern of substantial hardships for women and children. Somehow the elimination of grounds, fault, and consent, and the institution of gender-neutral standards for financial awards, were having unanticipated and unfortunate consequences.

The major unintended result of the no-fault reforms has been widespread economic disruption for divorced women and their children. The new rules for alimony, property, and child support end up shaping radically different economic futures for divorced men, on one hand, and for divorced women and their children on the other. My research reveals that women and the minor children in their households (90% of the children live with their mothers after divorce) experience a sharp decline in their standard of living after divorce. Their standard of living drops 73% in the first year after divorce. In contrast, their ex-husbands experience a rise in their standard of living—an average 42% increase in the first year after divorce (Weitzman, 1985: 337-340).

These findings are echoed by a 1987 report of the California Senate, that concluded "women and children suffer a marked decline in their standard of living after divorce, with older homemakers and mothers with young children experiencing the greatest hardship. Many of these women end up living in poverty or near poverty" (California Senate, 1987: 1).

Why have these supposedly "enlightened" legal reforms had such devastating effects? How could laws that were designed to create more equitable settlements end up impoverishing divorced women and their children?

One reason is that the court's interpretation of "equality" in divorce settlements often produces unequal results by ignoring the very real inequalities that marriage creates for men and women. It also ignores the economic inequalities between men and women in the larger society. Thus a woman who has been homemaker and mother during marriage may not be "equal" to her husband at the point of divorce. Rules that treat her as if she is equal (in the mistaken belief that she can quickly enter the labor force and become the economic peer of her husband), simply serve to deprive her—and their children—of the support they need.

A second reason is that an ostensibly equal division of property is not in fact equal when women have the responsibility for child care in nine out of ten divorces that involve children (Weitzman, 1985: 215-261). To divide the property equally between husband and wife typically means that one-half of the family assets are awarded to one person, the husband, while the other half are left to an average of three people, the wife and two children. In addition, judges often interpret the equal division rule as requiring the forced sale of the family home. This increases the disruption, dislocation, and distress in the lives of many women and children.

A third factor is that the elimination of grounds, fault, and consent have reduced women's bargaining leverage. Because the wife was usually the "innocent" party under the old law, she was in a stronger position to negotiate property and support for herself and her children (in return for her agreement to file for and obtain the divorce her husband wanted).

A final cause of the economic disparity between divorced men and women lies in the courts' failure to understand the changing nature of property in our society. In many cases, the major assets of the marriage are not divided equally. In fact, new forms of marital property are often not divided at all. This is because courts often ignore the husband's career assets—his enhanced earning capacity, his pension, professional license, and health insurance—and fail to award a wife a share of these valuable new forms of property.

The unintended economic consequences of the legal changes in divorce provide one major theme of this article. The second major theme traces the effects of no-fault divorce on the institution of marriage.

THE TRANSFORMATION OF MARRIAGE

No-fault divorce has not only redefined the rules for divorce, it has also transformed the legal rules for marriage. No-fault divorce has recast the legal rights and responsibilities of husbands and wives and the legal relationship between parent and children. As a result, it is creating new norms and new expectations for marriage and family commitments in our society.

A divorce provides an important opportunity for a society to enforce marital norms by rewarding the marital behavior it approves and by punishing transgression. It does this by handing out legal rewards and penalties, and by ordering people to pay for their transgressions in dollars and cents.

Consider, for example, the issue of alimony. If a divorce court awards alimony to a 50-year-old woman who has spent 25 years as a homemaker and mother, it is reinforcing the value of her domestic activities by rewarding the woman's devotion to her family. (It may also be punishing the husband for abandoning his wife in middle age.) But if, by contrast, the divorce court denies the wife alimony, and tells her that she must instead get a job and support herself, it is undermining the value of her domestic activities and penalizing her for investing in her family, home, and children at the expense of her own career. (The court is also releasing the husband from his traditional responsibility for his wife's support.) When divorce courts make these decisions, they are revealing and enforcing new expectations for husbands and wives. Although these expectations are being applied retroactively in divorce decrees, they necessarily suggest new expectations for marriage as well.

These expectations are not confined to those who experience divorce themselves. Awareness of the consequences of divorce affects the aspirations and intentions of those who are about to enter marriage. And it affects the behavior of men and women who are already married. A law that penalizes a woman for the years that she spends as a homemaker and mother sends a chilling message to married women who want to give priority to their families and children. It warns them that they had better not forego their own career advancement because they will suffer greatly if their marriage dissolves. This is a powerful threat in a society with a high divorce rate, especially when the no-fault no-consent laws of many states give a woman no choice about whether her marriage will dissolve.

Of course, the new norms provide an equally sobering message to the man who gives priorities to his wife and children. And these messages were evident to the men and women we interviewed. For example, one Los Angeles surgeon complained that all the sacrifices he made "to work like a dog . . . and earn the money so my kids and wife could have everything they wanted" were ignored in the present legal system of divorce. As he put it,

> Now, she walked out on me, and what do I get? Nothing. Nothing. And what does she get? She gets half of my house, half of my pension . . . [and so on]. For what, I ask you? For running off with a jerk psychologist. That's my reward?

THE RESEARCH

This research on the social and economic effects of the divorce law reforms involved the collection and analysis of five types of data:

—systematic random samples of about 2500 court dockets over a ten-year period;

—in-depth face-to-face interviews with 169 family law attorneys;

—in-depth face-to-face interviews with 44 family law judges;

—similar interviews with a sample of English legal experts; and

—comprehensive personal interviews with 228 divorced men and women about one year after their legal divorce.

This research design is unusual in that it uses a variety of sources. It does not rely solely on lawyers and judges (as legal scholars tend to do) or solely on divorced men and women (as sociologists and psychologists tend to do). It also has the advantage of a systematic data base in the random samples of divorce decrees drawn from court records. Although most of the data were collected in California, the findings are relevant to the entire United States because the major features of the California law have been adopted by most other states.

This chapter focuses on the in-depth interviews with 44 superior court judges who were hearing divorce cases in San Francisco and Los Angeles in 1975, questionnaire responses of 26 judges at a statewide family law conference in 1981, and a comparative sample of 27 legal experts in England (interviewed in 1980 and 1981).

THE ROLE OF THE JUDGE

Judges have the opportunity to structure equal or unequal results for men and women in three spheres: by dividing marital property, by awarding (or denying) alimony, and by awarding (and enforcing) child support. While only a minority of all divorce cases are actually contested and "decided" by a judge, judicial decisions in these cases establish the norms for negotiations in noncontested cases (so that most divorce settlements are structured in the shadow of judicial rulings).

In the pages that follow, we will examine the pattern of case outcomes in three spheres: property, alimony, and child support.

MARITAL PROPERTY

Historically, there have been two distinct legal systems governing the property of married couples in the United States: 42 states have the separate property system, based on the English common law, which segregates the assets of the husband and wife into two categories: "his" and "hers." Each spouse retains all the property he or she earns or inherits during the course of the marriage.

In contrast, in the eight community property states, like California, all property acquired during marriage is "theirs." The community property system assumes that all property acquired during marriage is "earned" by the joint efforts of the two spouses and it, therefore, belongs to both of them.

The two systems also differ in their approach to division of property upon divorce. In most separate property states, the starting point for dividing marital property is typically one-third of the property to the wife and two-thirds to the husband (if he was the one who earned it). In a community property system, the starting point is a 50-50 division of the property, one-half to the wife and one-half to the husband.

THE DIVISION OF PROPERTY

Before 1970, when every state had a fault-based system of divorce, property awards were often linked to findings of fault in both types of legal regimes. The innocent party typically received a greater share of the property than the guilty party.

One of the major innovations of California's 1970 legal reform was the institution of a fixed no-fault standard for dividing property: it *required* judges to divide the property acquired during marriage *equally* upon divorce—half to the husband, half to the wife. The equal division standard was seen as fair—and "protective" of wives—because it guaranteed each spouse one half of the jointly accumulated property.

Surprisingly, the equal division rule has reduced the wife's share of the property in California. That is because California wives were usually the "innocent" plaintiffs under the old fault-based divorce law, and they were, therefore, typically awarded more than half of the marital property. In 1968, wives were awarded more than half (60% or more) of the property in both San Francisco and Los Angeles divorce cases. Most of the awards allowed the wife to keep the family home, which was often the family's most valuable asset. By 1972, without the old lever of fault, the wife's share of the property dropped to exactly 50%.

THE PROBLEM OF THE FAMILY HOME

The major impact of the equal division rule has been on the disposition of the family home. Today more homes are being sold so that the proceeds can be divided equally: the number of cases in which there was an explicit court order to sell the home rose from about one in ten in 1968 to about one in three in 1977 (Weitzman, 1985: 78). Those wives who do manage to keep the family home typically have other property they can trade for their husband's share of the home—such as an interest in their husband's pension.

Surprisingly, the presence of minor children in the home has not deterred judges from ordering it sold. Our data reveal that 66% of the couples who were forced to sell their homes had minor children. These sales mean residential moves that disrupt children's school, neighborhood, and friendship ties, and create additional dislocations for children (and mothers) at the very point at which they most need continuity and stability. The emotional upheaval is underscored by a quote from a typical respondent who was ordered to vacate her home in three months so that it could be sold:

> I begged the judge.... All I wanted was enough time for Brian [her son] to adjust to the divorce.... I broke down and cried on the stand . . . but the judge refused. He gave me three months to move 15 years of our lives— right in the middle of the school semester . . . my husband's attorney threatened me with contempt if I wasn't out on time . . . he also warned me not to interfere with the real estate people—in my house—he said if I wasn't cooperative in letting them show the house when they wanted to, he'd "haul me into court for contempt." . . . It was a nightmare. . . . The most degrading and unjust experience of my life.

When we asked judges about their decisions to force the sale of the family home, they offered three explanations: it permitted a "clean break" between parties, it did not unduly hamper the husband by tying up his equity in the house, and it relieved the "burden" on the wife.

Most California judges stressed the husband's "right" to "his half" of the family property. Given that the home is the only substantial family property in many divorce cases, its sale was seen as necessary to give the husband the money he would need to start a new life. As one California respondent explained:

> You have to be fair to the husband. If you award a house to a woman when it is the only asset, you are then faced with the man who asks, "Why am I not entitled to the present enjoyment of the community asset that we have?" "Why should I stand still for deferred enjoyment?" He wants to start a new life. He doesn't want to hang around waiting for his equity. And, by law, he has a right to that equity.

In justifying the sale of the family home other judges asserted that a sale and clean break would make life "easier" for the wife. Many of them said that the wife was "better off" without a home that tied her down to old neighborhoods and children's schools and children's friends, that locked her into the suburbs and restricted her personal, social, and economic options.

But our interviews revealed that their "solution" was causing much more hardship. It was much worse for a mother and children to be evicted from their neighborhood and its social supports. The forced sale of the family home intensified the disruption, dislocation, and distress in the postdivorce lives of mothers and children.

The disposition of the family home in California is quite different from what is seen as the "equitable" solution in England. Among the English experts we interviewed, the first priority was given to preserving the family home for the children. For example, in responding to a typical case in which the home was the only family asset, one barrister explained the way the English courts would approach this case:

> First, let's make sure the children are looked after . . . the children have always lived in that house . . . you want to finish a child's schooling.

Similarly, a solicitor predicted:

> The wife would get the house because she has to make a home for the children, and the children come first—you don't want their home to be disrupted. You want to stabilize the situation for them.

The underlying principle in the English approach is that "children come first" because they are the most vulnerable members of the divorcing family and they most need societal protection. As one English judge said: "It's my job to protect the children."

In contrast to the English emphasis on the children's welfare as the court's first priority, the "interests" of children were rarely mentioned in the California interviews. Marital property was defined solely in terms of the relative rights of the husband and wife, and it was divided between the two of them.

It is not only children and their mothers who suffer from the forced sale of the family home. Some of the most tragic victims are older homemakers who not only lose their residence of 25 or 35 years, but also lose their whole social structure in a forced move to the other side of town. As one woman described her reaction:

> I had lived in that home for 26 years and my three children still considered it their home. But the judge ordered it sold. . . . He said he had to follow the letter of the law. . . . I married at a time when a woman who spent 30 years of her life raising a family was worth something . . . but in the eyes of

the court I was merely "unemployed." No one would rent me an apartment because my only income was $700 a month spousal support and landlords said that was "unstable" and "inadequate." Two months later my husband's attorney took me into court for contempt because I hadn't moved.... He said I was interfering with the sale of the house.... The judge gave me ten days to get out.... I am still outraged. It is a total perversion of justice. I was thrown out of my own house.

Significantly, the California legislature did not intend that the family home be sold in order to meet equal division requirement. Indeed, a 1970 Assembly Committee report specifically states that a temporary award of the home to the spouse who has custody of minor children should be seen as a valid reason to delay the division of property:

> Where an interest in a residence which serves as the home of the family is a major community asset, an order for the immediate sale of the residence in order to comply with the equal division mandate of the law would, certainly, be unnecessarily destructive of the economic and social circumstances of the parties and their children [California Assembly, 1970].

The California appellate courts have upheld the rationale for maintaining the family home for minor children when a sale would have an adverse economic, emotional, or social impact on them.

Fran Leonard, attorney for The Older Women's League, echoes these thoughts in asserting the importance of a similar delay to allow older homemakers to retain their homes:

> For the older woman, especially a homemaker (the sale of the family home) is a major cruelty. Upon divorce, she loses her husband and her occupation—then all too often, her home. This nearly comprises her universe. Unlike her spouse, she may have no credit history, no income aside from alimony, and almost no prospects of recovering her lost earning capacity. The chances of her ever buying another home are almost nil. Yet all too commonly the court orders the home sold, in order to divide its value. Attorneys frequently favor this, because their fees can be paid out of escrow.... Instead older women should try to keep the family home [Leonard, 1980: 9].

But despite the legislative and judicial authority for exempting the home from the immediate equal division of community property, the judges we interviewed in 1974-1975, 1981, and 1983 attested to the prevailing pattern of ordering the home sold and the proceeds divided upon divorce. While some judges were willing to leave the home in joint ownership for "a few years," very few were willing to let it remain unsold until small children attained majority. Even fewer were willing to make an exception for an older woman who, they asserted, didn't "need" the home anymore (even if her college-age children considered it their home as well).

Once again, the responses of the English judges reveal a very different approach. Their first priority is to provide the older housewife with the home or a comparable home so that she can maintain her life without grave hardship. The English perspective is based on the assumption that after a long marriage, a husband has a responsibility to provide for his ex-wife for the rest of her life. To ensure that this responsibility is met, the English courts often require an older (and well-to-do) husband to provide her with more than housing and support during his life; he is also required to purchase an insurance policy or annuity to compensate his ex-wife for the widow's benefits she forfeits by getting divorced.

CHANGES IN THE NATURE OF PROPERTY: THE IMPORTANCE OF CAREER ASSETS

The courts are not, in fact, dividing property equally. This is partially a result of major changes in the nature of property that have occurred in our society. Husbands and wives are increasingly investing in careers and human capital—most particularly in the husband's education and career. The new property resulting from this kind of investment is often the family's major asset. Yet this property is not typically divided equally upon divorce. In fact, in many states it is not divided at all. It is simply presumed to belong to the husband. But if the law allows men to retain their career assets—their professional licenses, their health insurance, and their earning capacities—then their wives are not in fact being awarded an equal share of the joint property, despite the equal division rule.

Career assets is the term I coined to refer to the tangible and intangible assets that are acquired as a part of either spouse's career or career potential. The term *career assets* includes two types of assets: investments in one's "human capital" (one's ability to earn a living in the future), and the benefits and entitlements of employment (such as pension and retirement benefits, medical and hospital insurance, and entitlements to company goods and services). Many of these assets have been acquired in the course of a marriage in the same manner as traditional assets are acquired, and they are often the most valuable assets the couple owns.

Consider these facts: We found that the average divorcing couple has only $20,000 in fixed assets when they divorce. Yet the average couple can earn more than the value of their assets in less than one year (Weitzman, 1985: 60). This means that the value of the couple's career assets—indeed the value of their earning capacity alone—is much greater than the value of their physical property.

These data have important policy implications. If one partner builds his or her earning capacity during the marriage, while the other is a homemaker and parent, the partner with the earning capacity has acquired the major asset of the marriage. If the earning power—or the income it produces—is not divided upon divorce, the two spouses are left with very unequal shares of their joint assets.

An awareness of this inequity was echoed over and over again in our interviews. As one veteran of a 30-year marriage to a college professor explained:

> We married at 21, with no money. . . . When he was a graduate student, I worked as a secretary and then typed papers at night to make extra money. When he became an assistant professor I "retired" to raise our children, but I never stopped working for him—typing, editing, working on his books. . . . My college English degree was very useful for translating his brilliant ideas into comprehensible sentences. . . . My name never appeared on the title page as his co-author, where it belonged, only in the dedication or thank you's. . . . There's more, lots more—the hours mothering his graduate students, hosting department parties, finding homes for visiting professors. . . . I was always available to help. . . . I got $700 a month for three years. The judge said, I was "smart and healthy enough to get a job." I am to "report back like a school girl" in 3 years. Never mind that I am 51. . . . Never mind that I had a job and did it well and am old enough to be entitled to a pension. . . . It's not that I regret my life or didn't enjoy what I did. But it was supposed to be a partnership—a fifty-fifty split. It isn't fair that he gets to keep it. It isn't fair for the court to treat it as his. . . . I earned it just as much as he did.

Career assets are also of great importance for younger couples. In many cases, one spouse's professional education or license is the only asset acquired during marriage. The issue arises when one spouse, usually the wife, supports the other's professional education and training with the expectation that she will share the fruits of her investment through her husband's enhanced earning power. If they divorce soon after the student spouse completes training, the young couple typically has few tangible assets because most of their capital has been used to finance the student's education.

In a landmark case in 1985, a New York Court of Appeals took this position and ruled that a medical license obtained during marriage is marital property (whose value must be divided at the time of a divorce).

That case, the O'Brien case (1985) involved a 9.5-year marriage in which Loretta O'Brien worked as a school teacher in Guadalajara, Mexico, to support her husband in medical school. Mrs. O'Brien, who knew no Spanish when the young couple moved from New York to Mexico, learned the language and found work teaching kindergarten and tutoring English. Three months after Michael O'Brien received his medical license, he sued for divorce. Mrs. O'Brien's reaction to the New York court's decision echoes a recurrent theme in our interviews. She said, "It means that people can't just use you and walk out on you whenever they feel like it" (*New York Times*, 1985).

What, then, are our conclusions about the extent to which property is being divided equally or equitably upon divorce? Given that career assets are typically acquired during marriage in the same manner that other marital property is acquired, and given that these assets are, along with the family home, often the most valuable assets a couple own at the time of the divorce, if the courts do not recognize some or all of these assets as marital property, they are excluding a major portion of a couple's property from the pool of property to be divided upon divorce. In addition, if the courts treat these assets as the property of only the major wage earner, they are in most cases allowing the husband to keep the family's most valuable assets. It is like promising to divide the family jewels equally, but first allowing the husband to keep all the diamonds.

The husband's career assets are "the diamonds" of marital property. Without them, the property cannot be divided equally or fairly.

ALIMONY: THE NEW TRENDS

The second area in which the new divorce laws attempt to treat men and women equally is in maintenance awards, or what is typically referred to as alimony or spousal support. The old divorce laws assumed that husbands were responsible for the financial support of their former wives. The reformers thought that that was inappropriate. They pointed to women's increased participation in the labor force, and assumed that women were now equally capable of supporting themselves—and their children—after divorce.

The California data reveal several changes in the pattern of alimony awards, reflecting these new standards (Weitzman, 1985: 163-164). First, in accord with the new law's goal of making the wife self-sufficient after divorce, there has been a shift from permanent alimony awards, awards based on the premise of the wife's continued dependency, to time-limited awards. Between 1968 and 1972, permanent alimony—

awards labeled permanent, until death or remarriage—dropped from 62% to 32% of the alimony awards in Los Angeles County. By 1972 (and in subsequent years), two-thirds of the alimony awards were transitional awards for a limited and specified duration. The median duration of these fixed-time awards was 25 months, or about two years. Thus the average award carries an expectation of a short transition from marriage to self-sufficiency.

Second, the standards of the new law have dictated a greater reliance on the wife's ability to support herself. Economic criteria, such as the wife's occupation and predivorce income, are, therefore, more important than the old standards of fault and innocence.

Although it is reasonable for courts to consider a wife's ability to support herself, it is shocking to see how little "earning capacity" is necessary to convince a judge that a woman is capable of self-sufficiency. We found countless wives with low earning capacities and limited and marginal employment histories who were denied spousal support altogether because judges assumed they were capable of supporting themselves.

The irregular work histories of many divorced women leave a lot of room for judicial discretion in deciding whether any individual woman is "capable of engaging in gainful employment at the time of the divorce." A judge may conclude that a woman who was employed during the first three years of her marriage but has not worked in the last 16 years is immediately capable of self-sufficiency. Similarly, a judge may decide that because a woman has done volunteer work at a hospital she can now obtain a paid job there, or that because a woman has spent three months a year in an accounting office during the tax season, she is now capable of earning an equivalent salary 12 months a year.

Because few women in longer marriages have held full-time, long-term jobs, their "employment histories" tend to be ambiguous. Judges tend to gloss over the ambiguities in assessing a woman's ability to get a job and be self-sufficient. Consider the following two statements from judges we interviewed:

[The Judge is referring to a case just presented in court.] The best thing for her is to get right out and get a job—earn her own money—and make her own life.
[Q: What kind of job do you think she can get?] Oh, anything. She can get a job in a store selling . . . clothes . . . or whatever. . . . There are lots of jobs out there, just read the want ads.
[Q: What about that woman? What kind of a job do you think she might find?] She said she used to work as . . . a . . . oh, what did she say? In an office or something—a bookkeeper or something like that. Well, that's a

good job. She could probably get good hours, too . . . and be able to pick up her kids after school, as she was worried about that.

[The judge is referring to a woman who testified that she had not taught for 20 years and did not have a California teaching credentials]. Just because she's been married twenty years doesn't mean she can be a sponge for the rest of her life. If she was once a teacher, she can always get a job teaching. Maybe she'll have to work as a substitute for a while, or at a not so fancy school, but just because she hasn't taught in twenty years doesn't mean she can't teach. She is a teacher.

Both cases suggest how easily judges can read evidence of employability in a diversity of situations and conclude that a woman does not need support. Yet neither of these women had been employed since the early years of marriage, and both of them had spent most of their married years raising children. They still had children at home (both of them were now in their late forties). The first woman had no formal training as a bookkeeper, but had worked as one many years earlier. The second woman had not held a paid teaching job for 20 years—of a 22-year marriage (which the judge apparently misheard as 20 years)—but had taught on a volunteer basis in the adult education program at her church.

How realistic is it to assume that these women can easily find well-paid full-time jobs and become self-supporting? If they are like most divorced women we interviewed—especially those in their late forties who had been career homemakers and mothers—it is totally unrealistic.

Many employers do not recognize homemaking skills as having a market value. They only recognize "recent paid work experience" and even with such experience, older women are unwanted in today's labor market. Consider the difficulties that most of the older women we interviewed faced:

There is no way I can make up for twenty-five years out of the labor force. . . . No one wants to make me president of the company just because I was the president of the PTA.

The judge told me to go for job training—but no training can recapture twenty-seven years of my life. I'm too old to start from the beginning and I shouldn't have to. I deserve better.

Professor Herma Kay suggests that judges were affected by the feminist movement in the early 1970s, and were using women's demands for equality as a justification for denying and terminating alimony (Kay, 1978). Along the same lines, attorney Riane Eisler quotes a California judge who described his colleague's attitudes as "What they [divorcing women] need is to go to work, so they can get themselves liberated" (Eisler, 1977: 46).

The result of these standards is that 85% of the divorced women in the United States are presumed capable of self-sufficiency and denied any alimony whatsoever (U.S. Census).

Although alimony has always been rare (because it has been, for the most part, confined to the wives of middle-class and upper-middle-class men, and these couples always constituted a small minority of the divorcing population), the awards and the length of the awards have been drastically cut under the new divorce laws. (In California, these awards average $370 a month in 1984 dollars—Weitzman, 1985: 171).

Instead of the old law's assumption that these women need permanent alimony to enable them to continue to share their husband's standard of living (which they, of course, helped to build), the new laws create an expectation that they *will become independent and self-sufficient soon after the divorce.*

THE GAP BETWEEN THEORY AND REALITY: YOUNG MOTHERS AND OLDER HOMEMAKERS

In theory, alimony is still supposed to be available for women with custody of young children and older homemakers incapable of self-sufficiency. However, we found that alimony awards to mothers of children under six had dropped more than any other group of women since 1970. Today, only 13% of the California mothers of preschool children are awarded spousal support (Weitzman, 1985).

Why does the need to care for young children appear to have so little effect on alimony awards? Two-thirds of the Superior Court judges we interviewed see the goal of making the wife self-sufficient as more important than supporting the custodial parent. As they put it, it is "good for a divorced woman to earn money instead of being dependent on her former husband," "work is a healthy form of rehabilitation that will help her build a new life," and "combining work and motherhood is now normal in our society." Although many of the young mothers we interviewed shared these sentiments and wanted to be self-sufficient, the economic reality of their low earnings and the need to support their children compelled their need of support from their former husbands.

The judges are always balancing the interests of children against their concern for the father and his need for his income. When they can justify her work as "healthy and good for her" and when they can overestimate her earning capacity, they can justify allowing the husband to keep most of his income for himself. As one respondent protested:

Why am I and my son worth so much less than he is? . . . It's because the judge looks at him and thinks he needs it—but I can get by. . . . He gets a company car and the privilege of eating out whenever he wants to—I have the privilege of food stamps. . . . I've never lived like this before in my life . . . it's degrading and it's not fair.

Our empirical analysis of the judges' actual awards reveals that the husband is rarely ordered to part with more than one-third of his income to support his wife and children. He is, therefore, allowed to retain two-thirds for himself while his former wife and children, typically three people, are expected to survive on the remaining one-third.

One reason for the disparity is that the judges we interviewed gave first priority to the husband's needs. They expressed great sympathy for the plight of divorced men and regarded the income of most divorced men as too low to support two households adequately, too low to provide even half of the support for the husband's children who are in the custody of their former wives. They therefore decide that it is "better" to leave most of the family's postdivorce income with the husband—viewing it as "his" rather than "theirs." Most judges place an "equal" burden of support on men and women without regard to the fact that the parties' capacities to support that burden are clearly unequal and, especially if there are children, unequal burdens after divorce.

SELF-SUFFICIENCY STANDARDS AND THE OLDER HOMEMAKER

A second group of women who are hurt by the new law's standard of self-sufficiency are the older homemakers who have been housewives and mothers throughout marriages of long duration. Although many more women in this category are awarded spousal support, *one out of three is not.*

It is not surprising to find that the women who feel most betrayed by the legal system of divorce are those older homemakers who are denied alimony. As one woman said:

You can't tell me there's justice if someone uses you for twenty-five years and then just dumps you and walks out scot-free. . . . It's not fair. It's not justice. It's a scandal . . . and those judges should be ashamed of themselves sitting up there in their black robes like God and hurting poor people like me.

When we compare the postdivorce incomes of long-married husbands and wives, we find that wives are expected to live on much smaller amounts of money, and are economically much worse off, than their former husbands. For example, wives married 18 years or more with predivorce family incomes of $20,000 to $30,000 a year have, on the average, a median income of $6,300 a year after the divorce. Their husbands, in contrast, have a median income of $20,000 a year—even if we assume that they are paying the full amount of alimony and child support the court ordered. The result is that the postdivorce income of these wives is 24% of the previous family income, whereas the average postdivorce income for their husbands is 87% of that standard (Weitzman, 1955: 190).

Once again, the judges approach these cases mindful of the husband's need for "his income" and his limited capacity to support two families. And, once again, it is clear that the judges simply misunderstand the economic reality of the wives' job prospects. In our interviews, the judges assured us that most of these women would "be able to find jobs." But they did not interview the women a year later, as we did, and did not hear about the women who applied for 50 jobs without success, or those who could only find jobs at the minimum wage (after long marriages to professional men).

As one woman said:

> It's so hard to start at the bottom when you've been a respected member of
> the community for years. . . . I just never realized that the respect and
> admiration and civic work doesn't count for anything in the job mar-
> ket. . . . and it certainly doesn't help pay my rent.

As this example suggests, women who have few marketable skills cannot make up for 20 or 25 years out of the job market. Most end up in low-paying jobs, living in greatly reduced circumstances, often on the edge of poverty (Leonard, 1980).

Obviously, the problem is not limited to California. Consider the case of Edith Curtis, a 55-year-old Idaho woman who applied for state unemployment compensation after her divorce from a college professor. Edith Curtis' two-year job search and 75 applications proved "fruitless to a shopworn and obsolete housewife . . . with a thirty-year-old B.A. in English and a lack of salable skills" (Chase, 1985). She was finally offered and accepted a job as a fast-food cashier, part-time, at the minimum wage (Chase, 1985).

No wonder the older homemaker typically feels betrayed by the new laws. She was promised, by both her husband and our society—her contract, if you prefer, both implied and expressed—that their marriage was a partnership and that he would share his income with her. Instead, the courts have changed the rules in the middle of the game—after she has fulfilled her share of the bargain (and passed the point where she can choose another life course).

CHILD SUPPORT

My research uncovered two major problems with child support: low awards and inadequate enforcement. Let us consider each of these in turn.

THE AMOUNT OF CHILD SUPPORT

The U.S. Census shows that the average award for two children in the United States is less than $200 a month—much less than half of the cost of raising two children (U.S. Census, 1983). In California, the average child support award was less than the average cost of day care alone.

Ironically, young mothers have a greater need for support from their ex-husbands after divorce—just at the point where judges are telling them to make do with less. Most custodial mothers have to take over many of their husband's family responsibilities and face greater burdens and greater expenses as single parents.

Yet, it is very rare for any court to order more than 25% of a man's income in child support or more than 32% of a man's income in combined child support and alimony. Even though judges say that their typical award is closer to one-half of the husband's income, the data from the analysis of court dockets and the interviews with divorced persons shows that the real proportion is quite different. Instead of a 50-50 division of the husband's income, the typical award is one-third for the wife and two children to two-thirds for the husband. Among upper-income men, it is one-fifth to four-fifths: men who earn $50,000 or more a year retain an average of 81% of their net incomes for themselves (Weitzman, 1985: table 24).

The implications of awarding one-third of the family income to the wife and children and leaving two-thirds for the father are immediately apparent when we look at the distribution of family income graphically, as shown in Figure 4.1

What do the current child support awards mean in terms of standards of living? Figure 4.2 shows that if they had to live on the child support the court ordered, 73% of the California men could live comfortably after making the payments, while only 7% of the women and children would be living at the same level—even if the support were *paid in full.* Almost all of the women and children—fully 93%—would be living below the poverty level.

A related issue is whether most divorced fathers can afford to pay the child support ordered by the court. The answer is an unequivocal yes. Whether one considers the percentage of the supporter's income, or the

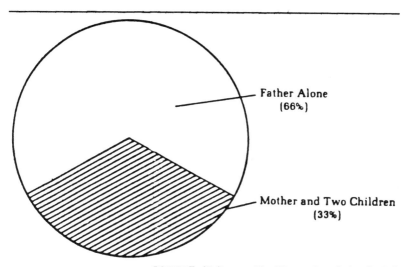

SOURCE: Weitzman, *The Divorce Revolution* (1985).

Figure 4.1   Division of Family Income after Divorce

standard of living he has after paying, the vast majority of divorced fathers can pay child support and still maintain a relatively comfortable standard of living.

Significantly, both divorced men and divorced women agree with this conclusion. When asked, "Can you (or your ex-husband) afford to pay the child support the court ordered?," fully 80% of the women and 90% of the men say yes. Thus both men and women see the award as reasonable in terms of the husband's ability to pay. Only a small minority felt the awards were excessive.

Along the same lines, when asked about their satisfaction with the amount of child support awarded in their case, the vast majority (91%) of divorced men *see the awards as reasonable* in terms of their income. Only 9% of the men say they were dissatisfied. (As might be expected, a larger percentage of the women, 36%, are dissatisfied with the amount of child support awarded and see it as inadequate.)

In summary, the data point to three conclusions. First, the amount of child support ordered is typically quite modest in terms of the father's ability to pay. Second, the amount of child support ordered is typically not enough to cover even half the cost of actually raising the children. Third, the major burden of child support is typically placed on the mother even though she normally has fewer resources and much less "ability to pay."

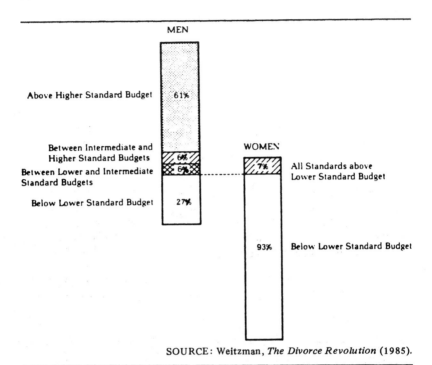

SOURCE: Weitzman, *The Divorce Revolution* (1985).

Figure 4.2   Income Standards of Divorced Men and Women If Men Pay all Court-Ordered Support and Women Live on Support (Based on Weighted Samples of Interviews with Divorced Persons; Los Angeles County, California, 1978)

SUPPORT ENFORCEMENT: ONE VIEW OF THE BENCH

Even though child support awards are modest to begin with, they are frequently not paid because many divorced fathers simply ignore court orders (U.S. Census data show that fewer than half of the fathers fully comply with court orders to pay child support [U.S. Census, 1983: 1].

Surprisingly, this is not because father cannot "afford" to pay. In California, we found that men who earn between $30,000 and $50,000 a year were just as likely to fail to pay child support as those who earn less than $10,000 a year (Weitzman, 1985: 267). The result is that the mother, who is the primary custodial parent in 90% of the divorce cases, is left with the major burden of supporting her children after divorce.

The typical child support order calls for the father to send the mother a check every month or every pay period. It is up to the mother to keep track of the checks and to try to obtain the money when the checks are late or are for less than the full amount ordered. This puts the burden of collection on the mother, who typically has few resources to begin with. As one mother explained:

> Each time I went to court I lost a day's pay, and I had to pay my lawyer for his court rate. We had to wait two hours for the case to be called, and [my ex-husband] got a postponement to get his papers together.... The next time he was sick.... Then he changed attorneys.... Each time the judge said he had a right to have his side represented ... but I couldn't afford it anymore. They let him get away with murder.

In most jurisdictions, judges have the options of ordering payments through the courts of ordering automatic wage assignments.

The judges, however, rarely take advantage of these options. They say it's an "additional bureaucratic impediment for the man" and they do not want to "embarrass" men, especially middle- and upper-class men. This leaves the burden of collecting support on the mother. As one woman described it:

> It's outrageous. The law gives him full control. He decides if he wants to pay or not.... No one monitors him.... He has the money but wants to make me call to ask for it.

JUDICIAL ATTITUDES AND PRACTICES

Three judicial practices are the subject of dissatisfaction among custodial parents who have tried to secure enforcement of child support orders: the judges' excessive leniency, their failure to order wage assignments, and their willingness to waive arrearages.

(1) Excessive leniency. Many mothers complained of judges' excessive leniency, which put the entire burden of doing without on the women and her children:

> My husband put on a big act in court saying he wasn't working and had no money ... but he works at the same plant as my brother-in-law and he has seen him there every day.... The judge let him get away with all that sweet talk about how he cared about his children. [Q: What did the judge do?] He told him to come back in a month with his pay stubs ... then he [the husband] didn't show and we had to start all over again.... Meanwhile, how am I supposed to buy food? With his promises?

Those women who went before a judge to secure enforcement were typically frustrated by the process. They were likely to feel that the judge was unsympathetic and impatient with their request. As one reported:

> The court didn't want to hear it about all I had been through trying to make him pay. The judge said to me, "Say it concisely." He didn't want to

hear how many times I had to go to his house to get the money. He didn't want to hear about my daughter left crying on the street because he didn't pick her up for the school picnic.... He was so patronizing... and I was so bottled up with anger and frustration I couldn't even talk.

(2) Reluctance to order wage assignments. Wage assignments have proven most effective in securing compliance. Yet the vast majority of California judges are reluctant to order them. In the 1977 random sample of court records, only 5% of the cases with a child support award had a wage attachment. (This includes wage attachments established with the award as well as those added within the first year after the divorce.) For alimony orders, the figure was 3%.

Senator Paula Hawkins of Florida reported a similar low incidence of wage assignments on the part of Florida judges:

An alarming discovery was that many of the courts responsible for enforcement were unaware of the variety of enforcement techniques available to them. For example, many of the judges were not aware that Florida State law permitted the courts to impose mandatory wage assignments on non-AFDC as well as AFDC recipients if the absent parent missed two or more payments. Even worse, many judges who were aware of the provision were very reluctant to use it [Hawkins, 1984: 15].

Unlike the Florida judges who said they were unaware of the law, the California judges we interviewed were well informed (and were aware that *the law required* wage assignments when support was two months overdue). But they chose not to follow the law.

Consider these two experiences which were typical of the women we interviewed:

The D.A. who tried to help me was very nice but he said it was like banging his head against a brick wall to get the judge to act.... When we went before the judge he said my husband had not yet violated *his* order (only the orders of the other two judges). So *he* had to give him a chance to comply with *his* order first.

I said, "The law says the judge is supposed to order a wage assignment." He [the D.A.] said "Yes, but this judge doesn't know what he's doing."

What is surprising about these responses is that at the time we conducted these interviews, the California law *required* judges to order a wage assignment if the man had not paid support for *two* months. Yet, even when presented with a case in which the father was five months in arrears, one-third of the judges said they would *not* order a wage attachment.

Even more telling are the judges' responses to the question, "How many wage assignments have you ordered in the past six months?" The average was only one or two wage assignments per judge over the six-month period, and more than one-quarter of the judges said they had *never* ordered a wage assignment. When one considers that there were about 36,000 divorce cases heard in Los Angeles County each year, and that the Los Angeles County judges (and commissioners) are a "specialized bench" assigned to hear only family law cases, it is evident that these judges heard thousands of noncompliance complaints during this six-month period. Yet they ordered wage assignments in only a tiny fraction of the cases—less than one in a hundred.

If, as Dean Pound said, "the life of the law is in its enforcement," it is clear why the child support laws make a mockery of the legal system.

Apparently California judges were not alone in failing to enforce the law. As noted earlier, Senator Paula Hawkins reported that Florida judges were also unwilling to use the enforcement procedures provided by the law, and Blanche Bernstein, former head of Social Services in New York City, reported the same pattern among family court judges in New York City (Bernstein, 1982).

When asked directly about the law that required wage assignments, more than one-third of the California judges said they disapproved of it. Their most common explanations were that it "took away judges' discretion" and "could jeopardize a man's job." The New York City judges who refused to enforce a similar law argued that it was unconstitutional, a view that was rejected by that state's highest court (Bernstein, 1982).

(3) Excusing arrearages. The third complaint about current judicial practice is that many judges are willing to excuse arrearages (money owed for past-due child support). As one woman reported:

> The judge said he could pay off the arrearage (of $12,000) at the rate of $20.00 per month ... with no interest or anything ... It's outrageous—he gave him 50 years to pay me back! ... But I'm stuck paying interest on the money I borrowed to keep the kids alive.

Most of the judges we interviewed said they often decreased or "forgive" large arrearages. Their explanations included not wanting to make payments too difficult ("It would be a financial hardship for a man to make back payments in full"); wanting to give the father a break so that he can get on the right track; and trying to look to the future, not the past (after all, some judges reasoned, "The children have managed to survive"). The implicit message in the judges' treatment of arrearages is that fathers are rewarded for noncompliance by having their debt reduced or forgiven.

In no other area of the law do judges retroactively adjust court orders and arbitrarily dismiss debts. Although relief from some debts is permitted if a person is bankrupt, child support obligations are not dischargeable in bankruptcy. They have a special status and cannot be forgiven. This is because the law recognizes that they have a *higher* claim and deserve greater respect than other debts. In light of the special status of support obligations, it is unconscionable for family court judges simply to "forgive" them.

A final (but less common) complaint was that judges were too weak on enforcement because they "never show they mean business" by sending seriously delinquent fathers to jail. This observation is accurate. The judges we interviewed were willing to use jail "as a threat" but were very reluctant actually to sentence anyone to jail—even after years of noncompliance.

Only two of the Los Angeles County judges we interviewed considered jail an appropriate sanction. As one of them said, "You don't see the money until the slammer door opens."

In view of these attitudes, it is not surprising to find that 45% of the Los Angeles County judges said that during the past six months they *had never jailed a single father* for noncompliance. The remaining 55% said they had sentenced an average of two men to jail during that period.

When these practices are read in light of what we now know about noncompliance rates with child support awards (which must involve at least 6000 seriously delinquent cases a year), it is easy to see why many men believe they can ignore child support orders with impunity. The present legal system provides virtually *every incentive* for fathers not to pay child support.

And in the end, the children are the tragic victims of the present system of inadequate and unpaid child support. Even though the typical child support award provides less than half the cost of raising a child, chances are that the noncustodial father will not pay it, and the legal system will do nothing about it. Current estimates of noncompliance with child support orders range from 60% to 80% (Cassetty, 1978: 3). These are appalling statistics for a society that purports to place such a high value on the welfare of its children (Cassetty, 1978: 3).

In summary, this research reveals that a majority of divorced fathers have the ability to pay court-mandated child support without seriously jeopardizing their own standard of living. A majority also believe they *should* pay. Yet two-thirds of the divorced women we interviewed said that they did not regularly receive the child support that had been ordered by the courts.

In large part, men do not pay because enforcement of child support awards is so lax that noncompliance rarely incurs a penalty. Lawyers, judges, and court personnel do not use the law to sanction defaulting fathers. The burden for securing payment, therefore, falls on the custodial mother, who is already disadvantaged by time and monetary constraints. In addition, the present custody rules may create additional pressures on mothers to accept a lower support award in order to secure and retain custody.

Increased public recognition of the national disgrace of unpaid child support has been growing in recent years. As Representative Dan Coats of Indiana said in the 1983 Congressional hearings on child support:

> The burden for mothers in providing economic and emotional security for the family is nearly an overwhelming task but even more complicated when they don't receive adequate child support from the fathers.
>
> It is our responsibility to do what we can do to alleviate this shameful child support record. I think ultimately we are faced with a task of reawakening our population to the importance of accepting and fulfilling the responsibility of caring for children that are brought into this world. That responsibility does not end upon separation or divorce but continues to an even greater degree. Fathers have both a legal and moral obligation to provide child support, and we should do what we can to insure that that is done [House Hearings, 1983: 84].

THE ECONOMIC AND
SOCIAL CONSEQUENCES

The major economic result of the divorce law revolution is the systematic impoverishment of divorced women and their children. They have become the new poor.

The net effect of the present rules for property, alimony, and child support is severe financial hardship for most divorced women and their children. They experience a dramatic decline in income and a drastic decline in their standard of living. Even women who enjoyed comfortable middle- and upper-class standards of living during marriage experience sharp downward mobility after divorce.

On the average, in the first year after divorce, men experience a 42% improvement in their standard of living, while women and their children experience a 73% decline. How can women cope with such severe deprivation? Every single expenditure that they take for granted—clothing, food, housing, heat—must be cut to one-half or one-third of what they are accustomed to.

It is difficult to absorb the full implications of the statistics. What does it mean to have a 73% decline in one's standard of living? When

asked how they survived this drastic decline in income, many of the
divorced women said that they themselves were not sure. It meant
"living on the edge" and "living without." As some of them described it:

> We ate macaroni and cheese five nights a week. There was a Safeway
> special for 39 cents a box. We could eat seven dinners for $3.00 a week....
> I think that's all we ate for months.

> I applied for welfare... It was the worst experience of my life.... I never
> dreamed that I, a middle class house wife, would ever be in a position like
> that. It was humiliating . . . they make you feel it. . . . But we were
> desperate, and I *had* to feed my kids.

Even those who had relatively affluent life-styles before the divorce
faced hardships they had not anticipated. For example, the wife of a
dentist sold her car "because I had no cash at all, and we lived on that
money—barely—for close to a year." The wife of a policeman told an
especially poignant story about "not being able to buy my twelve-year-
old son Adidas sneakers." The boy's father had been ordered to pay $100
a month child support but had not been paying. To make up that gap in
her already bare-bone budget, she has been using credit cards to buy
food and other household necessities. She had exceeded all her credit
limits and felt the family just couldn't afford to pay $25 for a new pair of
Adidas sneakers. But, as she said a year later:

> You forget what it's like to be twelve years old and to think you can't live
> without Adidas sneakers.... and to feel the whole world has deserted you
> along with your father.

EXPLAINING THE DISPARITY BETWEEN HUSBANDS AND WIVES

How can we explain the strikingly different economic consquences of
divorce for men and women? How could a law that aimed at fairness
create such disparities between divorced men and their former wives and
children?

As detailed in the preceding pages, the explanation lies first in the
inadequacies of the court's awards that we have discussed; second, in the
expanded demands on the wife's resources after divorce; and, third, in
the husband's greater earning capacity and ability to supplement his
income.

Because the wife typically assumes the responsibility for raising the
couple's children, her need for help and services increases as a direct
result of her becoming a single parent. Yet, at the same time that her
need for income and more financial support is greatest, the courts have
drastically reduced her income. Thus the gap between her income and
her needs is wider after divorce.

In contrast, the gap between the husband's income and needs narrows. Although he now has fewer absolute dollars, the demands on his income have diminished. While he loses the benefits of economies of scale, and while he may have to purchase some services (such as laundry and cooking) that he did not have to buy during marriage, he is much better off because he is no longer financially responsible for the needs of his ex-wife and children. Because he has been allowed to retain most of his income, he can afford these extra expenses and still have more surplus income than he enjoyed during marriage.

In this regard, it is also important to note the role that property awards play in contributing to, rather than alleviating, the financial disparities between divorced women and men. Today, when the family home is commonly sold to allow an "equal" division of property, there is no cushion to soften the financial devastation that low support awards create for women and children. Rather, the disruptive costs of moving and establishing a new household further strain their limited income— often to the breaking point.

The final explanation for the large income discrepancy between former husbands and wives lies in the different earning capacities of the two adults at the time of the divorce. Women are doubly disadvantaged at the point of divorce. Not only do they face the male/female income gap that affects all working women, they also suffer from the toll the marital years have taken on their earning capacity. (One-third of the working mothers who are employed full-time cannot earn enough money to support themselves and their children above the poverty line in the United States today [Bates, 1983: 6].)

Thus marriage—and then divorce—impose a differential disadvantage on women's employment prospects, and this is especially severe for women who have custody of minor children. The responsibility for children inevitably restricts the mother's job opportunities by limiting her work schedule and location, her availability for overtime, and her freedom to take advantage of special training, travel assignments, and other opportunities for career advancement.

The discrepancy between divorced men and women has been corroborated by other research. Sociologist Robert Weiss and economist Thomas Espenshade found parallel disparities in the standards of living of former husbands and wives after divorce, and Weiss corroborates the finding that the greatest reduction in postdivorce income is experienced by women who shared higher family incomes before the divorce (Weiss, 1984; Espenshade, 1979). Census Bureau data also document the disparities in both income and standards of living of men and women after divorce. In 1979, the median per capita income of divorced women who had not remarried was $4152, just over half of the $7886 income of divorced men who had not remarried (U.S. Census, 1981).

The situation of divorced women with young children is even more grim. The median income in families headed by women with children under six years of age was only 30% of the median income for all families whose children were under six (U.S. Census, 1980). Thus, for the United States as a whole, "the income of families headed by women is at best half that of other families; the income of families headed by women with young children is even less, one-third of that of other families" (National Center on Women and Family Law, 1983).

SOCIETAL CONSEQUENCES

The rise in divorce has been the major cause of the increase in female-headed families, and that increase has been the major cause of the feminization of poverty. Sociologist Diana Pearce, who coined the phrase "feminization of poverty," was one of the first to point to the critical link between poverty and divorce for women. (Pearce, 1978).

Contrary to popular perception, most female-headed single-parent families in the United States are not the result of unwed parenthood: they are the result of marital dissolution. Only 18% of the nearly ten million female-headed families in the United States are headed by an unwed mother; over 50% are headed by divorced mothers, and the remaining 31% by separated mothers (Weitzman, 1985).

When a couple with children divorces, it is probable that the man will become single but the woman will become a single parent. And poverty, for many women, begins with single parenthood (Pearce, 1978).

Consider these statistics:

—half (54%) of the children in single-parent mother-headed families are living below the poverty line (U.S. Census, 1985: 26-29).
—80% of the single-parent mother-headed families are the result of divorce and separation.
—one-third of all poor children in the United States live with parents who are divorced or separated (U.S. House of Representatives, 1987).

Such statistics led a 1987 California Senate Task Force to conclude that "there is a direct relationship between the operation of the current legal system of divorce—and, more specifically, the inadequate and poorly enforced awards of child and spousal support and the unequal division of community assets—and the resulting impoverishment of women and children" (California Senate, 1987: 2).

The well-known growth in the number of single-parent, female-headed households has been amply documented elsewhere. (The 8% of all children who lived in mother-child families in 1960 rose to 12% by 1970, and to 20% by 1981.) Also well documented is the fact that these mother-headed families are the fastest growing segment of the American poor.

In recent years, there have been many suggestions for combating the feminization of poverty. Most of these have focused on changes in the labor market (such as altering the sex segregation in jobs and professions, eliminating the dual labor market and the disparity between jobs in the primary and secondary sectors, eradicating the discriminatory structure of wages, and providing additional services, such as child care, for working mothers) and on expanding social welfare programs (such as increasing AFDC benefits to levels above the poverty line, augmenting Medicaid, food stamp, and school lunch programs, and making housewives eligible for social security and unemployment compensation).

A third possibility, which has not received widespread attention, is to change the way that courts allocate property and income at divorce. If, for example, custodial mothers and their children were allowed to remain in the family home, and if the financial responsibility for children were apportioned according to the means of the two parents, and if court orders for support were enforced, a significant segment of the population of divorced women and their children would not be impoverished by divorce.

CHILD POVERTY AND ECONOMIC HARDSHIP
FOR CHILDREN OF DIVORCE

Not surprisingly, the children of divorce often express anger and resentment when their standard of living is significantly less than that in their father's household. They realize that their lives have been profoundly altered by the loss of "their home" and school and neighborhood and friends, and by the new expectations their mother's reduced income creates for them. It is not difficult to understand their resentment when fathers fly off for a weekend in Hawaii while they are told to forgo summer camp, to get a job, and to earn their allowance. That resentment, according to psychologists Judith Wallerstein and Joan Kelly, is "a festering source of anger":

> When the downward change in the family standard of living followed the divorce and the discrepancy between the father's standard of living and that of the mother and children was striking, this discrepancy was often

central to the life of the family and remained as a festering source of anger and bitter preoccupation.

The middle-class children of divorce may also feel betrayed by their disfranchisement in their parents' property settlement. Because the law divides family property between the husband and wife and makes no provisions for a child's share of the marital assets, many children feel they have been unfairly deprived of "their" home, "their" piano, "their" stereo set, and "their" college education. The last item is indicative, for children's taken-for-granted expectations about the future are often altered by divorce. For example, one mother reported that the most upsetting thing about the divorce was her son's loss of the college education he'd been promised. His father, who had always pressed him to follow in his footsteps at Dartmouth, told him that a private college was out of the question: he would have to stay home and take advantage of the low tuition at the state college. While his father could still "afford" to send his son to Dartmouth, his priorities had changed.

Inasmuch as about 1.2 million children's parents divorce each year, the 30% who receive no support from their fathers adds up to 360,000 new children each year. Over a ten-year period, this amounts to 4 million children. If we add to these the approximately 3 million over the years who receive only part of their child support (or receive it only some of the time), we find a ten-year total of 7 million children deprived of the support to which they ere entitled. Remembering that fewer than 4 million children are born each year helps put all these figures in perspective.

The failure of absent parents to provide child support has taken an especially severe toll in recent years because of sharp cutbacks in public programs benefiting children since 1979. The Children's Defense Fund shows that children's share of Medicaid payments dropped from 14.9% in 1979, to 11.9% in 1982, despite a rise in the child proportion among the eligible. The Aid to Families with Dependent Children (AFDC) program has also been sharply cut back. In 1979, there were 72 children in AFDC for every 100 children in poverty, but only 52 per 100 in 1982 (Children's Defense Fund, 1984).

It is not surprising to find a strong relationship between the economic and psychological effects of divorce on children. Economic deprivation following divorce has been linked to increased anxiety and stress among American children. Mounting evidence also shows that children of divorce who experience the most psychological stress are those whose postdivorce lives have been impaired by inadequate income. For example, Hodges, Tierney, and Buchsbaum (1984) find "income inadequacy" the most important factor in accounting for anxiety and depression among preschool children in divorced families. When family income is adequate, there are no differences in anxiety-depression levels between children in divorced families and those in intact families. However, "children of divorced families with inadequate income had substantially higher levels of anxiety-depression." Hodges, Wechsler, and Ballantine also find significant correlations between income and adjustment for preschool children of divorce (but not, interestingly, for preschool children of intact families).

HOW WE CAN EQUALIZE DIVORCE?

We do not have to return to a fault-based system of divorce to alter the economic results of the present system, for the hardships of the present system are not inevitable. What is required to alleviate them is a commitment to fairness, an awareness of the greater burdens that the system imposes on women and children, and a willingness to require fathers to shoulder their economic responsibility for their children.

There are four groups that deserve our special attention. First, there are *the children of divorce* who need more financial support and more effective means of securing the support they are awarded. The goal of child support awards should be to equalize the standards of living in the custodial and noncustodial households; children are entitled to share the standard of living of their higher-earning parent.

In addition, all support awards should include automatic adjustments for cost of living increases and more effective and automatic methods of assuring payment. The 1984 federal law, which provides for wage assignments, income tax refund intercepts, national location efforts, and property liens and bonds that will reach self-employed fathers, is an important step in the right direction.

College-age children of divorce also need "child" support past age 18 if they are full-time students and financially dependent.

The children of divorce also need the protection of orders maintaining their residence in the family home. When these rules are optional, as they are in California, their use depends on judicial discretion, and they are often ignored. What works best are laws that require judges to maintain the family home for children after divorce.

The children of divorce would also benefit from a primary caretaker presumption for sole custody awards, and laws that allow joint custody only upon agreement of both parents (Weitzman, 1985). Such clear standards for custody awards would make it more difficult to use children as "pawns" in divorce negotiations, and would reduce both the threat and the use of custody litigation in order to gain financial advantages in property or support awards. Given that custody litigation and the prolonged hostility it typically generates are likely to have an adverse psychological and financial impact on the welfare of children, custody laws that designate clear priorities and minimize litigation are clearly preferable.

Second, *the long-married older housewife* merits special attention. If she has little or no experience in the paid labor force because she has devoted herself to her husband, home, and children in the expectation of sharing assets the family built, she needs rules that require, rather than allow, judges to redistribute the husbands' postdivorce income to *equalize the standards of living in the two households.*

This recommendation rests on the same principle that underlies community property rules: it is the assumption that marriage is an equal partnership in which all the assets should be shared. This principle is strongly supported by the divorced men and women interviewed in this study (Weitzman, 1985). They viewed the sharing of income through alimony—or whatever name we choose for income transfers after divorce—as the means for providing the wife with her share of the fruits of their joint endeavors. These sharing principles are fundamental elements in the "marital contract" that most married couples agreed to and lived by during marriage.

Older women should not be measured by the new standards of equality and self-sufficiency after divorce. It is both impractical and unfair to expect women who married and lived most of their lives under a different set of social and legal rules to be forced to find employment and to support themselves. They have earned an interest in their husband's income for the rest of their lives and require a legislative presumption of permanent (i.e., continuing, open-ended) support.

Women who divorce after long marriages should also be entitled to remain as members in their husbands' health insurance plans, to share their pension and retirement benefits, and to maintain their home. If the family home and the husband's pension are the only major assets of the marriage, the older wife should be allowed to retain her home without forfeiting her share of the pension.

In summary, we need "grandmother clauses" for the long-married older women who married and lived their lives under the traditional rules. It is unfair to change the rules on them in the middle of the game.

The third group that merits a new approach are *the mothers who retain major responsibility for the care of minor children* after divorce. Whether the custody award is labeled "sole custody," or "joint custody," or even "joint physical custody," if this woman assumes most of the day-to-day caretaking, she requires a greater share of the family's resources. These include the continued use of the family home (which should be viewed as part of the child support award rather than as an unequal division of property) and a significant portion of her ex-husband's income so that the two households maintain, insofar as practical, equal standards of living after divorce.

Because employment will play a critical role in the postdivorce lives of younger divorced mothers, and thus in their ability to contribute to their children's and their own support, they should be awarded full support in the early years after divorce to enable them to maximize their long-range employment prospects. This means generous support awards and balloon payments immediately after divorce to finance their education, training, and career counseling. Insofar as possible, every effort should be made to provide them and their children with full support in the transitional years so that forced employment does not interfere with their training and child care.

The fourth group that requires special attention are those of *the transitional generation—women who divorce in their forties.* Many of these women have been employed during marriage and have also raised children who are now approaching maturity. Yet, they have given priority to their families and their husbands' careers nonetheless. It is manifestly unfair to hold them to the new standards of self-sufficiency at the point of divorce as the courts do now. The means of bringing them to parity are less clear. But we can go a long way toward achieving more equality of results by assuring them an equal share of the fruits of the marital partnership (with an equal share of their husband's career assets, including his enhanced earning capacity); support to maximize their employment potential with additional training, counseling and education; and, where appropriate, compensation for the detriment to their own careers.

Although these recommendations may sound ambitious, it is significant that most of them—especially those related to children, older housewives, and custodial mothers—have been introduced as legislative proposals by the California Senate Task Force on Family Equity in 1987 (California Senate, 1987: 5-8).

THE ROLE OF JUDGES

Given that all these policy recommendations focus on legislative reforms, one might ask whether judicial education and continuing education of the bar might not provide equally useful routes to bring about change? One hopeful indication of the prospects for change through judicial education seminars comes from my own experience.

When I first began presenting the data from this research, the findings were greeted with some skepticism. Each judge insisted that he (the overwhelming majority of judges who hear family law cases are male) was not awarding low amounts of alimony and/or child support. Further, most judges insisted that they were not awarding a large proportion of the family income or property to the husband.

I soon learned to begin my talks by presenting a few hypothetical cases and asking the judges to set awards for Ann Thompson, a 53-year-old housewife, and Pat Byrd, a young mother of preschool children. After collecting and tabulating their responses in front of the audience (i.e., their awards of child and spousal support, and their disposition of the family home), we proceeded to "trace out" the implications of the awards they had just made. The results of their awards were compared to the costs of raising children, to state welfare and poverty levels, and to the husbands' disposable income after divorce. Women's job prospects and average wages were examined, and the probable postdivorce income of husband and wife were compared.

When it became clear that awards that seemed fair in the abstract— awards that would "allow" a man to keep "enough" of his income and yet effect an "equal" division of family income and assets—actually served in these concrete cases to disadvantage women and children severely, the judges were more receptive to the notion that they should reconsider the consequences of their decisions and begin to think about what awards-setting standards might lead to more equitable results.

While this suggests the potential benefits of judicial education, it is clearly not a panacea. For there is a pervasive pattern of sex-based assumptions and practices in the judiciary that was observed throughout our research: judges' open disregard of the law requiring them to order wage attachments for fathers who are not paying child support; their willingness to forgive the arrearage on past-due child support because it "unfairly burdens" the father; their readiness to attribute earning capacity to an older housewife; and their assumption that it is fair to divide family income so that the wife and children share one-third, while the husband keeps the other two-thirds for himself (Weitzman, 1985: 292-293, 302, 188-189, 264-267, 273). These assumptions and practices make one hesitate to rely on any prescription that seeks to change judges instead of changing the law itself.

It is also impossible to ignore the implicit sex bias in the way many judges define what is reasonable or unreasonable. For example, judges rarely grant a wife's request for a forced sale of the family business so that she can obtain her share of the equity, because they see an overriding interest in preserving the "husband's" business intact (Weitzman, 1985: 97-101). However, when a husband requests an immediate sale of the family home so he can cash out his share of the equity while the wife seeks to delay the sale to ensure housing for the children, the judges tend to see the overriding interest as, again, the *husband's* need for *his* share of the equity (Weitzman, 1985: 81-92). In the first case, they tell the wife that it is reasonable to make *her* wait for her share of the equity, but in the second case, they say it is unreasonable to make a husband wait for his share.

Consider also what judges consider a reasonable arrangement for the management and control of a family business or closely held "family" corporation. Here the judges typically acknowledge that to compel divorced spouses to manage an ongoing business jointly would be disruptive and impractical; rather, *one* person has to be empowered to make the final decisions. They, therefore, award the business management and control (as well as outright ownership, in come cases) to one spouse, invariably the husband (Weitzman 1985: 97-101). They simply overlook the *wife's right* to share equally in the control of a business or company that she partially owns.

However, when the same issues are raised about joint child custody, judges see no problem about compelling divorced spouses to cooperate in an ongoing relationship to make decisions. Nor do they see the impracticability of divided authority, or the disruption that this may cause for children. Rather, they focus on the *father's right* to share parental authority.

Finally, consider judicial attitudes toward the goodwill value of a business or a profession. Many judges frankly admit that they are reluctant to recognize the goodwill in a profession because it would be too difficult for the husband to raise the capital to "buy back his wife's share" (Weitzman, 1985: 123-124). However, when an older housewife who has spent 20 or 30 years in the family home points out that it is virtually impossible for her to raise the capital to buy out her husband's share of the home, judges say her practical difficulties are irrelevant (Weitzman, 1985: 81-84).

These attitudes underscore the need for the type of explicit laws and judicial directives that have been suggested above.

Several other recommendations on the judiciary were originally suggested by attorneys in our sample and have been reiterated at virtually every meeting I have had with attorneys and bar association groups. The first is for a specialized judiciary with an interest and expertise in the family law area. It is openly acknowledged that many

California judges are political appointees with primary experience in criminal courts. They have no interest or experience in family law and they resent hearing divorce cases and being assigned to the domestic relations calendar. Such judges may "endure" the assignment but make no effort to keep up with recent case law developments or to master the body of knowledge necessary to make competent judgments. Thus attorneys complain of having to educate judges in the course of presenting their cases, and of facing judges who do not want to bother to read briefs or hear case law precedents.

It is, therefore, recommended that judges assigned to family law cases have prior experience, knowledge, and interest in family law. In addition, courts could hire special commissioners with such expertise. Because these recommendations may be at odds with the current system of judicial appointments and the structure of the courts in many counties, an alternative is to require *mandatory judicial education before* judges are assigned to hear divorce cases. In addition, once a judge is assigned to the domestic relations calendar, continuing education courses, on an annual basis, should be mandatory.

As the 1987 California Senate Task Force concluded: "the high volume, complexity, and impact on people's lives of family law cases require an educated, fair, and efficient family law judiciary. Continuing judicial education on family law, while not a panacea, is necessary to eliminate gender bias and sensitize judges to the economic consequences of their decisions" (California Senate, 1987: II-2).

Along with the need for a specialized bench and for compulsory judicial education, there is clearly a need for more judges to be assigned to hear family law cases. These cases now compose one-half of all the cases in most counties, yet they are typically rushed through the judicial process because they are assigned only one-tenth (or less) of judicial time. Because the judges who are assigned to domestic relations can rarely handle the entire caseload of pending divorces, it is common practice in many counties to assign divorce cases that require more than a half-day or day of court time to the "master calendar," where they are given the next available superior court judge. It is, as one attorney put it, "like playing Russian roulette with my client's future because we can be assigned to a judge who doesn't have a clue about family law, hasn't heard a case in 3 years, and has never dealt with a complicated pension case in his life."

This appalling situation would also be alleviated by the establishment of a specialized family law bench with knowledgeable, experienced, and interested judges who participate in annual judicial education programs. In addition, sufficient judicial personnel should be assigned to the family court so that all of the divorce cases can be heard by those judges.

A final suggestion for the judiciary involves awards of attorneys fees and legal costs. Attorneys frequently cited the difficulties they face in obtaining awards for appraisers' and experts' fees when they represent the lower-earning or unemployed spouse. Although the law allows judges to award attorneys' fees and legal costs, judges typically award only a fraction of the costs requested or refuse to award any fees at all. This puts a greater burden on the attorney who represents the lower-earning spouse, or the spouse who has less access to family resources, who is usually the wife. An attorney's vigorous representation of the interests of the lower-income spouse is undermined if the attorney does not have the money to pay for depositions, investigative accountants, and independent appraisals. (These are serious handicaps when added to the initial handicaps of a spouse who typically has less knowledge of the family's finances.) Thus it is urged that judges be encouraged to award attorneys' fees and legal costs to the attorney representing the lower-earning spouse so that person is not disadvantaged in the legal process.

CONCLUSION

The no-fault revolution in divorce law took a major step forward by reducing the acrimony and hostility in the legal process of divorce, but because it did not provide economic protection for women and children, it failed to achieve its loftier goals of fairness, justice, and economically based equality.

Divorce today brings financial disaster for too many women and for the minor children in their custody. The data reveal a dramatic contrast in financial status of divorced men and women at every income level and every level of marital duration. Women of all ages and at all socioeconomic levels experience a precipitous decline in standard of living within one year after divorce, while their former husbands' standard of living improves. Older women and women divorced from men in the higher-income brackets experience the most radical downward mobility.

These economic changes have drastic psychological effects on the children of divorce. The sharp decline in mothers' standard of living forces residential moves with resulting changes of schools, teachers, neighbors, and friends. Mothers pressured to earn money have little time and energy to devote to their children just when they are needed most. Moreover, when the discrepancy in standard of living between children and father is great, children feel angry and rejected and are likely to share their mother's feelings of resentment.

These findings make it clear that, for all its aims at fairness, the current no-fault system of divorce is inflicting a high economic toll upon women and children. The time has come for us to recognize that divorced women and their children need greater economic protection, and to implement the legal changes necessary to achieve that goal.

We do not have to tolerate the hardships that the present legal system inflicts to achieve the long-range goal of equality; true equality cannot evolve while these abuses persist. Nor do we have to return to the traditional fault-based legal system to obtain economic settlements that better protect dependent wives and children.

The lesson of this experience is not that the goals of the divorce law reforms were unworthy, but rather that the means used to achieve them were not appropriate or effective. But now that the data are in, and the inequities in the present system are evident, the paths before us are clear. The challenge that lies ahead is to provide true equality in divorce—equality of results.

REFERENCES

Bates, Thomas E. (1983) Bates Brief. (Briefing paper prepared for California Assemblyman for hearings on "The Feminization of Poverty," San Francisco, April 8, 1983, mimeo)

Bernstein, Blanch (1982) "Shouldn't low income fathers support their children?" Public Interest 66.

California Assembly (1970) Assembly Committee on the Judiciary. Report on Assembly Bill No. 530 and Senate Bill No. 252 (The Family Act). Assembly J. 785, 787 (Reg. Sess. 1970).

California Senate Task Force on Family Equity (1987) Final Report, June 1, 1987. Sacramento, CA.

Cassetty, Judith (1978) Child Support and Public Policy. Lexington, MA: D. C. Heath.

Chambers, David (1979) Making Fathers Pay. Chicago: University of Chicago Press.

Chase, Marilyn (1985) "The no-fault divorce has a fault of its own, many women learn." Wall Street Journal (January 21): i (col. 1).

Children's Defense Fund (1984) American Children in Poverty. Washington, DC: Author.

Eisler, Riane Tennenhaus (1977) Dissolution: No-Fault Divorce, Marriage and the Future of Women. New York: McGraw-Hill.

Espenshade, Thomas (1979) "The economic consequences of divorce." Journal of Marriage and the Family 41: 615.

Hawkins, Paula (1984) Statement in Hearing before the Committee on Finance, United States Senate, Ninety-Eighth Congress, Second Session, January 24-25. Washington, DC: Government Printing Office.

Hodges, William F., Carol W. Tierney, and Helen K. Bushbaum (1984) "The Cumulative Effect of Stress on Preschool Children of Divorced and Intact Families." Journal of Marriage and the Family 46: 611-629.

House Hearings (1983) Statement in Hearing before the Subcommittee on Public Assistance and Unemployment Compensation of the Committee on Ways and Means, U.S. House of Representatives Ninety-Eighth Congress First Session, July 14, 1983, Serial 198-41. Washington, DC: Government Printing Office.

Hunter, Nan (1983) "Women and Child Support," in Irene Diamond (ed.) Families, Politics, and the State. New York: Longman.

Kay, Herma Hill (1978) Personal communication.

Leonard, Frances (1980) The Disillusionment of Divorce for Older Women. Gray Paper No. 6. Washington, DC: Older Women's League.

Matter of Farmer (1984) New York Law Journal (N.Y. City Family Court) (January 16): 13 (col. 2).

National Center on Women and Family Law (1983) "Sex and economic discrimination in child custody awards." Clearinghouse Review 16: 1132.

Norton, Arthur [U.S. Bureau of the Census] (1984) Interview (March).

Pearce, Diana (1978) "The Feminization of Poverty: women, work and welfare." Urban and Social Change Review.

Shields, Laurie (1981) Displaced Homemakers—Organizing for a New Life. New York: McGraw-Hill.

U.S. Bureau of the Census (1985) "Money Income and Poverty Status of Families and Persons in the United States: 1984." Current Population Reports, Series P-60, No. 149. Washington, DC: Government Printing Office.

U.S. Department of Commerce, Bureau of the Census (1980) "Families maintained by female householders 1970-1979." Current Population Reports, Series P-23, No. 107. Washington, DC: Government Printing Office.

U.S. Department of Commerce, Bureau of the Census (1981) "Money Income of Families and Persons in the United States: 1979." Current Population Reports, Series P-60, No. 129. Washington, DC: Government Printing Office.

U.S. Department of Commerce, Bureau of the Census (1983) "Child Support and Alimony 1981." Current Population Series Reports, Series P-23, No. 127. Washington, DC: Government Printing Office.

U.S. House of Representatives (1987) Opening statement of Congressman George Miller, Chairman, Select Committee on Children, Youth and Families. June 19, 1986. Hearings on "Divorce: The Impact on Children and Families." Washington, DC: Government Printing Office.

Weiss, Robert S. (1984) "The impact of marital dissolution on income and consumption in single-parent households." Journal of Marriage and the Family 28: 615.

Weitzman, Lenore J. (1985) The Divorce Revolution: The Unexpected Social and Economic Consequences for Women and Children in America. New York: Free Press.

5

FEMALE OFFENDERS:
PATERNALISM REEXAMINED

Meda Chesney-Lind

After years of almost total neglect, the female offender has, over the last decade, been the subject of considerable attention. While recognition of the importance of studying the female criminal was clearly long overdue, the last decade's fascination with women's crime had little to do with an interest in rectifying scholarly or programmatic oversight. Instead, most public, and a good deal of the scholarly, discussion was focused on the question of whether the women's movement had inspired a female crime wave (Adler, 1975; Simon, 1975). Simply stated, this perspective argued that because of increasing female participation in the labor force and liberalizing attitudes about women's place, women were committing more criminal acts and were no longer limiting themselves to the traditionally female crimes of theft and prostitution.

Because of the widespread public acceptance of this "liberation hypothesis," the results of studies that examined whether or not there has been an increase in female crime, particularly in the area of traditionally masculine crimes, as a result of the women's movement should probably be briefly reviewed. Such a summary is particularly vital because the data clearly show that the number of women offenders coming into the criminal justice system has increased dramatically over the last ten years. Between 1974 and 1984, for example, the number of girls and women arrested increased by 203% (FBI, 1975, 1985) and the number of women in prison jumped 258% (considerably steeper than the male increase of 199%). Women now account for a greater percentage of the total prison population than they did a decade ago (4.5% compared to 3.5% in 1974) (Bureau of Justice Statistics, 1982, 1985). The number of women in jail has also been climbing steeply. Between 1978 and 1983, the number of women in jail increased 165% (compared to a male increase of 140%), and women now account for 7.1% of the jail populations compared to 5.9% in 1978 (Bureau of Justice Statistics, 1984). Are these dramatic increases a reflection of changes in women's involvement in serious crime?

Darrell Steffensmeier and his associates have probably undertaken the most exhaustive evaluation of the liberation hypothesis utilizing both official and unofficial measures of the level of crime. In one of these, Steffensmeier (1980a) examined the pattern of female criminal behavior for the years 1965-1977 and concluded that "females are not catching up with males in the commission of violent, masculine, male-dominated, serious crimes (except larceny) or in white collar crimes" (Steffensmeier, 1980a: 1080). He did note female arrest gains in the Uniform Crime Report categories of larceny, fraud, forgery, and vagrancy but, by examining these gains more carefully, he demonstrated that they were due almost totally to increases in traditionally female criminal activities such as shoplifting, prostitution, and naive check forgery (fraud). He also suggested that changes in enforcement patterns (such as increased willingness of stores to prosecute shoplifters, the widespread abuse of vagrancy statutes to arrest prostitutes combined with a declining use of this same arrest category to control public drunkenness, and the growing concern with "welfare fraud") might well explain changes in female arrests without any necessary changes in the number of women involved in these activities.

A look at recent arrest data also fails to support the notion that women are committing more serious offenses than they did a decade ago. Essentially, the dramatic increases in arrests of women for nontraditional offenses that characterized the 1960s and early 1970s were not sustained into the 1980s. Arrests of women for violent Part One offenses increased only 10.4% between 1975 and 1984 (FBI, 1985: 167) compared to a 160.7% increase between 1960 and 1974 (FBI, 1975: 184). Indeed, arrests of women for murder and robbery actually declined during the last decade.

Studies of the characteristics of female offenders also fail to support the liberation hypothesis. Instead, they found them to be largely low-income minority women who have committed "traditionally female" crimes such as theft or prostitution (Crites, 1976; Figueira-McDonough et al., 1981; Chesney-Lind and Rodriguez, 1983). A look at the employment history of female offenders also fails to support any notion that increased occupational opportunities led to their criminal misconduct. On the contrary, women in prison who had been employed were working in low-skill occupations (often temporary or part-time in nature) (Figueira-McDonough et al., 1981).

Indeed, careful students of women's crime, like Jane Chapman (1980) suggest that it is economic discrimination rather than liberation that best explains the character of women's crime. And if real changes in women's crime have been occurring during the last 20 years, most of the evidence points to increases in the number of women committing these traditionally female crimes—particularly larceny (Nagel and Hagan, 1983; however, see Steffensmeier, 1980). To explain this, Giordano, Kerbel, and Dudley (1981) suggest that the severe economic discrimination all women confronted in the decade past was particularly hard on young, single, minority women perhaps propelling them into these property crimes.

During the last decade, a quieter debate, carried on primarily within the academic community, concerned the issue of the "chivalrous" treatment of female offenders (Anderson, 1976). Compelling evidence supported the hypothesis that girls, at least, did not appear to be the recipients of lenient treatment (Chesney-Lind, 1973; Kratcoski, 1974; Datesman and Scarpitti, 1977). Studies of the treatment of adult offenders, on the other hand, seemed to support the notion that women were treated chivalrously by the courts (Baab and Furgeson, 1967; Nagel and Weitzman, 1971; Simon, 1975). Most of these influential studies examined only felony case processing and looked only at sentencing (usually whether or not the offender was incarcerated); finally, they were generally unable to control for the effects of important legal variables (such as prior record) in case processing. During the last decade, research that corrected some of these shortcomings has been undertaken and the results indicate a less benign and more complex pattern of judicial behavior.

For good or ill, much of the public interest in crime has now shifted to other topics, and those concerned about the needs of the female offender once again confront considerable apathy. This state of affairs is ironic given that dramatic increases in the number of women in the justice system make concern about her situation more necessary than ever.

This chapter will review the kind of justice girls and women who are brought into the criminal justice system can expect to receive. This discussion will show that empirical support for the long accepted chivalry hypothesis is far weaker than most assume. Instead, evidence is stronger for a position that the courts have in the past and continue to act "paternalistically" (Moulds, 1978) in response to women's largely trivial offenses. That is to say, a considerable number of studies indicate that judges and other court personnel continue to act in ways that enforce girls' and women's obedience to traditional gender role expectations either in place of or in addition to the law. Consequently, women who are obedient to parents, married, have children, are economically dependent, and respectable may receive preferential treatment when compared to their female counterparts who do not possess those traits and whose crimes do not challenge fundamental components of the female sex role. Nor does there appear to be much change in this pattern as a result of greater attention to women's issues. Finally, the chapter will review the policy implications of these findings.

GIRLS AND JUVENILE COURTS

Though it is largely unrecognized, the juvenile justice system's treatment of girls may well constitute one of the clearest examples of institutionalized sexism in contemporary society. This pattern is largely a product of the juvenile court's ability to take youth into custody for a variety of noncriminal, "status" offenses as well as for criminal acts. These uniquely juvenile offenses include such activities as "running away from home," truancy, curfew violation, being a "person in need of supervision," "minor in need of supervision," being "incorrigible," "beyond control," in need of "care and protection," or engaging in "injurious behavior."

While these offenses have long been criticized as unconstitutionally vague and over-broad (Katz and Teitelbaum, 1977), their special meaning for young women has received less attention. In 1984, status offenses accounted for about 25% of all girls' arrests (as compared to 29% in 1975), but only about 7% of boys' arrests (compared to 8.9% in 1975). Although these declines are doubtless meaningful, arrests of girls for certain status offenses (notably running away) actually increased between 1983 and 1984 (FBI, 1985: 166-171). Examination of official court populations also shows that a large proportion of girls are charged with status offenses. In the United States, for example, 40% of the girls in court in 1975-1977, but only 15% of the boys, were charged with these offenses (Black and Smith, 1981). Ten years earlier, about half of girls and about 20% of boys were referred to court for these offenses (Children's Bureau, 1967). These data do seem to signal a drop in female status offense referrals, though not a dramatic one.

For many years, statistics showing large numbers of girls arrested and referred for status offenses were taken to be representative of the different types of male and female delinquency. However, self-report studies of male and female delinquency do not reflect the dramatic differences in misbehavior found in official statistics. Specifically, it appears that girls charged with these noncriminal status offenses have been and continue to be significantly overrepresented in court populations. For example, Figueira-McDonough (1985) analyzed self-reported delinquency behavior on the part of 2000 tenth-graders and concluded that "there is no evidence of greater involvement of females in status offenses" (1985: 277; see also Teilmann and Landry, 1981).

The most persuasive argument for such differences between unofficial and official rates of female delinquency is that the juvenile justice system's commitment to the notion of the state as parent has encouraged abuse of the status offense category. The language of status offenses invites, according to one student of the court, "discretionary" application of their provisions and "allows parents, police, and juvenile court authorities, who ordinarily decide whether PINS proceedings should be initiated, to hold girls legally accountable for behavior—often sexual or in some way related to sex—that they would not consider serious if committed by boys" (Sussman, 1977: 183).

Studies examining court processing of girls and boys, particularly those examining early court records, consistently found that because court officials participated in a double standard of juvenile justice, girls charged with status offenses were often more harshly treated than their male or female counterparts charged with crimes (Cohn, 1970; Chesney-Lind, 1973; Datesman and Scarpitti, 1977; Kratcoski, 1974; Schlossman and Wallach, 1978; Sheldon, 1981). Girls were also more likely to be held for long periods of time in often brutal detention centers, and they were overrepresented, compared to their percentage of arrests, in both training school and detention center populations (Conway and Bogdan, 1977).

Some recent studies (Teilman and Landry, 1981; Clarke and Koch, 1980; and Cohen and Kluegel, 1979) have found little evidence that female status offenders were more harshly sanctioned than their male counterparts once the effects of a variety of extralegal and legal variables were accounted for. Reviewing these studies more closely, however, reveals that some of the variables these studies control for are such things as "detention status" and even, in the case of the Stevens and Koch study, "the child's family structure," "source of referral" (whether a police officer or a parent), and support of the family. What may be happening is that these studies are statistically segregating those elements in the juvenile justice system that make women uniquely vulnerable to harsh sanctions, and then concluding there is no evidence of bias against women.

But, more to the point, other current research has failed to find evidence that girls and boys charged with status offenses are treated equally. Sheldon and Horvath (1986) found in a study of youth referred to court in Las Vegas that females referred for status offenses were more likely than males referred for these offenses to receive formal processing (i.e., a court hearing). Girls were also more likely to be detained than boys. Boisvert and Wells (1980: 232) found a "significant difference" in the types of status complaints brought against males and females in Massachusetts in the mid-1970s. Males, the researchers found, were more likely to be defined as "stubborn children" while females were more likely to be defined as "runaways." Moreover, males were more likely to have engaged in criminal misconduct. Finally, girls were far more likely than boys to be removed from their homes on a first referral to court for status offense: 46.3% compared to 17.2% (though this pattern eroded with subsequent referrals) (see also Mann, 1979).

Regardless of how one reads the research, though, the data are clear that their status offense category has historically legitimized a double standard of juvenile justice with large numbers of girls being brought into the juvenile justice system and harshly sanctioned for essentially noncriminal offenses. It remains to review what has happened to this historic pattern during a decade characterized by widespread criticism and review of the juvenile justice system's handling of status offenders.

DEINSTITUTIONALIZATION AND JUDICIAL PATERNALISM

In the mid-1970s, correctional reformers had become concerned about juvenile courts' abuse of the status offense category and, largely as a result of this, the Juvenile Justice and Delinquency Prevention Act of

1974 was passed. The act required that states receiving federal delinquency prevention monies begin to divert and "deinstitutionalize" their status offenders and, despite erratic enforcement of this provision, girls were the clear beneficiaries of the reform effort. Incarceration of young women in training schools and detention centers across the country fell dramatically. Between 1974 and 1982, for example, the number of girls admitted to public detention centers in the United States fell by 45% with an equally dramatic decrease in female admissions to training schools (Krisberg et al., 1985). Encouraging, too, were studies of court decision making that found less clear evidence of discrimination against girls in parts of the country where serious diversion efforts were occurring (Moeller, 1982).

However, while there may be some evidence in some parts of the country that girls are receiving more equal treatment, it is still likely that they are being placed in training schools for less serious offenses than their male counterparts. Otherwise, as Rosemary Sarri (1983: 392) has suggested, a far steeper decline in the incarceration of female youth in training schools should have been observed. Indeed, Hoffman (1981) noted that nearly half of the girls committed to Oregon's training schools between 1977-1980 were incarcerated for misdemeanors, but only 16% of the males were incarcerated for misdemeanors. In contrast, over a third of the males (34.1%) but only about a tenth (11.8%) of the females were incarcerated for Class A felonies.

Another study (Burbeck, 1978) suggests that this may, in fact, be a national pattern. Burbeck's research examined a national sample of adjudicated and committed delinquents. Examining the relationship between severity of sanction and seriousness of offense for which the juvenile was committed, he discovered that, for males, increases in the severity of the commitment offense was associated with an increase in the severity of the sanction. For girls, on the other hand, no correlation was found between commitment offense and severity of sanction. In short, while incarcerations of girls is declining in the United States, young women still appear to be incarcerated for far less serious offenses then their male counterparts. Additionally, the sharp declines in female commitments to U.S. training schools that were observed in the 1974-1975 interval (where a decline of 47.6% decline was noted) were not seen in the 1980s. Between 1979-1982, only a 4% decline was observed (Krisberg et al., 1985: 22).

These patterns could be partially explained by research that suggests that because of federal deinstitutionalization, the bias against girls may be less overt. Mahoney and Fenster (1982) found, in their courtroom observations, that many of the girls being taken into custody for crimes had actually exhibited behavior that would earlier have been classified as status offenses. Girls who have, for example, broken into their own parents' homes and taken food and clothing to enable them to prolong their runaway status were being charged with burglary (Mahoney and Fenster, 1982: 229).

This reclassification of female status offenders into female criminals has occurred during a period characterized by a "get tough" mood on juvenile crime, and some observers (Curran, 1984) suggest that this transition has been particularly hard on female offenders because their behavior was being statistically redefined as criminal at precisely the time that courts were increasingly likely to process these cases formally and punish them more harshly.

Taken together, these studies suggest that the juvenile justice system has responded to attempts to divert and deinstitutionalize status offenders in a less than enthusiastic fashion. There are indications, for example, that in some jurisdictions, relabeling of girls has occurred, and that elsewhere girls are still being incarcerated for less serious offenses than boys. These concerns notwithstanding, the gains of the deinstitutionalization movement are undeniable; dramatic reductions in female incarcerations did occur despite all the problems with implementation. This is a significant victory for all who favor deinstitutionalization, but it is, unfortunately, an extremely fragile one. Specifically, the reforms enacted in the past decade are increasingly criticized and, in certain parts of the country, being reversed.

RETHINKING REFORM

Court officials, particularly Juvenile Court Judges, have always been extremely critical of deinstitutionalization efforts (see Hurst, 1975). Not surprisingly, then, while there were great hopes when the Juvenile Justice and Delinquency Prevention act was passed, a 1978 General Accounting Office report (GAO, 1978) concluded that the Law Enforcement Assistance Administration (the agency given the task of implementing the legislation) was less than enthusiastic about the deinstitutionalization provisions of the act. Much of this reluctance was a product of the LEAA's recognition that the DSO provisions irritated virtually everyone in the juvenile justice system. Juvenile court judges, the report specifically noted, "often believe that status offenders are just as bad as delinquents and should be treated as such" (GAO, 1978: 10).

Just how deep the resentment was became clear a few years later. During the House Hearings on the extension of the act in March 1980, Judge John R. Milligan representing the National Council of Juvenile and Family Court Judges argued as follows:

> The effect of the Juvenile Justice Act as it now exists is to allow a child ultimately to decide for himself [sic] whether he [sic] will go to school, whether he [sic] will live at home, whether he [sic] will continue to run, run, run, away from home, or whether he [sic] will even obey orders of your court [United States House of Representatives, 1980: 136].

Ultimately, the judges were successful in narrowing the definition of a status offender in the amended act so that any child who had violated a "valid court order" would no longer be covered under the deinstitutionalization provisions of the act (U.S. Statutes, 1981). This change, which was never publicly debated in either the House or the Senate Hearings, effectively gutted the act by permitting judges to reclassify as delinquent a status offender who violated a court order. This meant that a young woman who ran away from a court-ordered placement (a halfway house, foster homes, and so on) could be relabeled a delinquent and locked up.

Moreover, the national Advisory Committee formed to advise the Office of Juvenile Justice and Delinquency Prevention (and included Judge Milligan) had just issued a report entitled *Serious Juvenile Crime: A Redirected Federal Effort* (NAC, 1984) in which it is argued that the federal government should never have gotten involved in the status offender issue. Seeking to "transform the federal effort against delinquency," the report's authors urge federal attention be shifted to "crime committed by the serious, violent or chronic offender" (NAC, 1984: 15). Ironically, the report also criticizes the extensive focus on status offenders as discriminatory against minority and poor youth (a position developed by Robert Woodson while a fellow with the American Enterprise Institute) (U.S. Senate, 1981: 410) while never once mentioning the significant role played by deinstitutionalization in reducing sexism in juvenile justice.

It is also worth mentioning that in certain parts of the country, changes in routine processing of status offenders was strongly resisted. Juvenile justice by geography is an important factor in the mixed success in curbing the abuses of the status offender category. Regional variations, and specifically initiatives by some jurisdictions to reinstitutionalize status offenders, deserve attention. In Hawaii, for example, the Honolulu Police Department initiated an antitruancy drive that resulted in a dramatic (414%) increase in youth arrested for this offense between 1981 and 1983 (Ikeda, Chesney-Lind, and Kameoka, 1985). During the summer of 1983, the department initiated a curfew program. In announcing the program to the media, a police captain explained that he had noticed groups of teenage girls sitting at certain spots along his jogging route. "You can tell they aren't from here . . . they are young but not innocent . . . not the kind we want in Hawaii" (Pressly, 1984). Both this program and the Anti-Truancy Program were initiated while the state was receiving funds from the federal government for deinstitutionalization of status offenders, and detention of status offenders during the period increased by 12% (the state has since been declared ineligible). Hawaii is not alone; policymakers in Washington, California, Ohio, North Carolina, and Florida are also advocating for increased authority to arrest and detain status offenders (Krisberg et al., 1985: 7). These could be bellwether states for a new view of the status offender.

This is particularly likely in view of the fact that strong criticism of deinstitutionalization has come from the Office of Juvenile Justice and Delinquency Prevention itself. In a recent report, "Runaway Children and the Juvenile Justice and Delinquency Act: What Is the Impact," case studies (all involving young girls) purporting to illustrate problems with deinstitutionalization were presented in detail. Interviews with police officers and a few youth workers expressing frustration with the law are also presented. One of these will suffice. "The job of getting runaways off the street has been made 'almost impossible' by current law" is the report's summary of an interview with a New York detective. It continues

> Some of the runaways with whom he maintained regular contact have been at large for several years. Even though he may know where they are and the dangers they face, he is virtually powerless. He may be able to take them off the street for a few hours, but he is unable to stop them when they decide to return [OJJDP, 1985: 7].

In the report's introduction, Alfred Regenery, then Administrator of the Office of Juvenile Justice and Delinquency Prevention, suggested that the blanket application of the deinstitutionalization provision has had "darker consequences." Specifically, "running away is legal. The question which needs to be asked is whether or not it is in the best interest of children to afford them such a right" (OJJDP, 1985: 2).

It does not take great wit and keen foresight to conclude that those who oppose deinstitutionalization are mounting a strong effort to divert federal attention away from status offenders, and, at the same time, suggesting that perhaps the entire effort to deinstitutionalize might have gone too far. And, though girls' potential victimization while on the streets is often used to support such a view, a look at the juvenile justice system's treatment of young women in trouble makes it clear that, for girls, such an approach would be a disaster. Institutional sexism has haunted the juvenile justice system since its inception and has survived despite the substantial, though indirect, attempts at reform represented by the JD act of 1974. The historical evidence is clear that court officials, when confronted with angry parents and the vague language of the status offense categories, tend to fall back on attitudes that result in a double standard of juvenile justice. If further erosion of the victories of the deinstitutionalization movement is not prevented, the world is likely to see, once again, the jailing of large numbers of young women "for their own protection."

WOMEN AND THE COURT

Considerable interest has also been focused, over the last decade, on the differential treatment of the adult female offender within the criminal courts. Here, unlike the situation of the female delinquent, the literature has always been more abundant though not necessarily consistent. The oldest and probably predominant view on the issue holds that women are the recipients of preferential or "chivalrous" treatment if they are drawn into the criminal justice system (Pollak, 1961; Nagel and Weitzman, 1971; Simon, 1975). Another body of literature suggests that, once the effects of a variety of variables known to influence sentencing are controlled, the advantage enjoyed by women seems to disappear (Chiricos, Jackson, and Waldo, 1972; Ekstand and Eckert, 1978; Green, 1961; Hagan, 1974; Hagan and O'Donnel, 1978; Simon and Sharma, 1979; Ghali and Chesney-Lind, 1986). Other studies that controlled for the effects of these variables, however, have found support for the view that women receive more lenient treatment than their male counterparts (Baab and Furgeson, 1967; Curran, 1983; Frazier, Bock, and Henretta, 1983; Gruhl, Welch, and Spohn, 1984).

This section will first undertake a brief review of this often confusing literature so that reasons for contradictory findings can be identified. Then, recent research results that indicate that the treatment of adult women by the criminal justice system is more complex than has been previously assumed will be summarized (Nagel, Cardascia, and Ross, 1982; Kruttschnitt, 1982; Daly, 1986; Nagel and Hagan, 1983). This discussion will reveal that approaches to court responses to female crime that look simply for evidence of lenience or severity may actually obscure complex and meaningful differences in the judicial response to male and female defendants. Indeed, a growing literature suggests that judges and other court personnel may be considering information that speaks less to a woman's guilt and more to her conformity to traditional gender role expectations when making decisions about female defendants. Finally, the policy implications of this research will be briefly discussed.

CHIVALRY RECONSIDERED

Most of the early efforts, as well as a considerable number of contemporary research studies, that systematically explore the effects of gender on judicial decision making appear to support the hypothesis that women are treated leniently (Pollak, 1961; Gibbens and Prince, 1962; Baab and Furgeson, 1967; Nagel and Weitzman, 1971; Simon, 1975; Moulds, 1978; Curran, 1983). However, a number of these research efforts, particularly the early studies, are flawed because they could not control for a number of legal variables (such as prior record) known to affect judicial decision making. Moreover, many of the more recent studies (which often corrected this defect) examined only felony cases and then looked only at sentencing (rather than the entire sequence of decisions that affect case outcome). Even when examining sentencing severity, many of these studies utilize only "in/out" distinctions that may be misleading.

Perhaps best known of the early studies, and a good example of the sorts of results that are obtained when researchers fail to consider the role played by prior record, is Nagel and Weitzman's (1971) analysis of national data collected to analyze procedures for providing attorneys to indigent defendants. Examining the experience of criminal defendants charged with either grand larceny or felonious assault, they found that fewer women when compared to men were sentenced to jail, more women than men were held less than two months before trial, and more received suspended sentences or probation. They concluded that the courts were treating women "paternalistically" (by which they meant leniently) rather than punitively.

Neither their widely cited research, nor the work of Simon (1975) that concluded that women received "preferential treatment," was able to control on a number of important variables known to affect judicial outcome (notably prior record). However, some research efforts that have controlled for important legal variables still concluded that women are being treated more leniently than men at least at some level of criminal justice processing (Baab and Furgeson, 1967; Moulds, 1978; Swigert and Farrell, 1977; Frazier, Bock, and Henretta, 1983; Curran, 1983; and Gruhl, Welsh, and Spohn, 1984). Virtually all of these studies examined only felony case processing (the exception is Frazier, Bock, and Henretta, 1983) and many, though not all, considered only the sentencing decision.

One of the most thorough of the studies that found evidence of preferential treatment was that conducted by Curran (1983) on the processing of felony cases in Dade County Florida. Curran used multiple regression to examine judicial processing at four levels (negotiations, prosecution, conviction, and sentence). She examined the effects of nonlegal variables (race, age, and occupational status) as well as legal variables (number of prior arrests, offense seriousness, and total number of counts) and she examined these in three different time periods. In general, she reported that none of these variables was particularly successful at predicting sentencing (an important point), and that sex was not important at the negotiation, prosecution, or conviction levels.

At the sentencing level, however, sex did play a role with women receiving more lenient sentences. Examining this finding further, she found a significant interaction effect between sex and age that indicated that females were indeed treated more leniently than some males (younger males) but not all males. Stated differently, she concluded that "younger males receive more harsh treatment than older males and all females" (Curran, 1983: 52).

Findings similar to Curran's were reported by Gruhl, Welch, and Spohn (1984) in their regression study of felony case processing. They found that while there was no sex difference in guilty pleas or conviction rates, women were more likely to have their cases dismissed and were less likely to be incarcerated. The authors also attempted to see if race of defendant affected the paternalism pattern and were somewhat surprised to note that while being white confers advantages on male defendants, "white women were prosecuted and incarcerated more often than either black or Hispanic women" (Gruhl, Welch, and Spohn, 1984: 465).

Frazier, Bock, and Henretta's work (1983) represents one of the few pieces of research that found paternalism in nonserious offenses. In this instance, the authors examined all cases adjudicated during the early 1970s in Florida judicial district. Controlling only for whether or not the charge was a misdemeanor or a felony, they found that males were more likely to be the recipient of a harsh sentence (measured by this research only by incarceration). The effect was diminished by the inclusion of other sociodemographic and legal variables, but it was still statistically significant (Frazier, Bock, and Henretta, 1983: 312). They also found that probation officer's recommendation played a substantial role in this process and because these court officials were, in their words "influenced by traditional ideas about gender roles," they tended to avoid recommending incarceration for women. In a related study based on the same data set (Bishop and Frazier, 1984), however, the authors found no evidence of differential treatment by gender in charge reduction considerations.

In summary, most of the recent research that finds evidence for preferential treatment for female defendants finds it only among those charged with serious offenses. Moreover, the studies find it most consistently only at the sentencing stage, particularly when severity is measured only by whether or not the defendant was incarcerated. The fact that so many of these studies examine only felony case processing points up a problem. Experienced researchers in the area have called for research efforts that include less serious offenses and for work that actually tracks the movement of causes through all levels of the criminal justice system (Hagan, 1974; Steffensmeier, 1980b; Parisi, 1982). Steffensmeier (1980b) specifically called for consideration of police and lower court decision making "since the overwhelming majority of women (and even men) are arrested and processed for minor kinds of crimes" (1980b: 348).

Indeed, a number of rigorous studies, many of which examined decisions other than sentencing or considered decisions in less serious cases, have found less support for the notion that women are treated chivalrously or leniently (Green, 1961; Chiricos, Jackson, and Waldo, 1972; Goldkamp, 1979; Hagan and O'Donnel, 1978; Simon and Sharma, 1979; Figueira-McDonough, 1982; Ghali and Chesney-Lind, 1986). One of the best of these (Simon and Sharma, 1979) used 1974 PROMIS data for Washington, D.C., and controlled for a variety of legal and nonlegal variables. Using multiple regression, the authors examined criminal justice processing at the level of prosecutorial and court decision making for a considerable array of offense categories (including both misdemeanor and felony arrests in 15 crime categories). These researchers found, like Curran, that the model they employed explained only a small portion of the variation but, unlike her, they found that sex was of virtually no predictive value (Simon and Sharma, 1979: 35). Specifically, while they found "very slight" evidence that women might have their cases dismissed by the prosecutor, sex was not a useful predictor when they turned to a consideration of whether the court dismissed the case. At trial, they found that sex did not play a role in either findings of guilt or in the decision to incarcerate (Simon and Sharma, 1979: 33).

Ghali and Chesney-Lind (1986) examined the processing of males and females charged with a similarly broad range of offenses and found even less evidence of chivalry, particularly in the processing of minor offenses. The research examined the impact of gender on criminal justice decision making at three distinct levels (police, prosecutor, court) for all Part One arrests (which include both misdemeanor and felony arrests for the following offenses: murder, forcible rape, robbery, burglary, larceny theft, and auto theft) in Honolulu during 1979-1980. The results indicated that sex may, indeed, play a role at some stages of criminal justice processing but that the results are not consistent in direction. At the earliest stages of criminal justice processing (the decision to forward for prosecution and whether to prosecute), there appears to be a disadvantage associated with being female. Specifically, after accounting for the individual's age employment and marital status, the type of crime and prior criminal history, arrested females were more likely than arrested males to be prosecuted. Arrested males are more likely than females to be released pending further investigation, or to be released as the victim declines prosecution.

At the district court level, which generally handles the less serious cases, little evidence of preferential treatment was found. This finding is important because those charged with larceny were significantly more likely to be female. Women were, in fact, more likely to enter a guilty plea at arraignment. While this is not a judicial decision, its impact can hardly be termed preferential. Finally, there was no evidence that the court's decision on pretrial dismissal, trial outcome, or sentencing was affected by the defendant's sex. At the level of circuit court (which handles felonies), the defendant's gender played no role in determining the outcome of the arraignment and plea stage. Sex was also not a factor in trial outcome (guilt or innocence). Sex does appear to influence the type of sentence, however. Consistent with previous research, females appear more likely to receive probation than males with identical sociodemographic characteristics who have been convicted of identical crimes.

In general, the evidence for lenient treatment is usually found in those studies that only consider sentencing, rather than other stages in court processing, and only examine the most serious cases. When other steps in the process are considered or when less serious crimes are considered, the advantage enjoyed by women seem to dissipate. This is important given that the vast majority of women are in court for minor offenses, and given that there are significant decisions made on cases before sentencing occurs. For example, Figueira-McDonough (1982), in taking a closer look at two generally hidden judicial processes, charge reduction and sentence reduction (plea bargaining), found women disadvantaged at both of these stages of the criminal justice process largely because these activities tend to be reserved for crimes with low female representation. As a consequence, she found that women were "less able to bargain and more willing to plead guilty" (1982: 22).

With reference to findings that women charged with more serious offenses seem to be treated more leniently by courts, it is possible that greater attention should be given to the details of the offense. Most sentencing studies employ a methodology that may obscure important differences in the defendant's culpability (Daly, 1985). For example, Ward, Jackson, and Ward (1968) found that women charged with robberies were either accessories or partners in 80% of the cases (see also Fenster, 1977).

With reference to another serious crime, murder, a study of the Women's Correctional Center in Chicago (Lindsey, 1978) revealed that 40% of the women serving time for murder or manslaughter had·killed their husbands or lovers who repeatedly beat them. Brown's (1985) research on these types of murders documents what a major role brutal and escalating abuse plays in women's murder offenses and notes that public perception to the contrary, many of these women are sentenced to prison for first degree murder. It is clear that sentences in these types of murders may reflect the mitigating circumstances in the case—a pattern that might well look like judicial lenience unless the case were closely scrutinized.

JUDICIAL ENFORCEMENT OF GENDER ROLES

Both Parisi (1982) and Nagel and Hagan (1983), in their reviews of the studies on the effect of gender on sentencing, noted that there is some evidence that women who are charged with "nontraditional," manly offenses are not the beneficiaries of chivalry (the "evil woman" hypothesis). While this seems somewhat contradicted by research results that found evidence of greater lenience toward women charged with felonies, the finding appears frequently enough to warrant further study. It is possible, for example, that women charged with specific kinds of nonfeminine violent behavior are, in some of these studies, merged with nonviolent felony offenders. Less widely recognized is the significant role played by extralegal variables, particularly variables that consider the woman's respectability, marital status, or sexual behavior, in case processing. The following studies demonstrate how these nonlegal considerations seem to enter into judicial decision making.

Examining sentencing patterns in a typical New York Court for a wide range of cases (excluding prostitution, rape, and abortion), Ilene Nagel and her associates (Nagel, Cardascia, and Ross, 1982) found that although males were generally more likely to receive a harsher sentence, there were considerable differences in the manner in which the court responded to male and female defendants. First, they determined that while the severity of the offense (whether the crime was a felony or a misdemeanor) was strongly related to the likelihood of a male spending time imprisoned, this variable had no significant effect for females. But, while seriousness of offense was not important in female sentencing, they did find a strong adverse effect for females charged with personal crimes (as compared to property crimes) (see also Fenster, 1977). And they noted that marital status, a variable not significant among male defendants, had a strong effect on the probability of a woman being sentenced to prison, with married women experiencing preferential treatment.

Bernstein's findings with reference to the existence of a form of judicial paternalism that does not result in a consistent pattern of judicial leniency have received recent confirmation by Candace Kruttshnitt, who, in her research on women probationers in California (1982), found that women who were economically dependent upon someone else and were "respectable" (i.e., no records of prior psychiatric care, drug or alcohol use, employer censorship, and peer deviance) received less severe dispositions than did their independent, "freer," and less respectable counterparts. Indeed, a woman's degree of respectability appeared to be as significant as previous involvement with the law. Fenster (1977), in her study of co-defendants, also found that marriage (even to a co-defendant) tended to shield the woman, though not the man, from harsh punishment; and, in contrast to some evidence that children shield women from punishment (see Daly, 1986), single women with children were more harshly punished than their married counterparts.

Much the same pattern was found by Farrington and Morris (1983) in their regression study of 408 persons found guilty of various types of theft in Cambridge. The authors found no evidence of leniency toward females once they controlled for the fact that women had committed less serious offenses and were less likely to have been convicted previously. They also found that while for men the most important factor in sentencing was seriousness of offense, for women it was "current problems," which the authors defined as "social, domestic, financial, drugs or alcohol" problems (Farrington and Morris, 1983: 257). Also important in woman's sentencing, though not in male sentencing, was the woman's marital status with women who were divorced or separated receiving relatively severe sentences. Women who were found guilty of acting with others and women who came from "deviant family backgrounds" were also sanctioned more harshly. For men, such variables were not important in sentencing; for them, legal variables played a more distinct role though judges did consider current problems and age in male sentencing.

SEXISM OR RATIONAL SENTENCING

Some might suggest that considerations of nonlegal variables in sentencing (marriage, employment status, drug dependency, and so on) is appropriate because a judge is attempting to assess the likelihood that the individual will be able to avoid future criminal behavior (stability). It has also been observed that because of women's generally less severe prior records, judges arrive at a consideration of nonlegal variables earlier (Kruttschnitt, 1984: 227).

Two issues arise in this regard. First, the evidence is fairly clear that judges respond to different factors in a person's background depending upon gender. Interviews with judges reveal that for men, the chief criterion appears to be employment, whereas for women it appears to be marriage and children (Daly and Morris, 1985). These come uncomfortably close to the traditional breadwinner/housewife dichotomy in gender roles. Added to this, however, is the fact that nonlegal considerations appear, in the case of women's offenses, to be as important, if not more important, than the crime involved. It is also interesting that one study that studied this form of paternalism over time (Kruttschnitt and Green, 1984) found that attention to women's "economic dependence" was particularly evident during years that were characterized by public protest and media coverage of the women's movement (1969-1971) (Kruttschnitt and Green, 1984: 547). In general, then, the evidence is not clear that court attention to women's conformity to traditional sex-role expectations benefits all women. Instead, the pattern appears to be reserved for those women whose characteristics most closely resemble those of the stereotypical "good wife."

THE OLDEST PROFESSION

With reference to women's respectability, it is odd that so many studies of judicial processing routinely ignore prostitution and other "trivial" offenses particularly because these offenses account for a substantial portion of women's crime and may play a major role in women's criminal careers (Chesney-Lind and Rogriguez, 1983). Although formal arrests for prostitution accounted in 1984 for only 4.5% of women's arrests, prostitution is the only arrest category where arrests of women outnumber men (in this regard, it is the adult equivalent to the runaway status offense category for girls); moreover, arrests of women for prostitution increased by 123.9% between 1975 and 1984 (the greatest increase in women's arrests) (FBI, 1985: 167).

Field studies of prostitution (Carmen and Moody, 1985; LaFave, 1969) indicate that women are routinely harassed by police, that they are often swept up simply because they are "known" as prostitutes, and that they are occasionally brutalized by law enforcement officers. Other research (Miller and Graczkowski, 1985) documents the fact that male prostitutes are not similarly treated by police officers. Finally, while efforts in some jurisdictions to punish male patrons as well as female prostitutes have led to changes in the law, they have not succeeded in changing arrest patterns or discrimination against women after arrest. Research in these jurisdictions has shown that police resistance to punishing male patrons resulted in few men being arrested and, after arrest, male patrons were released more quickly than female prostitutes

(Bernat, 1984a, 1984b). Once in court, women charged with prostitution were often held in detention longer than permitted by law before appearing before a judge and were then processed in batches and coerced into guilty pleas (Carmen and Moody, 1985).

PATERNALISM OR PROPORTIONALITY

Even when examining the evidence of preferential treatment of women being sentenced for felonies (particularly when measured· as imprisonment), some (Parisi, 1982; Steffensmeier, 1980b; Daly, 1986; Daly and Morris, 1986) argue that judicial behavior at this point could be less an expression of chivalry than "practicality" given that so many female offenders are single mothers and imprisonment of such a caretaker may cost the taxpayers a substantial amount of money.

To this notion, one might also add *proportionality*, given that sentencing women to jail or prison might, in fact, be a harsher sentence as conditions in these facilities are rarely equivalent to those found in male facilities (Sims, 1978; Chesney-Lind and Rodriguez, 1983; Shaw, 1982). Additional support for the proportionality explanation in women's less severe sentences may also be found by looking more closely at the content of women's serious crimes. Women who kill, for example, may well be responding to long histories of abuse and women charged with other serious offenses could well have been only accessories. However, given the fact that most females are arrested, prosecuted, and tried for less serious offenses, the research results suggest that sweeping generalizations about the preferential treatment of women before the bar of justice are largely inaccurate. Instead, the evidence seems to be fairly clear that at most steps in the judicial process, women, particularly those being processed for trivial offenses, are not treated leniently. It also seem disturbing that some studies find judges responding to different factors when sentencing men and women. These studies suggest that women before the bar of justice may be treated differently depending upon their conformity to a traditional female sex role that requires that they be married, sober, nonviolent, and sexually respectable.

CONCLUSION

Despite the considerable attention the female offender received in the last decade, the study of women's crime is still in its infancy. For this reason, it is clearly too early to attempt to summarize rather complex judicial responses as either lenient or harsh. It does seem clear, though, that while public discussion of the need for changes in women's traditional roles has occurred in virtually all segments of society, there is little evidence that these debates have affected judicial decision making in the handling of girls and women who come before them. Instead, both girls and women who find their way into the criminal justice system continue to be the recipients of a special kind of justice, a justice that is clearly not gender blind. Indeed, there is considerable evidence that it may occasionally function in ways to enforce women's obedience to traditional gender roles.

Although evidence for this form of judicial involvement in reinforcing women's place as well as, and sometimes in place of, the laws can be found in both the juvenile and the adult systems, it is clearly a greater problem in the juvenile system. Juvenile court policies seem to encourage all in the system to overlook criminal misconduct of girls who conform to traditional sex-role expectations, but to respond harshly to girls who deviate from sexual and behavioral components of the female sex role. Stated baldly, this has resulted in a double standard of juvenile justice that has been surprisingly resistant to the last decade's attempts to divert and deinstitutionalize status offenders.

Within the adult system, a more complex pattern is apparent. Evidence of lenient sentencing of women charged with felonies has been found rather consistently, particularly when the judge is confronting a decision to incarcerate. This lenience is, however, sensitive to a woman's conformity to traditional female attributes and harsher treatment may be in store for adult women who cannot provide evidence of their obedience to the standards of womanhood (marriage, economic dependence, children, and "respectability"). Less consistently, there seems to be evidence of the harsh punishment of the "evil woman"—the adult woman who has committed a traditionally masculine crime. Finally, and most important, those studies that examine less serious offenses find that women charged with these offenses are not treated leniently. Given that the vast majority of women are charged with these minor offenses, this finding suggests that many women in court are not handled gently.

Attention must also be drawn to the important policy issues that the recent literature on the female offender reveals. The deinstitutionalization of status offenders has meant a dramatic decrease in the incarceration of girls, but this victory is shallow and jeopardized by shifts in federal policies toward delinquent youth and more punitive attitudes toward criminals. Adult women have also been the victims of this latter trend. Tougher national sentiments have resulted in the passage of mandatory sentencing and career criminal legislation that has unquestionably resulted in dramatic increases in the incarceration of both men and women. Thus even if the treatment of men and women has been relatively evenhanded during the last ten years, judges have been sentencing women to prison in record numbers.

The irony is that at a time when the needs of the female offender have never been more acute, many groups concerned about women's issues have shifted their interest and regard to the female victims of crime. While women's victimization is undeniably important (and in fact related to women's crime), it is equally important that the growing number of women who are appearing before the bar of justice be assured of fair and equal treatment.

REFERENCES

Adler, F. (1975) Sisters in Crime. New York: McGraw-Hill.

Anderson, E. (1976) "The chivalrous treatment of the female offender in the arms of the criminal justice system: a review of the literature." Social Problems 23: 349-357.

Baab, G. W. and W. Furgeson (1967) "Texas sentencing practices: a statistical study." Texas Law Review 45 (February): 471-503.

Bernat, F. B. (1984a) "New York state's prostitution statute: case study of the discriminatory application of a gender neutral law," in C. Schweber and C. Feinman (eds.) Criminal Justice Politics and Women: The Legal Aftermath of Legally Mandated Change. New York: Haworth.

Bernat, F. B. (1984b) "Gender disparity in the setting of bail," in S. Chanels (ed.) Gender Issues, Sex Offenses, and Criminal Justice: Current Trends. New York: Haworth.

Bishop, D. M. and C. E. Frazier (1984) "The effects of gender on charge reduction." Sociological Quarterly 25 (Summer): 385-396.

Black, T. E. and C. P. Smith (1981) A Preliminary National Assessment of the Number and Characteristics of Juveniles Processed in the Juvenile Justice System. Washington, DC: Department of Justice, Government Printing Office.

Boisvert, M. J. and R. Wells (1980) "Toward a rational policy on status offenders." Social Work 25, 3 (May): 230-234.

Brown, A. (1985) "Assault and homicide at home: when battered women kill," in M. J. Sakes and L. Saxe (eds.) Advances in Applied Social Psychology, Vol. 3. Hillsdale, NJ: Lawrence Erlbaum Associates.

Burbeck, T. (1978) "Sex discrimination in the disposition of incarcerated juveniles." Ann Arbor: University of Michigan Department of Sociology.

Bureau of Justice Statistics (1982) Prisoners at Midyear 1982. Washington, DC: Government Printing Office.

Bureau of Justice Statistics (1984) The 1983 Jail Census. Washington, DC: Government Printing Office.

Bureau of Justice Statistics (1985) Prisoners in 1984. Washington, DC: Government Printing Office.

Carmen, A. and H. Moody (1985) Working Women. New York: Harper & Row.

Chapman, J. (1980) Economic Reality and the Female Offender. Lexington, MA: Lexington Books.

Chesney-Lind, M. (1973) "Judicial enforcement of the female sex role." Issues in Criminology 8 (Fall): 51-70.

Chesney-Lind, M. and N. Rodriguez (1983) "Women under lock and key." Prison Journal (Women in Prison, I), 63, 2 (Autumn-Winter): 47-65.

Children's Bureau, Department of Health, Education and Welfare (1967) Statistics on Public Institutions for Delinquent Children, 1965. Washington, DC: Government Printing Office.

Chiricos, T. G., P. D. Jackson, and G. F. Waldo (1972) "Inequality in the imposition of a criminal label." Social Problems 19: 553-572.

Clarke, S. H. and G. G. Koch (1980) "Juvenile court: therapy and crime control, and do lawyers make a difference." Law and Society Review 14, 2 (Winter): 263-308.

Cohen, L. E. and J. R. Kleugel (1979) "Selecting delinquents for adjudication." Journal of Research in Crime and Delinquency (January): 143-163.

Cohn, Y. (1970) "Criteria for the probation officer's recommendation to the juvenile court," in Peter G. Garabedian and Donald C. Gibbons (eds.) Becoming Delinquent. Chicago: Aldine.

Conway, A. and C. Bogdan (1977) "Sexual delinquency: the persistence of a double standard." Crime and Delinquency 23, 2 (April): 131-135.

Crites, L. [ed.] (1976) The Female Offender. Lexington, MA: Lexington Books.

Curran, D. (1983) "Judicial discretion and defendant's sex." Criminology 21 (February): 41-58.

Curran, D. (1984) "The myth of the 'new' female delinquent." Crime and Delinquency 30, 3 (July): 386-399.

Daly, K. (1985) "Gender and conceptions of justice in the criminal court." Junior Faculty Fellowship Proposal, Yale University.

Daly, K. (1986) "Discrimination in the criminal courts: family, gender and the problem of equal treatment." (unpublished)

Daly, K. and M. Morris (1985) "Gender in the adjudication process: are judges really paternalistic toward women?" Presented at the American society of Criminology Meetings, San Diego, November 13-17.

Datesman, S. and F. Scarpitti (1977) "Unequal protection for males and females in the juvenile court," in Theodore N. Ferdinand (ed.) Juvenile Delinquency. Newbury Park, CA: Sage.

Ekstrand, L. E. and W. A. Eckert (1978) "Defendant's sex as a factor in sentencing." Experimental Study of Politics 6: 90-112.

Farrington, D. P. and A. M. Morris (1983) "Sex, sentencing and reconviction." British Journal of Criminology 23, 3 (July): 229-248.

Federal Bureau of Investigation (1975) Crime in the United States: 1974. Washington, DC: Government Printing Office.

Federal Bureau of Investigation (1985) Crime in the United States 1984. Washington, DC: Government Printing Office.

Fenster, C. (1977) "Differential dispositions: a preliminary study of male-female partners in crime." Presented to the annual meeting of the American Society of Criminology, Atlanta, Georgia.

Figueira-McDonough, J. (1982) "Gender differences in informal processing: a look at charge bargaining and sentence reduction in Washington, DC." Presented at the American Society of Criminology, Toronto, Canada.

Figueira-McDonough, J. (1985) "Are girls different? Gender discrepancies between delinquent behavior and control." Child Welfare 64, 4 (May-June): 273-289.

Figueira-McDonough, J. et al. (1981) Females in Prisons in Michigan, 1968-1987. Ann Arbor: School of Social Work, University of Michigan.

Frazier, C. E., E. W. Bock, and J. C. Henretta (1983) "The role of probation officers in determining gender differences in sentencing severity." Sociological Quarterly 24 (Spring): 305-318.

General Accounting Office (1978) Removing Status Offenders from Secure Facilities: Federal Leadership and Guidance Are Needed. Washington, DC: Author.

Ghali, M. and M. Chesney-Lind (1986) "Gender bias and the criminal justice system: an empirical investigation." Sociology and Social Research 70, 2 (January): 164-171.

Gibbons, T.C.N. and J. Prince (1962) Shoplifting. London: ISTD.

Giordano, P., S. Kerbel, and S. Dudley (1981) "The economics of female criminology," in Lee Bowker (ed.) Women and Crime in America. New York: Macmillan.

Goldkamp, J. S. (1979) Two Classes of Accused: A Study of Bail and Detention in American Justice. Cambridge, MA: Ballinger.

Green, E. (1961) Judicial Attitudes in Sentencing. New York: Macmillan.

Gruhl, J., S. Welch, and C. Spohn (1984) "Women as criminal defendants: a test for paternalism." Western Political Quarterly (September): 456-467.

Hagan, J. (1974) "Extra-legal attributes and criminal sentencing: an assessment of a sociological viewpoint." Law and Society Review 8 (Spring): 357-383.

Hagan, J. and N. O'Donnel (1978) "Sexual stereotyping and judicial sentencing: a legal test of the sociological wisdom." Canadian Journal of Sociology 3: 309-319.

Hoffman, T. (1981) "Sex discrimination in Oregon's juvenile justice system." Presented at the Spring Meeting of the Oregon Psychological Association, Newport, Oregon, May.

Hurst, H. (1975) "Juvenile status offenders." Speech delivered to the New Mexico Council on Crime and Delinquency, Albuquerque, New Mexico, June 20.

Ikeda, L., M. Chesney-Lind, and K. Kameoka (1985) The Honolulu Anti-Truancy Drive: An Evaluation. Honolulu: Youth Development and Research Center.

Katz, A. and L. H. Teitelbaum (1977) "PINS jurisdiction, the vagueness doctrine and the rule of law," in Lee H. Teitelbaum and Aidan R. Gough (eds.) Beyond Control: Status Offenders in the Juvenile Court. Cambridge, MA: Ballinger.

Kratcoski, P. (1974) "Delinquent boys and girls." Child Welfare 53 (January): 16-21.

Krisberg, B., I. M. Schwartz, P. Litsky, and J. Austin (1985) The Watershed of Juvenile Justice Reform. Minnesota: Hubert Humphrey Institute of Public Affairs.

Kruttschnitt, C. (1982) "Women, crime and dependency." Criminology 19 (February): 495-513.

Kruttschnitt, C. (1984) "Sex and criminal court dispositions: the unresolved controversy." Research in Crime and Delinquency, 21 (3): 213-232.

Kruttschnitt, C. and D. Green (1984) "The sex-sanctioning issue: is it history." American Sociological Review 49 (August;): 541-551.

LaFave, W. (1969) "Arrest: the decision to take a suspect into custody," in Lawrence M. Friedman and Stewart Macauly (eds.) Law and the Behavioral Sciences. Indianapolis: Bobbs-Merrill.

Lindsey, K. (1978) "When battered women strike back: murder or self-defense." Viva (September): 58-59, 66-74.

Mahoney, A. R. and C. Fenster (1982) "Female delinquents in a suburban court," in Nicole Rafter and Elizabeth Stanki (eds.) Judge, Lawyer, Victim, Thief: Women, Gender Roles and the Criminal Justice System. Boston: Northeastern University Press.

Mann, C. (1979) "The differential treatment between runaway boys and girls in juvenile court." Juvenile and family Court Journal 30 (May): 37-48.

Miller, E. and G. S. Graczkowski (1985) "Gender, sex and money: a comparative analysis of female heterosexual and male homosexual prostitution." Presented at the annual meetings of the American Society of Criminology, San Diego, California, November 16.

Moeller, R. A. (1982) "Gender bias in juvenile court court processing." University of Wisconsin-Milwaukee. (unpublished)

Moulds, E. F. (1978) "Chivalry and paternalism: disparities of treatment in the criminal justice system." Western Political Quarterly 31 (September): 416-430.

Nagel, I. H., J. Cardascia, and C. E. Ross (1982) "Sex differences in the processing of criminal defendants," in D. K. Weisberg (ed.) Women and the Law. Cambridge, MA: Schenkman.

Nagel, I. H. and J. Hagan (1983) "Gender and crime: offense patterns and criminal court sanctions," pp. 91-144 in Michael Tonry and Norval Morris (eds.) Crime and Justice: An Annual Review of Research, Vol. 4. Chicago: University of Chicago Press.

Nagel, S. S. and L. J. Weitzman (1971) "Women as litigants." Hastings Law Journal 23 (November): 171-198.

National Advisory Committee for Juvenile Justice and Delinquency Prevention (1984) Serious Juvenile Crime: A Redirected Federal Effort. Washington, DC: U.S. Department of Justice.

Office of Juvenile Justice and Delinquency Prevention (1985) Runaway Children and the Juvenile Justice and Delinquency Prevention Act: What is the Impact? Washington, DC: Juvenile Justice Bulletin.

Parisi, N. (1982) "Are females treated differently?" in Nicole Hahn Rafter and Elizabeth Stanko (eds.) Judge, Lawyer, Victim, Thief: Women, Gender Roles and the Criminal Justice System. Boston: Northeastern University Press.

Pollak, O. (1961) The Criminality of Women. New York: Barnes.

Pope, C. E. (1975) Sentencing of California Felony Offenders. Washington, DC: Criminal Justice Research Center.

Pressly, C. (1984) "Police are now picking up under-age visitors." Honolulu Star Bulletin (June 16).

Rottman, D. B. and R. J. Simon (1975) "Women in the courts." Chitty's Law Journal 23 (January): 171-181.

Sarri, R. (1983) "Gender issues in juvenile justice." Crime and Delinquency 29, 3 (July): 381-397.

Schlossman, S. and S. Wallach (1978) "The crime of precocious sexuality: female juvenile delinquency in the progressive era." Harvard Educational Review 48 (February): 65-94.

Shaw, N. S. (1982) "Female patients and the medical profession in jails and prisons," in Nicole Hahn Rafter and Elizabeth Stanko (eds.) Judge, Lawyer, Victim, Thief: Women, Gender Roles and the Criminal Justice System. Boston: Northeastern University Press.

Sheldon, R. G. (1981) "Sex discrimination in the juvenile justice system: Memphis, Tennessee, 1900-1917," in Marguerite Q. Warren (ed.) Comparing Female and Male Offenders. Newbury Park, CA: Sage.

Sheldon, R. and J. Horvath (1986) "Processing offenders in a juvenile court: a comparison of males and females." Presented at the annual meetings of the Western Society of Criminology, Newport Beach, February 27-March 2.

Simon, R. J. (1975) Women and Crime. Lexington, MA: Lexington Books.

Simon, R. J. and N. Sharma (1979) The Female Defendant in Washington, DC: 1974 and 1975. Washington, DC: INSLAW.

Sims, P. (1978) "Women in southern jails," in Laura Crites (ed.) The Female Offender. Lexington, MA: Lexington Books.

Steffensmeier, D. J. (1980a) "Sex differences in patterns of adult crime, 1965-1977: a review and assessment." Social Forces 58, 4 (June): 1080-1109.

Steffensmeier, D. J. (1980b) "Assessing the impact of the women's movement on sex-based differences in the handling of audit criminal defendants." Crime and Delinquency 26: 344-357.

Sussman, A. (1977) "Sex-based discrimination and the PINS jurisdiction," in Lee H. Teitelbaum and Aidan R. Gough (eds.) Beyond Control: Status Offenders in the Juvenile Court. Cambridge, MA: Ballinger.

Swigert, V. and R. Farrell (1977) "Normal homicides and the law." American Sociological Review 42: 16-32.

Teilmann, K. S. and P. H. Landry (1981) "Gender bias in juvenile justice." Journal of Research in Crime and Delinquency 18, 1 (January): 47-80.

United States House of Representatives, Committee on Education and Labor (1980) Juvenile Justice Amendments of 1980. Washington, DC: Government Printing Office.

United States Senate, Committee on the Judiciary (1981) Reauthorization of the Juvenile Justice and Delinquency Prevention Act of 1974. Washington, DC: Government Printing Office.

United States Statutes at Large (1981) Ninety-Sixth Congress, Second Session. Public Law 96-5 9-December 8, 1980. Washington DC: Government Printing Office.

Ward, D., M. Jackson, and E. Ward (1968) "Crime and violence by women," in Crimes of Violence 13, Appendix 17, President's Commission on Law Enforcement and the Administration of Justice.

III

WOMEN AS JUDGES, LAWYERS, ADMINISTRATORS, AND JURORS

There are serious practical costs to the quality of justice in our society and ultimately to our democratic principles in the exclusion of women as decision makers from our court system. Such exclusion assures that the process and outcome of justice reflect the views, values, and beliefs of only the male members of our society—less than half of the population. As the previous sections have shown, the result often works to the disadvantage of women. It is clear that decisions regarding the rights and treatment of women within a court system dominated by men often reflect patriarchal beliefs about women's role and nature.

While it is not the case that all males share these beliefs and all females reject them, absence of the female experience and perspective makes possible the kind of bias that was discussed in the preceding section. The male perspective is clearly dominant in the judicial response to wife abuse and can be seen in the seeming judicial insensitivity to the impact of divorce orders on women and their children. It is also apparent in the sentencing patterns of female offenders.

Thus the extent to which women are afforded access to the courts as decision makers has significant implications. As the following chapters make clear, however, equal access to positions within the court does not assure equal opportunity once in.

During the last decade, much progress was made in promoting the access of women to legal, administrative, and judicial positions within the court system. Title IX of the Civil Rights Act barring sex discrimination in schools receiving federal funds assured that women would have equal opportunity to study law. Women now constitute over 39% of the law students, up from 9% in 1970. Title VII of the Civil Rights Act prohibited sex discrimination in hiring, opening the employment doors to women who achieved their degrees. And the increase in litigation in our society combined with other social forces greatly expanded the number of legal positions available to those women. Between 1970 and 1984, the number of women lawyers rose from 11,000 (4%) to 104,000 (16%).

These factors also influenced the potential for women to become judges. From 1955 to 1978, the number of judicial positions increased 200% according to Cook. And the number of women eligible for these positions had increased as well.

Opportunities for women court administrators were also affected by the expansion of educational opportunities for women, the promotion of nondiscriminatory hiring practices, and the development of professional management positions within the court system.

This would suggest that the long history of discrimination against women who sought to become lawyers, court managers, and judges had ended. Part III explores that issue and finds that all is not well.

Cook leads off the discussion with an analysis of the opportunities for women on the bench, using a three-variable model. According to this model, the following three factors control the opportunities for women to become judges: the number of judicial positions available, the number of women eligible, and the willingness of the gatekeepers to hire women for the positions. She examines how each of these factors has operated to limit the full integration of women into the judicial ranks.

Hepperle utilizes the same model in examining appointments for women in the field of court administration. While women have moved into court management positions in greater numbers during the last decade, they have yet to move beyond mid-level. Her analysis suggests some unique factors that may influence equal employment opportunity for women in the courts.

Schafran follows with an analysis of the opportunities for women lawyers. While she finds a pattern of lack of access for women to particular types of work that have been associated with males or that carry particular benefits, Schafran focuses primarily on the treatment of female lawyers by male judges and peers. Her article is an important contribution to understanding how equal access to employment opportunity does not, by itself, assure that once hired, a woman will have equal opportunity either to function at an optimum level or to advance. Subtle and overt sexist behavior toward a woman by her male peers and judges can severely limit her effectiveness and upward mobility.

The final significant area in which the access by women to participation in the justice process has been historically restricted is in the jury system. As Mahoney recounts, women have only recently had equal access to participation on juries. But as with the other areas discussed in this section, equal access does not mean equal opportunity. Inclusion in the jury pool is only the first step in the process of becoming a jury member. Mahoney focuses on how the use of stereotypes of women acts to control or influence their actual selection for a jury.

It is clear from the chapters in this section that equal employment opportunity for women in the courts is yet to be realized. The assumption that the history of employment discrimination is behind us and that enforcement of EEO and affirmative action laws is no longer necessary belies reality. Only when women have become fully integrated as decision makers at all levels of the judicial system can we rest assured that justice for women and men in the courts will be free of gender bias.

6

WOMEN JUDGES IN THE OPPORTUNITY STRUCTURE[1]

Beverly Blair Cook

Only a preface can be written to the history of women on the bench in the United States. Since 1870 women gradually have desegregated every kind and level of court from Justice of the Peace to the United States Supreme Court.[2] However, the degree of integration has remained token for over 100 years.[3] In 1985 women held only 7% of the attorney judgeships (Fund for Modern Courts, 1985), a percentage which is disproportionate to the 16% in practice, the 40% in law school, and the majority status of women as citizens.[4] Women will exceed tokenism in the courts only if three simultaneous conditions take place—an increase in the number of judicial positions to be filled; an increase in the number of women eligible for judgeships; and an increase in the number of gatekeepers—those who select among candidates for law jobs—who are positively inclined to give women fair consideration.

The notion that women will fill legal positions, from the entry level to the most prestigious judgeships, in proportion to their presence in law school and the bar takes account of the eligibility factor only and does not fit the historical experience of women.[5] It is also not likely that women will "filter up" the court hierarchy in the contemporary period, as a mechanical theory would predict, because the attitude of gatekeepers does not become more favorable to women in direct relationship to the increase in number of judgeships or of eligible women. The availability of positions is as important as the eligibility of women, but these two conditions are also unrelated.

This three-variable model, offered to explain the status of women in the judiciary, centers upon the judicial opportunity structure of the set of linked positions that provide incumbents the opportunity to prove their eligibility for higher offices. For each position in an opportunity structure, there are gatekeepers who apply the customary and official rules to screen out candidates and to select among the most promising. These gatekeepers will ordinarily replace those retiring from positions— whether they are graduating seniors, professors, partners, prosecutors, or judges—with persons of "their own kind" from the next generation, unless several factors are present.

Focusing upon the judicial positions at the top of this opportunity structure, the first factor to consider is court size—or the total number of judgeships available and their distribution within courts and judicial districts. Second is the pool factor or the number of women qualified to apply to the gatekeepers for each judgeship. The pool of eligible women becomes smaller for each successive office in the opportunity structure to the extent that the gatekeepers at lower levels do not select women to get the training and experience for the next level. Third is the attitude of the gatekeepers toward the presence of women in the specific position they control. The general proposition that fits this model is that the number of women judges will increase as the pool of eligible women and the number of positions in the opportunity structure increase, and to the extent that the gatekeepers recognize the presence of eligible women for the positions and the legitimacy of their claims for those positions.

If a gatekeeper strongly favors the sex integration of the courts, then one might predict the presence of a token woman judge despite a small pool and few positions. Although such a token woman in a highly visible and powerful office may provide a "role model" for women, there must be a large enough pool of women entering the profession to recognize her as such. Because of the absence of such a pool of eligibles, the first women judges were often not replaced by other women or, at best, their seats became designated for a successor without any thought of considering women for a second position in the same court or judicial district. In the 1980s, however, there is a large professional base of women to emulate those who have reached the prestigious judgeships.

An active and successful women's movement provides an impetus for young women to focus their ambitions upon the legal profession and to exert pressure upon the gatekeepers to recognize their entitlement to compete for places in law schools. Without a women's movement and specialized organizations of women lawyers and judges, the pool of women eligible for law jobs would not increase and the gatekeepers would not be reminded of their claims. No direct relationship exists between a women's movement and the growth of the legal system, however. It was serendipitous that the movement for women's equality coincided with the expansion of law jobs during the period of the mid-1960s into the 1980s. The increase in number of judicial positions from 1955 to 1978 was over 200%. In contrast, the increase between 1925 and 1955, after the suffrage movement, was less than 10% (Whitehurst, 1977; Cook, 1983; Cook et al., 1986; Council of State Governments, 1935-1983). A women's movement stimulates two of the factors necessary for women to integrate the courts, but is not sufficient in the absence of new legal positions.

The concept of opportunity structure implies a hierarchy of offices, with many identical positions at the bottom that require fewer credentials and offer lesser rewards than the unique and scarce positions at the top that require more credentials and offer greater rewards. Inclusion of women at the lower rank is less unsettling to the legal system because lawyers and judges in the higher positions can supervise and monitor the behavior of practicing lawyers and lower court judges. Women may, therefore, intrude into the lower ranks without challenging male domination as they would if they took higher positions. The entrance of women at the bottom of a court system, therefore, does not necessarily imply future integration at the top.

A special concern of this chapter, then, is the presence of women at the top of the judicial hierarchy. Understanding why women are (or are not) able to move up the opportunity structure requires data on the number and percentage of women on these prestigious courts. Table 6.1 provides a list arranged by state of every woman who has served on a prestigious court in the United States. Twenty-two women are listed under the federal appellate court heading, and twenty are now serving. They constitute 11% of the total number of U.S. Supreme Court and Circuit judges. The first woman entered at this level in 1934; the second in 1968. In the federal trial judge category are 60 women appointed between 1928 and 1987; the 48 who are now in active status are 8% of the total now serving.[6] On the highest state courts there have been 40 women in 30 states and the District of Columbia.

Very few women judges were able to improve their status once they reached a prestigious court. Three of the state supreme court justices moved to federal judgeships (see Table 6.1). One federal district judge accepted appointment to her state's supreme court; three were elevated

TABLE 6.1
Women Judges on Prestigious Courts by State

State	Federal Appellate	Federal Trial	State Court of Last Resort
ALA			Janie L. Shores 1975-
ARZ	Sandra D. O'Connor* 1981- SCt Mary M. Schroeder* 1979- 9th	Mary Anne Richey* 1976-83 Dec	Lorna E. Lockwood* 1961-75 Dec CJ
ARK		Elsijane T. Roy* 1977-	Elsijane T. Roy* 1975-77 Int
CAL	Shirley Hufstedler* 1968-79 Res 9th Dorothy Nelson 1979- 9th Cynthia Hall* 1984- 9th	Mariana Pfaelzer 1978- CD Judith Keep* 1980- SD Marilyn Patel* 1980- ND Consuelo Marshall* 1980- CD Cynthia Hall* 1981-84 CD Pamela Rymer 1983- CD Alicemarie Stotler* 1984- CD	Rose Bird 1977-87 Def CJ
COL		Zita Weinshienk* 1979-	Jean Dubofsky 1979-87
CON		Ellen B. Burns* 1978-	Ellen A. Peters 1978- CJ
DEL		Jane R. Roth 1985-	
FLA		Susan H. Black* 1979- MD Elizabeth Kovachevich* 1982- MD Lenore C. Nesbitt* 1983- SD Patricia Fawsett* 1985- SD	Rosemarie Barkett* 1985-
GA	Phyllis Kravitch* 1979- 11th	Orinda Evans 1979- ND	
HAW			Rhoda Lewis 1959-67 Ret
ILL		Susan Getzendanner 1980- ND Illana D. Rovner 1985- ND Ann C. Williams 1985- ND Suzanne Conlon 1987- ND	

Continued

TABLE 6.1   Continued

| State | Federal | | State |
	Appellate	Trial	Court of Last Resort
IND		Sarah E. Barker 1984-	SD
IO			Linda Neuman* 1986- SD
KS	Deanell R. Tacha 1985- 10th		Kay McFarland* 1977-
LA		Veronica Wicker 1979- ED	
ME			Caroline Glassman 1983-
MD		Shirley B. Jones* 1979-82 Res	Rita C. Davidson* 1978-84 Dec.
MAS		Rya W. Zobel 1979-	Ruth I. Abrams* 1977-
MCH	Cornelia Kennedy* 1979- 6th	Cornelia Kennedy* 1970-79 CJ ED	Mary S. Coleman* 1973-82 Ret CJ
		Patricia Boyle* 1978-1983 Res ED	Dorothy Comstock-Riley* 1982-82, 1984-
		Anna Diggs-Taylor 1979- ED	Patricia Boyle* 1983-
		Barbara K. Hackett 1986- ED	
MN		Diana E. Murphy* 1980-	Rosalie Wahl 1977-
			M. Jeanne Coyne 1982-
MIS			Lenore Prather* 1982-
NJ		Anne Thompson 1979-	Marie L. Garibaldi 1982-
		Maryanne T. Barry 1983-	
NMEX			Mary C. Walters* 1984-
NY	Amayla Kearse 1979- 2d	Constance Motley 1966- Sr CJ	Judith Kaye 1983-
	Ruth Ginsburg 1980- DC	Mary J. Lowe 1978- SD	
		Shirley W. Kram 1983- SD	
		Mariam G. Cedarbaum 1986- SD	
		Genevieve Cline 1928-54 IT	
		Mary Alger Donlon 1955-56 IT	
		Jane A. Restani 1983- IT	

Continued

TABLE 6.1 Continued

State	Federal		State Court of Last Resort
	Appellate	Trial	
		Reena Raggi 1987- ED	
NoC			Susie M. Sharp* 1962-79 Ret CJ / Rhoda Billings 1986-
NoD			Beryl Levine 1985-
OH	Florence E. Allen 1934-66 CJ 6th Dec.	Ann Aldrich 1980- ND	Florence E. Allen* 1922-34
		Alice M. Batchelder* 1985- ND	Blanche Krupansky* 1981-82 Def
OK	Stephanie Seymour 1979- 10th		Alma Bell Wilson* 1982- / Yvonne Kauger 1984-
OR		Helen J. Frye* 1980-	Betty Roberts* 1982-86
PA	Delores Sloviter N 1979- 3d	Norma Shapiro 1978- ED	Anne X. Alpern 1961-61 Def
	Carol LosMansman* 1985- 3d	Sylvia H. Rambo 1979- MD	
		Carol LosMansman 1982-85 WD	
RIS			Florence K. Murray* 1979
SoC		Karen Henderson 1986-	
TEN		Julia S. Gibbons 1983- WD	
TEX	Carolyn Randall 1979- 5th	Sarah T. Hughes* 1962-85 Dec ND	Ruby Sondock* 1982-82 Int
	Edith H. Jones 1985- 5th	Mary Lou Robinson 1979- ND	
		Gabrielle McDonald 1979- SD	
UT			Christine M. Durham* 1982-
WSH	Betty B. Fletcher 1979- 9th	Barbara Rothstein* 1980- WD	Carolyn Dimmick* 1981-85
		Carolyn Dimmick* 1985- WD	Barbara Durham* 1985-
WVA		Elizabeth Hallanan* 1983- SD	
WIS		Barbara Crabb* 1979- CJ WD	Shirley Abrahamson 1976-

Continued

TABLE 6.1   Continued

State	Federal Appellate		Federal Trial	State Court of Last Resort
DC	Patricia Wald 1979- CJ	DC	Burnita Matthews C 1950- Sr	Catherine B. Kelly* 1967-83
	Helen Nies 1980-	Fed	June Green 1968- Sr	Julia C. Mack 1975-
	Jean G. Bissell 1984-	Fed	Joyce Green* 1979-	Judith W. Rogers 1983-
	Pauline Newman 1984-	Fed	Norma Johnson* 1980-	
	Susan Liebeler 1987-	Fed		
PR			Carmen Cerezo 1980-	

NOTE: * = prior judgeship; CJ = Chief Justice or Judge; Sr = Senior Status; Dec = deceased; Res = resigned; Ret = retired; Def = defeated; 2d = Second Circuit; DC = DC Circuit; Int = interim appointment; ND = northern district; MD = middle district; CD = central district; Fed = Federal Circuit created 1982, former Ct of Customs and Patent Appeals; IT = Court of International Trade. States with no women on prestigious courts over time are Alaska, Idaho, Indiana, Iowa, Kentucky, Missouri, Montana, Nebraska, Nevada, New Hampshire, South Dakota, Vermont, Virginia, and Wyoming.

to the federal Court of Appeals. The first woman on the U.S. Supreme Court, appointed in 1981, did not come up from a prestigious court. Unlike her male predecessors, she "skipped" a step in the opportunity structure to move directly from a state intermediate court of appeals (Cook, 1982; Cook et al., 1986). This willingness to ignore the opportunity structure pattern occurs only when the gatekeeper has determined to find a woman for a woman's seat; in this case, President Reagan was fulfilling a campaign promise (Cook, 1982). In appointing Justice O'Connor, he ended the period of exclusion and began the period of token status for women on the highest court.

The following section examines the relationship between the increase in the number of positions in the courts and the presence of women. The next section examines the steps in the opportunity structure to prestigious judgeships and the gatekeeping devices that control the movement of individuals from one position to a higher one.

THE COURT SIZE FACTOR

The court size factor represents the number of positions in the judiciary and the way they are clustered. More positions open up new opportunities for the formerly excluded, although an organization that does not grow or that operates through decentralized single offices reduces such opportunities. The huge growth in the number of judgeships in the United States, which occurred fortuitously at the same time as the modern women's movement, created a situation hospitable to the ambitions of women to participate in the courts. These new positions were established for federal circuit and district courts and for lower state courts. The courts of last resort at the top of the federal and state hierarchies did not increase in size. Thus the size factor helps women candidates only for subordinate courts.

The more offices, particularly at low levels, the more likely it is that some will be allotted to women by the appointing authority or by voters. The scarcer and more powerful judgeships attract the most intense interest and competition; men, the "insiders," have a much larger pool of eligibles actively pursuing such positions than do the female "outsiders." High court judges' power to make public policy means that the positions are valuable to those gatekeepers who want to maintain the status quo. Further, a great deal of attention can be given to the choice of the one chief justice or the one high court vacancy; such a spotlight means that gatekeepers must satisfy the traditional expectations of their constituents. In contrast, the many limited jurisdiction judgeships are less visible and powerful. Therefore, the gatekeepers can afford to invest less effort in trying to keep every position for the male insiders and can placate female outsiders with minimum distress to the system's stability.

The other aspect of size is the clustering of offices in a collegial court or in a judicial district. In the collegial courts, the presence of one outsider does not jeopardize control by the majority. One woman in a judicial district that contains many judges makes little difference in how the court looks to observers or in its policy output. A rural district with one judgeship will value that single office more highly than a metropolitan district with 20 or even 100 identical positions. For solitary and independent authority figures in a local community, the public expects the traditional, white male image in a judge. However, in a courthouse with many judges, restrained by a pyramid of superior judges and a staff of administrators, no judge has much importance and the inclusion of women does not jeopardize male dominance of the system.

The rate of turnover of judge incumbents also affects the acceptability of assigning such a position to a woman. With only one vacancy, a position appears unique. When several vacancies occur at the same time for the same office type in the same district, however, the assignment of one of those positions to a woman appears less threatening. A sudden increase in the number of positions presents the most advantageous situation for the female outsider. Such an increase occurs when a new court is inserted into the hierarchy, or an omnibus judgeship act creates a large number of new seats, and the same authority or gatekeeper fills the new seats within a short time period. Although President Carter deserves a great deal of credit for responding to the pressures of women lawyers and politicians for female nominees to federal court vacancies, his ability to do so without ignoring obligations to provide patronage to political party leaders was due to the passage of the 1978 Omnibus Judgeship Act (Berkson and Carbon, 1980; Goldman, 1979). President Reagan began responding to pressure for more women in federal judgeships only after his Omnibus Act positions became available. Although the appointment of women at the end of his first term has been attributed to Reagan's concern with the effect of a "gender gap" on his reelection (CQ Almanac, 1984), it is more likely related to the availability of positions. Carter selected women for 15% of his vacancies and Reagan for 10% during his first term.

Omnibus positions are not just vacancies but new positions. Therefore, the tradition of male incumbents often associated with particular public offices is not present. In the short run, they may also be perceived as "extra" positions to which old entitlements do not apply as strongly. Once a seat on a large court is assigned to a woman, those who want female representation can claim a new entitlement to that seat as a "woman's seat."

COURT SIZE AND TRIAL COURTS

The relationship between court size and women's access to judicial positions can be appreciated by examining the California trial courts in order of judge size on Table 6.2. The size range of courts is from the one-judge justice courts to the Los Angeles Superior Court with over 200 judges. As the size of the superior and municipal courts increases, so does the percentage of women on the bench; up to 11% on the Los Angeles Superior Court and 27% on the Los Angeles Municipal Court. The cutting point before a "woman's seat" is created seems to be 25 judges for superior court and 5 judges for municipal court.

The same table also reveals a relationship between the importance of the jurisdiction of the courts and the proportion of women judges. Even on multijudge courts, women find fewer places in the general than in the limited jurisdiction courts. Below the court size of 25, women do not

TABLE 6.2
Court Size and Women Judges: California in 1983

Number of Judges	GJ–Superior		LJ–Municipal		Rural LJ–Justice	
	N Courts	% Fem	N Courts	% Fem	N Courts	% Fem
200+	1	.11	0	–	0	–
50-199	1	.10	1	.27	0	–
25-49	5	.09	0	–	0	–
20-24	1	.00	3	.18	0	–
15-19	1	.00	2	.15	0	–
10-14	5	.03	7	.17	0	–
5-9	8	.02	19	.12	0	–
2-4	17	.00	43	.04	0	–
1	11	.00	10	.10	90	.03

SOURCE: Compiled from data in Arnold, 1983.
NOTE: GJ = general jurisdiction; LJ = limited jurisdiction.

exceed 3% on superior courts but reach 17% on municipal courts. No woman sits on a superior court with less than five judges. However, of the 10 single-judge municipal courts, one court has a woman; of the 90 one-judge justice courts, 12 have a woman judge. Given a pool of eligible women, the size of the trial court in combination with its power and rank in the opportunity structure explains the proportion of women judges.

COURT SIZE AND COLLEGIAL APPELLATE COURTS

Table 6.3 shows the relationship between court size and female presence on federal appellate courts. The percentage of women on appellate courts is slightly higher than on the trial courts, but this difference does not necessarily indicate more acceptance. Just one woman constitutes a substantial percentage of a court with five to nine seats. These percentages exaggerate women's share in the judiciary.[7] The appellate percentages for each circuit are artifacts of small court size, while the trial percentages based upon a much larger number better reflect the contemporary acceptance of women as judges. Women hold about 11% of the federal appellate court seats in contrast to about 8% on the trial level; but the appellate percentage is still within the bounds of tokenism.

Table 6.4 shows the relationship between size of state courts of last resort and the presence of women. On state courts of last resort, there is now or has been a woman on 32% of the small courts with three to five seats. Women have gained a place on 68% of those courts with six or

TABLE 6.3
Size of Federal Appellate Courts and Presence of Women in 1985

Court Size	N of Courts	N with Woman Judge	N of Judges	N and % of Woman Judges	
6	1	0	6	0	0
9-11	5	2	51	3	6%
12-16	7	7	83	12	15%
28	1	1	28	4	14%
Total	14	10	168	19	11%

SOURCE: Court and Judge lists in Federal Reporter 2d (West ed. 1985); 28 US Stat. Ann. 44.
NOTE: Includes 11 circuits, D.C. and Federal Circuit, and Supreme Court.

seven positions, and on 89% of those courts with eight or nine positions. There is a clear relationship between the amount of voting power wielded per seat on collegial courts—one-third on the smallest and one-ninth on the largest—and the generosity of the gatekeepers in distributing the judgeships.

The collegial feature of the appellate level, in which every vote is equal in weight, allows for some integration without risk to the status quo. Admission of one woman to a group that deliberates and decides by consensus or by majority vote is relatively safe. Every court system has at least one collegial court at the top of the hierarchy where a woman can be placed without giving her too much authority. This argument applies even where the court handles cases in panels, because the court can meet *en banc* to reconsider the panel decision.

Size very clearly makes a differences in the willingness of appointing authorities to place a woman on a bench, although custom may also prevent a governor from choosing a justice from an outside group (Adomeit, 1977). President Reagan's failure to nominate a woman to the circuit level until the last year of his first term may be understood as a court size problem. The courts of appeals with no women are the smaller courts: the First Circuit with six seats, the Eighth Circuit with ten seats, and the Fourth Circuit and the Seventh Circuit with eleven seats. He could place one woman on three of these courts without exceeding tokenism but had not done so by 1987.

To date, only a few collegial courts have two or more women sitting together. The federal courts with more than one woman are the Third, the Fifth, the Tenth, the D.C., the Federal, and the Ninth Circuit (where a panel of three women sat at least once). Except for the D.C. Circuit, each major party has one woman judge. The Second Circuit with 13

TABLE 6.4
Size of State Courts of Last Resort and Presence
of Women Ever Through 1986

Court Size	Number of Courts*	Number with Women Justices Ever	% Courts
3-5	19	6	32%
6-7	25	17	68%
8-9	9	8	89%
Total	53	31	58%

SOURCE: Regional Reporters (West ed. 1920-1985); *Book of States,* 1984-85, Judiciary Table 1.
*Includes two high courts in Texas and Oklahoma and the D.C. Court of Appeals.

judges is large enough to tolerate a second woman's seat, but the case types involve powerful interests and the pool of male eligibles is very large. Minnesota, Michigan, D.C., and Oklahoma have two women on their courts of last resort. In Minnesota, Rosalie Wahl was appointed by a Democratic governor and M. Jeanne Coyne by a Republican Governor. The women in Michigan and D.C. are also from different political parties.

The small court systems are less likely to have a woman on their appellate courts than the larger court systems. The size of the court system also seems to explain the historical timing of the introduction of the first woman justice to that court. Before 1980, 57% of those court systems with more than 500 judges had experimented with a female member on the court of last resort; 41% of the systems with 250-500 judges; 31% of those with 50-250 judges; and only 18% of the small systems.

THE SINGLE EXECUTIVE IN THE COURTS

The position of chief judge stands out from the other judgeships as more visible and powerful. Although for purposes of deciding cases, the chiefs have the same power as their peers, they enjoy considerable symbolic authority as leaders of the entire court system. In very large systems, such as the United States and California, the chief justice may affect public policy through administrative powers to direct the court bureaucracy, to chair court policy groups, and to assign judges to temporary service outside their own courts.

No woman has yet served as chief justice of the United States. However, Florence Allen reached the position of chief judge of the Sixth Circuit by seniority before her retirement and Patricia Wald now serves as chief of the D.C. Circuit. On the district level, Cornelia Kennedy was chief judge in Detroit and Constance Motley has just retired as chief judge in New York City. Both are large federal trial courts that require strong management. Barbara Crabb became chief judge in Madison (Wisconsin) when the court size grew from one to two judges; her presence on such a small court is in itself unusual.

Of the women who have ever sat on the highest state courts, five have served as chiefs. Where the judges choose their own chief, as they do in 17 states, women are present and, therefore, potentially available in Colorado, Michigan, Oklahoma, and Oregon. In only two states with this form of selection have women judges been chosen. Fellow justices selected Lorna Lockwood in Arizona and Mary Coleman in Michigan. In 11 states the chief takes a turn by seniority or rotation; and women now sitting will probably attain status as chiefs in Kansas, Mississippi, Utah, Washington, and Wisconsin. The chief justiceship is a separate position on the U.S. Supreme Court and in 23 states and the District of Columbia. Susie Sharp of North Carolina is the only woman elected chief by voters and Rose Bird the only woman chief justice removed by voters. Rose Bird of California and Ellen Peters of Connecticut are the only women appointed to the chief's seat by a governor.

Metropolitan trial courts also have chief judges who enjoy power and prerequisites greater than those of the other trial judges. In the federal system, the judges take the chief judge role in order of seniority. In many state courts, however, the chief is appointed by the chief justice or elected by peers. Very few women have served in this capacity in trial courts, although women have been designated to head important New York City courts by the state chief justice. The explanation is the same as for the inclusion of women in collegial legislative bodies and the exclusion of women from executive offices.

THE OPPORTUNITY STRUCTURE AND ITS GATEKEEPERS

An opportunity structure is a hierarchical set of positions in which any person ambitious for an important office usually serves consecutively, becoming visible and gaining credentials in each lower office to earn eligibility for higher office (Schlesinger, 1966; Jacob, 1984; Schmidhauser, 1979; Martin, 1982; Slotnick, 1984). The opportunity structure for a prestigious judicial office can be visualized as two parallel ladders, attached at every rung, one ladder consisting of private law jobs and the other of public law jobs. The largest number of positions are at the bottom of the ladders; every year there are thousands of new law school students and bar admittees. These entry positions are almost mandatory to achieve any of the higher positions, which are fewer in number at every step. It is not necessary, however, to serve as trial judge to reach the position of Supreme Court justice. Some judges have followed a public office route, taking staff positions in the prosecutor's office or the state attorney general's office before entering and moving up the court hierarchy. Other lawyers have taken professorships in law schools and partnerships in private law firms before moving to important judgeships.

There is a "fast track" to the prestigious courts, which is narrower and more difficult to follow than the broad track to the lesser courts. The backgrounds and professional experiences of members of the U.S. Supreme Court fit a narrow spectrum of the range of possibilities (Schmidhauser, 1979). The first woman on the Supreme Court fit the male pattern of elite university and law school training and partisan experience, but she had missed those opportunities barred to women during her professional life, such as the Rhodes scholarship, the U.S. Supreme Court clerkship, the U.S. Department of Justice office, and the elite law firm partnership (Cook, 1982). There is some evidence that the federal circuit judges follow a faster track than their colleagues on the district level (Slotnick, 1983). Like the U.S. Supreme Court justices, the circuit judges are more likely than the district judges to have attended elite law schools, to have earned honors there, to have accepted important clerkships, to have high status law practices, and to write and speak for elite audiences. The women appointed to the circuit level by President Carter had not followed that same pattern (Martin, 1982). Exceptions to the customary expectations for career experience were made for the first and token women on these courts. We do not yet know whether the entry of women will change the informal rules for male applicants or whether future women appointees will be required to show career preparations more similar to the historical pattern set by men.

There are gatekeeping arrangements at every level of the opportunity structure to provide and apply standards in selecting among candidates. The standards are not, by any means, ideal Weberian bureaucratic standards, but rather describe what the incumbents are like. The gatekeeping process produces more of the same kind in education, experience, personality, and family/friendship networks. Because women were formally excluded from the profession of law until 1869, it has been very difficult for women to present themselves as viable candidates at any entry point from law school admission to federal appellate vacancies (Weisberg, 1977).

ENTERING THE OPPORTUNITY STRUCTURE: TRAINING FOR THE BAR

The formal or informal qualification for the prestigious judgeships is membership in a state bar; therefore, entering the opportunity structure for the judiciary requires bar admission. During the nineteenth century when the few existing law schools were not able to produce the number of lawyers needed by society, preparation for the bar was unstructured and decentralized (Auerbach, 1976; Pound, 1953; Warren, 1911). An individual could "read law" with a practicing lawyer or a judge and take an exam made up by the local judge. The standards varied according to the local gatekeepers, but generally did not place onerous demands upon the applicant's time, money, or ability. Women could prepare for the bar in a protected, socially approved environment with their fathers or husbands. The first woman known to have won admission to a state bar, Arabella Mansfield in Iowa in 1869, studied law in her brother's office and passed the bar with her husband (Thomas, 1971). Her legal career also ended at this entry level. Even with the necessary credential, women lawyers in the last century had limited opportunities to appear in court, to find clients, to join law firms, or to attend bar association meetings.

In the twentieth century, law schools have gradually come to monopolize the training of potential lawyers, and control over entry to the opportunity structure has come into the hands of admissions committees at law schools. As the generalist gatekeepers in every county courthouse are replaced by specialists, law school professors, and administrators, the formerly broad-based entry points have narrowed. In the 1870s, very soon after women discovered that they could prepare for this profession with appropriate privacy in their own communities, the American Bar Association, founded in 1878, began its efforts to require a law degree for bar admission (Fossum, 1980). Women then had to enter the public world of higher education that, with few exceptions, excluded women, in order to earn a degree before taking the bar exam.

Due to the growing prestige of law schools in this century, in most states a law degree became an informal requirement for judgeships before it became a formal requirement for law practitioners. By excluding women or setting a low quota for their admission, elite law schools cut off women from opportunities for clerkships with appellate judges and from associate positions with elite firms. The revision in admissions policies of law schools since the 1960s has been nothing short of revolutionary. As Table 6.5 shows, from 1971 to 1986, the female share of approved law school seats increased fourfold from less than one-tenth to more than 40%. By 1990, the percentage of women law students nationally may reach equality. For the first time in American history there will soon be enough women with law degrees to take more than a token proportion of the judgeships.

From 1920 through 1930, the percentage of women in graduating classes of approved law schools was 6.8% (Hummer, 1979: table 4). A degree received from a night or part-time law school, which accepted women's tuition with the same alacrity as men's, was a weaker investment in future legal opportunities than a degree from a better school. Yet women had no option but to go where they were welcome. The same form of discrimination continues at a different level into the present; approved nonelite schools accept women in larger proportions than do elite schools. By the early 1980s, the elite law schools were just exceeding tokenism for women students (Epstein, 1983: table 3.2), while some approved nonelite schools were close to equality (see Table 6.6).

Of the 15 law schools ranked as elite by three or more evaluative reports, all now admit more than a token proportion of women, although only two give women competitive status. Those two are Northwestern with 45% female law students and New York University (NYU) with 47% in 1983. The acceptance of women students by NYU is not surprising as the law school established a reputation for its support of women before 1920. The first woman to reach a prestigious position in the judiciary—Florence Allen, who served on the Ohio Supreme Court and the Sixth Circuit—left the University of Chicago Law School after experiencing discrimination there and later recalled her good experience at NYU (Allen, 1956; Epstein, 1983). Twelve of the fifteen elite law schools admit less than the national average percentage of women.

As compared with the percentages of women admitted by nonelite schools in the same geographical area and with a similar sized student body, the nonelite schools have a higher percentage in all but two cases. Eight of the nonelite schools provide women with more than 40% of the available places. The average difference between the two groups of schools is 5.5%. This difference means that more men than women will have an advantage in moving onto the fast track of the legal profession,

TABLE 6.5
Percentages of Female Law Students, Supreme Court Clerks,
and Law Professors After 1970

Date	Approved Law Schools	Supreme Court Clerks	Law Professors
1971	9.4	3.0	2.9
1972	12.0	9.1	3.7
1973	15.8	3.0	4.7
1974	19.7	12.1	5.9
1975	22.9	9.1	6.9
1976	25.5	9.1	7.5
1977	27.4	21.2	8.6
1978	30.3	15.6	9.5
1979	31.5	18.8	10.5
1980	33.5	9.4	11.0
1981	35.0	25.0	–
1982	37.5	17.6	12.7
1983	38.0	21.2	13.5
1984	38.5	21.2	–
1985	39.0	24.2	–
1986	40.0	34.4	–

SOURCE: A Review of Legal Education in the United States-Fall 1983, Chicago, American Bar Association, Section on Legal Education and Admission to the Bar; *The Docket Sheet* 16 (January 1980); National Law Journal August 4, 1980: 3; August 10, 1981: 3; July 19, 1982: 3; August 15, 1983: 7; January 9, 1984: 1; Fossum, Women Law Professors, 1980 American Bar Foundation Research Journal 903, Table 2 at 906 (Fall 1980).

into the important apprenticeships as judge clerks or associates in elite firms, where lawyers win their credentials to enter the law jobs with prestige, power, and income. Graduation from a parochial law school sets the student on the path to a trial judgeship; but graduation from an elite school is a credential that facilitates entry to the appellate bench.

CLERKING FOR THE JUSTICES

After graduation from an elite law school, the next position on the fast track is a clerkship on a prestigious bench. Until recently, U.S. Supreme Court justices selected their clerks among law journal editors and honor students. Now the pool of eligibles draws from the law clerks serving on other prestigious courts, who were students the year before. By changing the focus of their recruiting, the justices have added another step to the opportunity structure. Making the ladder longer provides the justices with more experienced clerks but requires the potential applicant to please another mentor. The prospective clerk now needs a supportive and influential federal or state judge as well as law

TABLE 6.6
Law School Admissions by Sex:
Elite and Nonelite Practices, 1983

Elite Law Schools*	N	Fem %	Nonelite Matching Schools	N	Fem %
Harvard	1782	29.3	Boston	1286	38.8
Chicago	515	30.1	DePaul	1100	38.9
Michigan	1150	31.4	Wayne State	965	41.5
Columbia	955	31.6	Brooklyn	1292	44.7
Stanford	520	31.7	Golden Gate	848	46.9
Duke	555	33.0	Wake Forest	504	31.9
Yale	620	33.4	Bridgeport	740	40.5
Pennsylvania	700	34.1	Temple	1282	43.0
Virginia	1145	34.6	American	1267	39.5
Cornell	530	34.7	Albany	709	39.1
UCLA	1103	36.9	Southwestern	1500	39.0
Texas	1600	37.1	Houston	1174	43.1
UC-Berkeley	926	37.7	Santa Clara	932	43.2
Northwestern	575	45.0	Loyola	716	45.8
New York U	1115	47.1	St. John's	1177	34.9

SOURCE: *Prelaw Handbook* 1983-1984 (Law School Admission Council, 1983).
*As defined by E. Slotnick, *Western Political Quarterly* 36 (December 1983): 574, n. 6.

professor to receive consideration. For women who, against the odds, have matriculated and made their mark in an elite law school, this new practice means finding a prestigious judge without prejudice and with a positive inclination toward women clerks.

In finding their clerks, the justices appear to place particular confidence in certain circuits and judges. Over the five terms 1979 to 1983, the District of Columbia and Second Circuits provided more than half of all clerks for the Supreme Court. The circuits in which federal judges sponsored women for more than a token proportion of the selected clerks are the Seventh (40% female), the Ninth (30%), and the Fourth (20%). The Second, Third, Fifth, and District of Columbia Circuits provided token proportions of women clerks. Six women judges have sponsored women clerks—Shirley Hufstedler for Justice Marshall, Betty Fletcher for Justice Blackmun, Ruth Ginsburg for Justices Stewart and O'Connor, Amalya Kearse for Justice Powell, Pamela Rymer for Justice O'Connor, and Phyllis Kravitch for Justice Blackmun.

The total number of women clerks, beginning with the first one who served Justice Douglas in 1944, has been 87 through the 1986 term

(*National Law Journal*, 1980-1986). The total number of male clerks ever at the Supreme Court is estimated at more than 1500.[8] The number of women clerks per term was one in 1944, 1966, 1968, 1971, and 1973; three or four in 1972, 1974, 1975, and 1976. From 1977 to 1985, there were five to eight per term. The female proportion reached one-fourth in 1981, by happenstance the year Justice O'Connor joined the Court, and in the 1986 term jumped over one-third. The percentage of women law clerks on the Supreme Court did not increase in relation to the percentage of women law graduates. The percentage of clerks for the 1984 term matched 1974 law classes; for the 1985 term, the 1975 law classes; but for the 1986 term, the 1980 law classes. Even taking into account the lower percentage of women finishing at the elite schools from which clerks are drawn, there has clearly been some barrier to the preparation and consideration of women. However, the lag time is now shorter, due perhaps to the election of women as law review editors by students and a lesser reluctance of justices.

Unlike the more formal process of selecting students for law school, the screening of prospective clerks is highly personal and subjective, as managed by the justices or chosen surrogates. Aside from Justice O'Connor, only Justices Douglas, Marshall, and Blackmun have selected two women for the same term (out of the four clerks that most justices use). Justice Blackmun set a record in 1985, repeated in 1986, by choosing three women. None of the male justices averages one woman clerk per term for their respective tenures, although Justice Marshall comes close. In contrast, Justice O'Connor selected two women for the 1981, 1982, 1984, and 1986 terms and one woman for the 1983 and 1985 terms. The gatekeepers for the law clerk positions are the justices themselves or the law professor, judge, or small group of lawyers in whom they have personal confidence. The three women hired for the 1980 term attributed the underrepresentation of women to covert prejudices institutionalized by the system of channeling candidates to the justices (*National Law Journal,* August 4, 1980). Their complaint was against the gatekeepers.

LAW PROFESSORS IN THE OPPORTUNITY STRUCTURE

In the United States there is a direct link between clerkships and law faculty positions. Some women who served as Supreme Court clerks moved directly into teaching at elite law schools. About the same proportion of the female as the male clerks now become professors, but because of the small share of the positions at one step of the opportunity track such as the Supreme Court clerkship, only a small pool of eligibles for the next step on the law faculty is created. The personalized gatekeeping for the Supreme Court clerk contrasts to the formal procedures of search and screening for new faculty under the pressure of conformance to Title IX guidelines and procedures.

The proportion of women law professors is at the token level. Table 6.5 shows that the percentage of women on law faculties remains below 20% and that every year since 1971 the percentage has been one-third that of women law students. The percentage of women professors has increased in relation to the percentage of women in practice, but with the end of the period of expanding student bodies and new law schools, the percentage of women law professors is slipping behind as the percentage of practitioners continues to increase.

In 1950 five women and in 1960 eleven women were on the tenure track at approved law schools, less than 1% of the total number of tenure track professors. By 1970 the number of women had increased fivefold and the percentage just exceeded 2%, by 1979 it had reached 10.5% (Epstein, 1983: table 12.1; Weisberg, 1979). The elite law schools have fewer women on tenure track than the nonelite schools. In 1976, when the national average of female law faculty was 7.5%, of ten elite schools only NYU matched or exceeded that proportion (Epstein, 1983: table 12.2). In 1980, when the national average was 11%, NYU was still the only elite school exceeding the norm. By 1980 Chicago had chosen its first full-time woman professor, but Virginia and Pennsylvania did not increase their percentage of female faculty between 1974 and 1979.

The new and progressive schools just building their faculties in the 1970s hired more women than would be expected given the percentage of women in the bar. As late as 1974, one-fourth of law schools had all-male faculty; another fourth had a token woman (Fossum, 1980: 905-906). The percentage of law faculties with no women was 65% in 1970, 10% in 1976, and 2% in 1983; the percentage with six or more women was zero in 1970, 5% in 1976, and 17% in 1983 (Lauter, 1984). In 1979, 17% of the law schools had one woman and 80% had more than one woman (Fossum, 1980: 913). The period of exclusion was almost at an end and the period of tokenism well established.

The position of dean of a law school carries somewhat more honor and responsibility than the professorship. The female law school, Washington College of Law in D.C., had six women deans between 1898 and 1947. The number of women deans of sex-integrated schools can easily be counted: Miriam T. Rooney and Elizabeth F. DeFeis, Seton Hall;

Dorothy Nelson, University of Southern California; Judith Younger, Syracuse, now law professor at Cornell; Jean C. Cahn, Antioch; Soia Mentschikoff and Mary Doyle, University of Miami; Judith G. McKelvey, Golden Gate; Susan W. Prager, UCLA; Janet A. Johnson, Pace University; Barbara Black, Columbia University; and Marjorie Fine Knowles, Georgia State. Two of the law schools headed by a woman, UCLA and Columbia, are on the list of 15 elite law schools. The visibility of a law school dean means that when a public official is looking for a woman to appoint, the name of a woman dean of the appropriate political party and age will probably go on the screening list. Dorothy Nelson, now on the Ninth Circuit, was widely considered to be a candidate for the Stewart vacancy on the United States Supreme Court. However, as an "independent" who had been placed on the Court of Appeals by President Carter, her ideological credentials were not as good as Justice O'Connor's.

The presence of women as law deans or professors at the elite schools may improve the chances of women students to enter the fast legal track. These women may participate in the making of policy on admissions, in the choice of new students, in the advising of law reviews, and in the recommendation of graduates for clerkships and associate positions. They are likely to propose women students who might not be as visible to male faculty for these opportunities. Women students in turn demand more women faculty to provide role models and mentors. Because most of the judges on the prestigious courts have graduated from elite law schools, it is particularly important for women to play gatekeeping roles at the elite schools to monitor the fair treatment of women applicants and students, and thus create a pool of eligibles for future consideration for the prestigious courts.

LAW FIRMS

The new admission and placement practices of law schools, reinforced by Titles VII and IX of the Civil Rights Act of 1964, as revised in 1972, are beginning to have an impact upon the sex ratios of public and private law offices. Law schools, which select one-third of their student body every year, can change their sex composition quickly; in contrast, it takes a generation or more to equalize the sex ratio in the personnel of an organization with long tenure and little turnover. Just as women as "outsiders" first found places at unapproved and less elite law schools, they find opportunities to practice law in the less lucrative and visible law areas. Therefore, the impact of women law graduates is first found in the public defender and legal aid offices and other government positions with rapid turnover of young lawyers (Epstein, 1983: 99, 112-119). In the major law firms, young women may join the associate rank, where the seven year up-or-out policy allows for regular recruiting. But women are having a more difficult time reaching and integrating at the level of partner in the top law firms.

In the 250 largest law firms in the country in 1985, women claimed 30.5% of the associate positions (Stille, 1985). This percentage fit the law class sex ratio of seven years earlier. Women made up 6% of the total number of partners in these law firms, twice the percentage in 1981 but still 10 years behind the proportion of women in practice. The proportion of partners was slightly higher in Washington, D.C., where the largest number of women lawyers is concentrated. The connection between graduation from an elite law school and an invitation to join a prestigious law firm is not as close for women as for men. Women who have the necessary credential are not recruited as seriously as men.

Movement from one step to the next in the opportunity structure is much more difficult for women than men for two reasons—the number of women chosen and trained at one step provides a small pool of eligibles for the gatekeepers at the next step, and the actual minority status of women reinforces their cultural invisibility as viable candidates. For instance, a partnership in a well-established law firm is an important credential for those ambitious for a prestigious bench. The gatekeepers who choose only male or mostly male partners in private firms directly affect the opportunities of women for judicial office in a negative way.

TRIAL JUDGE POSITIONS

If women had equal opportunity for the positions that require a law degree, then one would expect the same percentage of women judges as women lawyers. One would also expect that the sex integration of the bar would be followed within a reasonable period of time by the sex integration of the courts. The gatekeepers for judgeships, however, kept their barriers high long after women penetrated the bar. Table 6.7 illustrates the time intervals from female eligibility to first presence on the state bench (Berkson, 1982: 29). The denial to women of the opportunity to take the step from bar to bench is dramatically illustrated by the 104-year interval between Mansfield's admission in Iowa and the presence of the first woman trial judge in Iowa. The longest wait for women to take a major trial judgeship after admission to the bar was 110 years in Missouri; the average period for all states is half a century.

TABLE 6.7
Time Intervals from Female Eligibility to First Presence on State Bench
(number of states and D.C.)

Time Interval	Bar to Trial Bench (years)	Bar to Appellate Bench (years)	Trial to Appellate Bench (years)
0-9 years	0	0	7
10-19	4	0	5
20-29	3	0	8
30-39	6	0	6
40-49	14	1	4
50-59	8	5	6
60-69	4	7	1
70-79	4	3	0
80-89	4	5	0
90-99	2	8	0
100+	2	8	0
not yet (1987)	0	14	14
Average interval	52 years	85 years	29 years

SOURCE: Time intervals calculated from dates of admission for first woman to state bar, Berkson (Table 1, 1982); Cook (Table 9.1, 1984).
NOTE: Trial Bench includes limited jurisdiction courts which require bar admission. Appellate Bench includes intermediate level.

For women and men, entrance to the bar was a necessary qualification for important judgeships. But the unwritten qualification for a judgeship was that the applicant be male. If women had received fair consideration, then there should be a relationship between the dates of admission to the bar by the states and the dates of first female presence on a major trial court. The insignificant relationship means that the dates of entry into the opportunity structure provide only a small part (10%) of the explanation for the delay—generations later—until women finally reached the state courts.

PRESTIGIOUS STATE COURTS

The period of time that elapsed in each state from women's entrance into the opportunity structure through the bar to their presence on the state's high courts provides a measure of the resistance of appellate level gatekeepers. The average time span from state bar to state appellate court was 85 years, the longest was 111 years in Maine. The 14 states that have never had a woman at this level are requiring even longer waiting periods of their women lawyers. In six of these states, women in the legal profession had already waited 80 or more years for the trial bench, but have not gained the appellate level—Missouri, Montana, Nebraska, New Hampshire, South Dakota, and Wyoming.

The progress of women as a class through the opportunity structure is very similar to the successive position-holding of individuals. One or more women have served as a state trial judge in every state that has accepted a woman on its supreme court. The average time lag between the presence of women on the trial level and the appellate level is 29 years. Pennsylvania provides a typical example—after the first woman was admitted to the bar an interval of 47 years elapsed before a woman served on a minor court, 58 years until a major trial court, and 78 years until the appellate bench.

The access of women to the highest court is predictable from women's presence on the trial court. The willingness of bar gatekeepers to admit women did not influence the gatekeepers at the trial level, as was demonstrated above, but entry to the trial court does improve women's chances for elevation. The dates of women's first presence on state trial courts correlate with the dates of women's first presence on the supreme court ($r = .58$), which means that one-third of the explanation for women's success rests with the pool of eligibles.

A few states excluded women from their courts until the late 1970s, when women won places on the major trial and appellate levels in quick succession. These states include Connecticut, Indiana, Iowa, Kansas, Maine, Minnesota, New Mexico, Utah, Washington, Wisconsin, and Washington, D.C. (Cook, 1984). The same woman was quickly elevated from the trial to the supreme court in Kansas, Utah, and Washington states.

PRESTIGIOUS FEDERAL COURTS

Admission to the state bar is a prerequisite for selection to the federal as well as to the state bench, but there is little relationship between the dates when women first join the state bar and when they claim a federal court judgeship. Of the 29 states and the District of Columbia with women on the federal benches, 16 had women judges on the federal bench before a woman reached the state's prestigious level (see Table 6.1). Six states with female federal judges—Georgia, Illinois, Indiana, Louisiana, Tennessee, and West Virginia—still do not have women on their state courts of last resort.

In those states where women showed their competence on state benches before winning the more prestigious federal posts, the longest waiting period was 27 years. The first serious woman candidate for the federal bench, Mabel Walker Willebrandt, worked assiduously from 1923 through the 1930s for a district seat in California (Brown, 1984). President Harding, before his last trip to the West Coast, had almost been persuaded by women leaders of his party to show women appropriate recognition before the 1924 election. However, his successor, President Coolidge, did not feel that the contributions of women to the party justified a federal judgeship. It was not until 1950 that President Truman rewarded Burnita Matthews with a district judgeship for the contributions she had made 30 years earlier in the suffrage movement (Cook, 1978).

Only four women have held prestigious state and federal positions in succession, thus using their credentials at one level of the opportunity structure to move to the next level. Florence Allen left the Ohio Supreme Court to accept President Roosevelt's appointment to the Sixth Circuit in 1934 and Elsijane Roy, daughter of a federal judge, served on the Arkansas Supreme Court before taking the district bench, from which her father had retired, in 1977. Patricia Boyle moved in the opposite direction in 1983, from the district bench in Detroit to the Michigan Supreme Court. Carolyn Dimmick served four years on the Washington Supreme Court and then went to the federal district court in 1985. About half of the women on federal courts first served on the less important state intermediate or trial court, and inside the federal hierarchy, only five women have been elevated: Alice M. Batchelder from Bankruptcy Judge to district judge in Ohio; Barbara Crabb from magistrate to district court in Wisconsin; Cynthia Hall from tax court to district court in Los Angeles and then to Ninth Circuit; Cornelia Kennedy from district court in Detroit to the Sixth Circuit; and Carol Los Mansman from middle district in Pennsylvania to the Third Circuit. The pool of women at the district level was too small prior to the Carter administration to provide any competition to the numerous male candidates for circuit level vacancies. With seniority accumulated after 1980, the Carter appointees will be available for elevation by the next Democratic president. President Reagan, having placed 21 female Republicans in federal district positions, selected two from this pool for elevation to the circuit bench.

MEASURING UNDERREPRESENTATION OF WOMEN IN THE OPPORTUNITY STRUCTURE

Women found a place on the nonprestigious courts much earlier than on the prestigious courts. Table 6.8 shows that before 1930 13 states had

TABLE 6.8
First Presence of Woman on Court by State and Time

Time Period	State Trial		State Appellate* (N)	Federal	
	Limited (N)	General (N)		Trial (N)	Appellate (N)
Pre-1930	13	2	1	1	0
1930-1949	12	8	1	0	1
1950-1969	9	9	6	2	1
1970-1986	17	28	29	24	10
not yet (1987)	0	4	14	24	39
	(%)	(%)	(%)	(%)	(%)
Pre-1970	67	37	16	6	4
1970-1986	33	55	57	47	20
not yet (1987)	0	8	27	47	76

NOTE: N = 50 states plus D.C.; first federal trial judge date is 1928 for Genevieve R. Cline of the Customs Court. Analysis from data compiled by Cook (1980, 1984).
*Intermediate and Court of Last Resort.

seated women on limited jurisdiction courts, two states on general jurisdiction courts, one state on its supreme court, and one state on a federal trial court. By 1950, over half the states had found places for women on their minor courts. But in 1987 more than one-fourth of the states did not have women on appellate courts, and almost half of the states did not have women on the federal trial courts located within their boundaries.

The analysis so far has looked at the treatment of women lawyers at different levels of the opportunity structure within the states. Another way of examining women's status in the courts is to aggregate the state data to the national level and compare across levels. Table 6.9 treats the percentage of women in the bar as the basic pool of eligibles and then reports the disparity between the number of judgeships expected and achieved. For 1925 and 1955 the comparison is between the percentage of women in the bar and those on the bench in the same year, because the percentage of women by age cohort did not vary. However, for the modern comparisons, the percentages of women in the bar in 1972 and 1978 are compared to the percentages of women on the bench five years later. The time lag is necessitated by the skewing of ages of women lawyers toward the younger cohorts. In 1975, 45% of women lawyers were under 30 and 53% under 35. In 1980, 75% of women lawyers were under 40 and half were under 33. Because most candidates for minor judgeships are at least 30 years of age, and those ready for prestigious courts closer to 50, at least a five-year time lag makes sense.

TABLE 6.9
Women on the Bench: Disparity from Pool of Women Lawyers

% Bar Female		Date	State Trial			State Appellate			Federal Trial			Federal Appellate		
Date	Fem %		N	Fem %	Disp	N	Fem %	Disp	N	Fem %	Disp	N	Fem %	Disp
1925	1.5	1925	4000	0.3	-49	350	0.3	-4	121	0.0	-2	45	0.0	-1
1955	3.0	1955	4150	1.3	-70	493	0.2	-14	250	0.4	-7	77	1.3	-1
1972	3.8	1977	9500	3.4	-34	806	3.6	-2	390	1.3	-10	106	0.9	-3
1978	9.4	1983	10500	5.6	-427	982	5.7	-36	541	7.6	-10	158	8.9	-1

SOURCE: Directory of American Judges, 1955; C. Whitehurst, *Women in America* (1977: Table 4.4); B. Cook, *Trial* (August 1983: Table 1).
NOTE: N = number of available judgeships; Fem % = percentage of women judges; Disp = disparity or number of positions held by men which the percentage of women in the bar predicts women would hold.

Across time, the relationship between the percentage of women in the bar and bench was closer for the prestigious courts than the lower courts. In 1925 female bar strength indicated that women could claim 20 more state trial seats but only one or two more federal and state appellate seats. The representation of women on state courts in relation to their bar presence actually improved between 1955 and 1977, while representation did not decline by more than a few potential positions on the federal courts.

From the 1970s into the 1980s, however, the state court gatekeepers did not choose women as judges in proportion to their increasing numbers in the bar. The number of seats on the state trial and appellate levels to which women have an unrealized claim increased tenfold. On the other hand, the Carter affirmative action policy and introduction of nominating commissions kept the level of underrepresentation steady on the federal courts.

The rapid transformation of law schools from male to integrated institutions is creating a large pool of women eligible for the bench in 1990 and later. A projection of the estimated 1985 percentage of women lawyers onto the 1990 bench, assuming no increase in court size, indicates that the state courts should select more than 1000 additional women trial judges. The figures are less startling for the prestigious courts—90 more women should go on the state appellate courts, 40 more on federal district courts, and 10 more on federal appellate courts. Unless the number of judgeships continues to increase, particularly at the trial court level, and the attitude of the selecting authorities toward women improves, it is not likely that the goal of a close correspondence of bar percentages and judge percentages will occur for women.

CONCLUSION

Women's token status in the courts has lasted over 100 years. Female success in achieving minority status in law schools will be translated to other positions in the judicial opportunity structure only over a long period of time, as the large student cohorts move into practice and politics. However, time is not the only barrier to integration. The opportunity structure includes positions in organizations outside of government that are resistant to the incursion of women. In particular, elite law faculties and major law firms lag behind the average for the profession in their acceptance of women as colleagues. Some of the positions in the opportunity structure are not open to competition of the kind involved in group admission to law schools or in large hirings by law bureaucracies. There is a strong element of subjectivity in the choice of junior colleagues as court clerks, as tenure track professors, and as new firm partners, and the men who hold the senior positions are not generally comfortable choosing young women at proteges.

There is nothing in this preface to the history of women on the bench that suggests that the increasing percentage of women at the bottom of the opportunity structure will automatically bring about integration at the middle or top of the court hierarchies. The resistance will be especially strong at the appellate level, where the number of positions is scarce and the power great. The number of women now sitting on these courts is token; yet opening up one seat to female candidacy and winning that seat for a specific individual costs a great deal of time, energy, and money of those involved in the effort. Gaining one woman's seat and one woman incumbent on a prestigious court has proved an expensive enterprise with a payoff more symbolic than real. When the addition of more women to a court means a real rather than a symbolic shift in the balance of power between the sexes, then the price attached to that seat will be considerably higher than the price attached to the token seat. Integration at the population ratio is far in the future.

NOTES

1. Reprinted by permission from Golden Gate University Law School Journal, Beverly B. Cook (1984) "Women Judges: A Preface to Their History," Women's Forum 14 (Summer 1984): 573-610. Table 6.1 has been updated, and the legal style revised to the social science format.

2. Women without law degrees who have served on nonattorney courts with minor jurisdictions are not covered in the body of this article because they lack the credentials to aspire to higher courts. The first woman judge, Esther Morris, a JP in Wyoming in 1870, was not a member of the bar (Gressley, 1971).

3. The definition of tokenism comes from the Kanter model of integration and denotes occupancy by members of a recognizable class of less than 20% of available positions. The first stage of the Kanter model is total exclusion; there is no historical record of an American woman judge before 1870. The second stage of token inclusion has lasted from 1870 to date. The third stage exists when the outsider class gain a minority status of between 20% and 40%, and the stage of integration occurs when the formerly excluded class controls 40% to 60% of the positions. Unlike any other "minority" group in the United States, women have the potential based upon their population percentage to integrate the courts and all other public institutions (Kanter, 1978).

4. The 6% figure is based upon my updated data file of women judges, created for 1977-1978 and 1982-1983 surveys of women judges (Cook, 1980, 1981, 1984). The percentage of women in practice has been variously estimated as 13% and 15%, depending upon whether women in the bar who are inactive are included or not. The figure for 1982 was 12% (see Cook, 1983: table 1). The percentage in law school was computed from data reported for ABA-accredited law schools (Association of American Law Schools, 1983).

5. For example, in 1920, with the passage of the suffrage amendment, women entered law schools, medical schools, and doctoral programs in larger numbers than previously with the expectation that they would be accepted as equals and share the rewards of professional status with men. By the end of the decade, the influx of women declined in the face of resistance to their presence (Hummer, 1979).

6. The National Women's Political Caucus (NWPC) keeps a running tally of women appointed to federal judgeships in its Washington, D.C., office (Ness, 1980).

7. The one woman supreme court justice in Rhode Island and the one in Utah, each on five-person courts, take 20% of the available seats, but are still a minority. Even in systems with no or few women at the trial level, such as Mississippi, Maine, Kansas, and Utah, a single woman may be present on the supreme court. The four women on the Ninth Circuit (from three states) take 17% of the positions. The two women on the Third Circuit hold 20%. The one woman on the U.S. Supreme Court holds 11% of the voting power and the one on the 11-person Sixth Circuit 9% of the seats. The First Circuit, in which each of the four judges enjoys 25% of the court power, has never had a woman judge.

8. This approximation is based upon the number of justices and the number of clerks allotted since the first male law clerk served Justice Horace Gray in 1882. Congress provided salaries for one law clerk for each justice in 1886. The associate justices may now select four law clerks per term, although not all choose to do so (Abraham, 1980).

REFERENCES

Abraham, Henry (1980) The Judicial Process. New York: Oxford University Press.

Administrative Office of the U.S. Courts (1940-1983) Annual Report. Washington, DC: Author.

Allen, Florence E. (1956) To Do Justly [autobiography]. Cleveland: Western Reserve University Press.

The American Bench (1985-1986) Sacramento: Regional Bishop Forster and Assoc.

Arnold, Kenneth J. (1983) California Courts and Judges Handbook. San Francisco: Law Book Service.

Association of American Law Schools (1980) Directory of Law Teachers. St. Paul: West Publishers and Foundation Press.

Association of American Law Schools (1983) Pre-Law Handbook. Law School Admissions Council.

Auerbach, Jerome (1976) Unequal Justice: Lawyers and Social Change in Modern America. New York: Oxford University Press.

Berkson, Larry (1982) "Women on the bench: a brief history." Judicature 65 (January): 286-293.

Berkson, Larry and Susan Carbon (1980) The United States Circuit Judge Nominating Commission: Its Members, Procedures, and Candidates. Chicago: American Judicature Society.

Brown, Dorothy (1984) Mabel Walker Willebrandt: A Study of Power, Loyality and Law. Knoxville: University of Tennessee Press.

Cook, Beverly B. (1978) "Women judges: the end of tokenism," ch. 4 in W. Hepperle and L. Crites (eds.) Women in the Courts. Williamsburg, VA: National Center for State Courts.

Cook, Beverly B. (1980) "Political culture and selection of women judges to trial courts," ch. 2 in D. Stewart (ed.) Women in Local Politics. NJ: Scarecrow Press.

Cook, Beverly B. (1981a) "The first woman candidate for the supreme court: Florence E. Allen," pp. 19-35 in The Supreme Court Historical Society Yearbook.

Cook, Beverly B. (1981b) "The selection of judges." Judges' Journal 20 (Fall 1981): 20-24, 50-52.

Cook, Beverly B. (1981c) "Will women judges make a difference to women's legal rights?" in M. Rendel (ed.) Women, Power, and Political Systems. London: Croon Helm.

Cook, Beverly B. (1982) "Women as supreme court candidates, from Florence Allen to Sandra O'Connor." Judicature 65 (January): 314-326.

Cook, Beverly B. (1983) "The path to the bench: ambition and attitudes of women in the law." Trial 19 (August): 49-55.

Cook, Beverly B. (1984) "Women on the state bench: correlates of access," ch. 9 in J. Flammang (ed.) Political Women: Current Role in State and Local Politics. Newbury Park, CA: Sage.

Cook, Beverly B., Leslie Goldstein, Karen O'Connor, and Susette M. Talarico (1987) Women in the Judicial Process. Washington, DC: American Political Science Association.

Council of State Governments (1935-1983) Book of the States.

Directory of American Judges (1955) Charles Liebman, Compiler. Chicago: American Directories.

Epstein, Cynthia (1983) Women in Law. New York: Anchor Books.

Flammang, Janet [ed.] (1984) Political Women: Current Role in State and Local Politics. Newbury Park, CA: Sage.

Fossum, Donna (1980a) "Women law professors." American Bar Foundation Research Journal 3 (Fall): 903-914.

Fossum, Donna (1980b) "Law professors: a profile of the teaching branch of the legal profession." American Bar Foundation Research Journal 3 (Summer): 501-554.

Fund for Modern Courts (1985) "The success of women and minorities in achieving judicial office." New York City: Author.

Goldman, Sheldon (1979) "Should there be affirmative action for the judiciary?" Judicature 62 (May): 488-494.

Gressley, Gene M. (1971) "Esther Morris," pp. 583-585 in Edward T. James (ed.) Notable American Women, 1607-1950, Vol. 2. Cambridge, MA: Harvard University Press.

Hummer, Patricia M. (1979) The Decade of Elusive Promise: Professional Women in the United States, 1920-30. Ann Arbor, MI: UMI Research Press.

Jacob, Herbert (1984) Justice in America. Boston: Little, Brown.

Kanter, Rosabeth Moss (1977) Men and Women of the Corporation. New York: Basic Books.

Kanter, Rosabeth Moss (1978) "Reflections on women and the legal profession." Harvard Women's Law Journal 1 (Spring): 1-17.

Lauter, David (1984) "Gender gap gets wider on law faculties." National Law Journal (January 9): 1, 9-11.

Lauter, David (1986) "Yale outpaces Harvard in clerkships." National Law Journal
    (March 24): 5, 34.
Martin, Elaine (1982) "Women on the federal bench: a comparative profile." Judicature 65
    (December-January): 306-313.
National Law Journal (NJL) (1981) "Survey of black and women lawyers." April 20.
National Roster of Women Judges (1980) Larry Berkson and Donna Vandenberg,
    Compilers. Chicago: American Judicature Society.
Ness, Susan (1980) Women and the Federal Judiciary. Washington, DC: NWPC
    Appointments Project.
Pound, Roscoe (1953) The Lawyer from Antiquity to Modern Times. St. Paul: West.
Schlesinger, Joseph (1966) Ambition and Politics. Chicago: Rand McNally.
Schmidhauser, John (1979) Judges and Justices. Boston: Little, Brown.
Slotnick, Elliot E. (1983) "Federal trial and appellate judges: how do they differ?" Western
    Political Quarterly 36 (December): 570-576.
Slotnick, Elliot E. (1984) "Gender, affirmative action, and recruitment to the federal
    bench." Women's Law Forum, Golden Gate University Law Review, 14 (Fall):
    519-571.
Stewart, Debra W. [ed.] (1980) Women in Local Politics. NJ: Scarecrow Press.
Stille, Alexander (1985) "Minorities and the law: in the firms." National Law Journal 23
    (December): 1, 6-10.
Thomas, Dorothy (1971) "Anabella Mansfield," pp. 492-493 in Edward T. James (ed.)
    Notable American Women, 1607-1950, Vol. 2. Cambridge, MA: Harvard University
    Press.
Warren, Charles. (1911) A History of the American Bar. Boston: Little, Brown.
Weisberg, D. Kelly (1977) "Barred from the bar: women and legal education in the United
    States, 1870-1890." Journal of Legal Education 28, 4: 485-507.
Whitehurst, Carol A. (1977) Women in America. Santa Monica: Goodyear.

7

FEMALE COURT ADMINISTRATORS: STUCK AT MID-LEVEL

Winifred L. Hepperle

The importance of court administrators has been grudgingly granted, but never fully recognized since the "profession" emerged in the 1960s. Then the federal government, through its Law Enforcement Administration Act (LEEA), made loan funds available for students to learn court administration, provided they promised to repay the debt with service in the courts. Many would-be administrators took advantage of the program. Several universities, notably, the University of Southern California, the University of Denver, and American University, plus one specialized school, the Institute for Court Management, provided the "education." Much of it was an ad hoc program combining public administration, business management, and a smattering of law cum judicial process. Course material, in the traditional sense, was unavailable; there was an emphasis on fieldwork, otherwise known as "see how the system works" and suggest reforms. Judges loved it because they thought it would provide a great new support system. On-the-job court clerks worried that they would be euchred out of a top job, after long years of patient toil and devotion. Special organizations emerged; specialized publications sprouted; "proper" reports proliferated.

With these developments came more interest and examination of the whole judicial process. Concern about judicial responsibilities was expressed by lawyers and legal organizations like the American Bar Association, by government agencies including legislatures and state judicial councils, and by public interest groups such as the ACLU and the League of Women Voters. They worried about cases were not being heard on a "timely basis," criminal defendants who could not afford legal representation, victims who were not consulted as to their opinions, juries that often did not reflect the community composition, and similar issues. In partial response to this need, there emerged the recognized, official position of court administrator: a skilled professional, trained to tackle these problems, under the supervision, of course, of the presiding judge.

Since then, the role of the court administrator has steadied. Some who were court clerks (pre-1960) have had the title updated to court administrator. Some who were in the ranks have advanced by completing a field course or supplemental seminar in court administration. Others have progressed through degrees in public administration, law, or specialty programs sponsored by the federal government and private institutions. A small proportion of women have moved up but only a few have managed to grab the plum, the title of court administrator.

This chapter looks at why that happened and why advancement has been slow for women.

WOMEN MANAGERS

According to the U.S. Department of Commerce, the American woman's share of managerial occupations increased sharply between 1970 and 1980 (U.S. Department of Commerce, 1984). While the rise was sharp, the percentages tell another story: the increase was from 18.5% to 30.5%. Even so, *Glamour* magazine reports that women are presently more aware of sex discrimination in the job market than before. Based on 800 interviews with women in late 1985, *Glamour* found 83% of the women say they have less opportunity to earn top salaries, as compared to 76% who felt that way in 1982. In addition, almost three-quarters thought their chances for job advancement were worse than a man's, compared to 69% who felt that way in 1982. The report noted further that women are still barred from senior management positions (*Glamour,* 1986). In the same vein, a 1986 poll in California showed that 77% of the women and 69% of the men believe that despite recent gains, it remains essentially a "man's world." University of California sociologist Alie Hochschild commented, "We know that over the last 10 years the education gap between men and women has almost disappeared, and yet the income gap between men and women has increased slightly" (*San Francisco Chronicle,* 1986b).

The U.S. Department of Labor confirms these feelings. In 1984, the median weekly earnings of men in executive, administrative, and managerial positions was $568, compared to women's earnings of $358 (U.S. Department of Labor, 1985).

Narrowing the focus to women as court managers, we examine what a court manager does, the qualifications needed for the job, the pay range, where men and women managers are now situated in the hierarchy and how they got there, and how they feel about it.

Two national organizations exist to foster professionalism at the trial court level: the National Association of Court Managers and the Conference of State Court Administrators. Other organizations support those engaged at the appellate level and similar organizations exist to advance other areas concerned with judicial administration including educators, planners, researchers, judges, and so on.

According to the National Association of Court Managers (NACA), a court manager's primary role is to oversee the administrative functions of the court, under the general direction of the Chief Judge. These functions are identified as management of personnel, fiscal affairs, court calendar, automated office systems, juries, space and equipment, public information, reports, records, research and advisory services, intergovernmental relations and secretariat services (*The Court Administrator*, n.d.). However, the primary tasks are budgeting, personnel, jury management, and case scheduling, all essentially comparable to management responsibilities in corporate organizations (Mays and Taggart, 1985).

In 1985 Mays and Taggart published the results of a comprehensive report entitled, "Local Court Administration: Findings From A Survey Of Appointed Managers." In compiling this "profile" of a local court manager, the authors noted several items that are relevant here. There is no accurate count of the number of court managers in the United States. Many "clerks" of court are not managers. About 55% are appointed court managers and almost all of them (82%) are selected by a single judge or body of judges. At lower salary levels, the proportion of females far exceeds that of males. One-half the women reported income lower than $25,000 per year, whereas 90% of the men earn more than this a year. Of all managers, slightly more than 60% have successfully completed college (4 years) and one-third hold postbaccalaureate degrees. Most court managers are males in the 31-50 age range. Most held court-related positions prior to their current appointment, and many work in the region of the country where educated.

These factors considered together mean that court managers resemble others in the courtroom work group—particularly attorneys and judges. While this similarity does not guarantee their acceptance, it does make them less *foreign* to the other actors in the adjudication process. [Coincidentally,] a full 60% of the managers revealed that judges, more than anyone else have been the most supportive group [Mays and Taggart, 1985, emphasis added].

Because there are no centralized statistical data covering employment on the management side of the court system (as distinguished from numbers and placement of judges) a variety of tactics were used to gather more specific information about court employees and what factors were relevant to advancement. This included contact with schools and professional organizations involved in court training programs, with selected court systems, and an informal survey of court administrators.

As to whether specific training in court administration, as distinguished from public administration, business, and so on, is particularly helpful to job advancement, limited data were made available by two organizations that provide such education. The University of Denver, College of Law, provides a curriculum leading to a M.S.J.A. (Master of Science, Judicial Administration). In the 15 years from 1970 through 1985, there have been 237 graduates, with 109 female and 128 male. Spot checks for the years 1975 and 1980 showed that about one-third of each class of 17 are presently employed in court administration. Of those 13 persons, 6 are female and 7 are male. The current salary range for the class of '75 ranged from $50,000 to $68,000 for the four males, and $54,000 to $68,000 for the two females. In the class of '80, four males earned from $28,000 to $34,000, and the three females earned from $27,000 to $43,000. These figures suggest a high dropout rate; about two-thirds of the classes sampled did not stay in court administration, but of those who did, the distribution and salary range was approximately equal between men and women.

The Institute for Court Management, on the other hand, is primarily concerned with advancing the education and professional standards of those already employed in court administration. The consequent differential between male and female graduates demonstrates this fact, and emphasizes that men are making efforts to qualify for higher-ranked jobs. Of a total of 454 graduates from 1970 to 1985, 381 were male, and 73 female. Information on salary and current occupation was not available (Hepperle, 1985).

Compare these figures to those of the Mays and Taggart survey of the membership of the National Association of Trial Court Administrators (now the National Association of Court Managers) indicating 58% were male and 42% were female, but also recall that women mainly occupy the lower salary positions.

Looking more closely at male/female manager employment, the following information was gathered:

As of 1986 in the U.S. court system, both the Clerk of the United States Supreme Court and the Administrator for the United States Office of the Court are male. Among the 13 Circuits there are four female court executive officers (8%); among 94 United States District Courts there are 10 female district court clerks (12%); and among 92 Bankruptcy Clerks of Court, at least 36 are female (39%). These numbers demonstrate the decline in percentage of female administrators as the rank and prestige of the court increases. In the 50 state court systems, there are six female state court administrators (12%).

Using California as an example of a state reputed to be "progressive" in its court administrative system, the following is a summary of the employment pattern in the major court administrative positions.

The Administrative Office of the California Courts has a total staff of 100. It has adopted a formal Affirmative Action plan. According to the 1986 Report, the job category of "officials and managers" comprised 13% of the work force. Of these 13 employees, three were female (23%). Note, however, that these are at the lower end of the scale, while men occupy the top six slots, including the position of director.

The clerk's office for the California Supreme Court is headed by a male. Each of the six Courts of Appeals has a clerk's office; all are headed by men.

The California statewide court of general jurisdiction is the Superior Court; there is one for each of the 52 counties. In most counties the position of superior court clerk is subsumed under the title of county clerk, usually an elective position with a wide range of authority. Many of the larger counties, and a few smaller ones, also employ an appointed court administrator. Of the 19 counties that employ a superior court executive officer, 16 are male and 3 are female. The California courts of limited jurisdiction are municipal courts (with a few rural justice courts) and each has a clerk/administrator. Of the municipal courts, 32% of the clerks are male, and 68% are female (Arnold, 1983).

Such sex segregation is not unique to courts; it cuts accross all employment areas. The National Research Council recommends a series of actions to achieve change, which would apply to the courts as well. These are: vigorous enforcement of laws now on the books; reduce sex stereotyping in education and job training: use of more varied referral sources in job recruiting; and provision for more abundant and improved child care.

The overall pattern makes it plain: in terms of authority, prestige, and income, the field of court administrators is dominated by men. A survey conducted by the author sought the individual views of selected male and female administrators now in the courts. Although there is no attempt to suggest statistical validity, because the respondents totaled only 36 (18 male and 18 female), some factors are worth noting. In terms of education, 90% of the males had a college degree, and 44% reported advanced training, compared to 53% of the women with college degrees and 18% who reported advanced training. Here, the male candidates appear more qualified. Similarly, there was a differential in salary range between men and women. The median male annual salary was between $35,000 and $45,000, while the female median was between $25,000 and $35,000. Note that 33% of the females earned under $25,000, while no males were in that bracket. Conversely, 33% of the men earned $45,000 or more, compared to 22% of the women in that range.

The respondents were asked to rank a series of statements pertaining to personal observations and reactions in the workplace using the usual one through five scale of strongly agree, agree, uncertain, disagree, strongly disagree. Men and women coincided on two issues: both "agreed" that they were recognized and respected for their individual work abilities; both "disagreed" that they were frustrated by lack of authority to do the job. Split votes resulted as follows: about equal proportions of both men and women were divided on whether they would like the challenge of a position with more responsibility; while most felt they were considered part of the management team, a greater proportion of women felt they were not.

About 66% of the women believed that judges had *not* challenged their authority as a manager, while only 22% of the men felt they had not encountered judicial challenge. One wonders if women encountered less challenge to their authority because they were less a member of the management team, or if this difference is a result of working styles, perceptions, or the judges' attitudes. On a different issue, there was a clear difference of opinion on the proposition that advancement in court administration is almost always based on merit. Slightly more than half of the men agreed, while two-thirds of the women were "uncertain" or disagreed with the concept that advancement is based on merit.

Questions about personal aspirations indicated that both men and women agreed that the power associated with being a manager was a motivating factor in their occupational role. Also, both agreed that they (individually) had a strong, positive self-concept, although a few women were not quite so certain. About 45% of both men and women agreed that their personal life suffers from the amount of time spent on the job.

Finally, comments were requested about the advantages and disadvantages of seeking a court manager position, as a male, and as a female. Men and women agreed that the main consideration was essentially one of stereotypes, particularly those held by judges, who often are the final voice in job selection. Words such as "authority," "credibility," "respect," and "hierarchy" were used to describe the judicial view of a male court administrator. Women were generally credited as being "flexible," "understanding," "concerned with detail," and "non-threatening" to males. There was a split of opinion as to the female ability to deal with a largely female staff. "Not being one of the guys" was recognized by both men and women as an impediment to advancement by women. Nevertheless, a small proportion of both men and women pointed out that a strong manager, whether male or female, should have no problems (Hepperle, 1985).

In 1977, a similar survey was conducted by this author (Hepperle and Hendryx, 1978). In brief, it indicated that men in court administration had a higher educational level, higher job classifications, and higher salary levels than women; much the same story then as now. As for upward aspirations, again the same story. Then: "there was a slight tendency toward resistance (to placing women in top administrative positions) by male judges." Now: "the main consideration was one of stereotypes, particularly those held by [male] judges." In 1977, while both men and women agreed that the women's movement had helped women achieve top administrative positions, many stated they believed it had not affected them personally or professionally. A similar question was not posed in 1985, but the tone of the 1985 comments again reflected a belief in the puritan work ethic, plus a degree of cynicism, as expressed by women: the unspoken belief that women are "worth less"; that a woman must be "daring and knowledgeable enough to take anyone to the wall who tried to do you in"; that "women are not fully recognized for their capabilities in this [geographical] work area."

WOMEN: AVENUES UP

Beverly Cook, in another chapter, has listed three criteria required if there is to be an expansion in the number of women judges. Adapted and modified for the purposes of this chapter, these criteria now read:

(1) The eligibility factor; or how many qualified females are available for a court administrator's job?
(2) The attitude of the gatekeepers; or will (mostly male) judges seek or accept a woman court administrator?
(3) The situational opportunities; or what growth or changes in the organization will open positions to females?

Qualified candidates: If the "available" pool includes all who "might be qualified"—because they are now employed in court management or semimanagement positions—the number of available women will exceed the number of available men. But, more narrowly and more realistically, among the persons who possess the requisite educational and experience credentials, there is a sharp differential, with a significant proportion of more qualified available men than women.

Gatekeepers: In the typical situation, the person or committee charged with recruiting and appointing a court administrator is a "select" group composed of judges (usually male) with an occasional representative from a related court unit, such as probation, personnel, or perhaps the local bar association. The quest, typically, is for a highly qualified person who has excellent references.

Given this scenario, the last act is clear. First, there will be few applications from "highly" qualified females. Second, most of those will fail to clear the hurdle of "references," given that the selection committee network is largely in the male domain. At present, only 12% of the state judiciary and 17% of the federal judiciary is female (Fund for Modern Courts, 1985).

Opportunities: While the total area of judicial administration has widened in the last 10 to 20 years, much of it has been in adjunct fields such as research, service and educational organizations, diversion programs, probation, sentencing alternatives, and so on.

Within the courts, most support staffs have increased to cope with the burgeoning caseload, but the number of senior or top positions has remained approximately the same. Thus women here face the same obstacle as men; as the opportunities diminish, the probabilities of advancement are reduced.

Horizontal transfer, from a related court field, is also difficult: the opening of top positions in a local court system are not widely advertised, and the gatekeepers often prefer to choose from the local ranks.

In some instances the Chief Judge has authority to select and appoint a court administrator. In that situation the position of such a policy level appointee might be exempt from employment regulations under Title VII of the Civil Rights Act of 1964, as amended, and subsequent legislation. (See next section.) This has the effect of narrowing the search process and increasing the selection power of the appointing person.

IMPACT OF NATIONAL POLICIES:
EQUAL EMPLOYMENT OPPORTUNITY (EEO) AND
AFFIRMATIVUE ACTION (AA) MANDATES

Equal Employment Opportunity (EEO) has been described as

a principle of employment policy that establishes the right of all persons to obtain work and to advance solely on the basis of merit, ability and potential, without discrimination on the basis of race, sex, or other legally irrelevant criterion. In general, EEO is used to characterize the attitudes and actions of an organization's administrators and supervisors who are authorized to make employment decisions.

Affirmative Action (AA), on the other hand, denotes an affirmative duty to act remedially, to correct employment practices that have effectively limited the employment opportunities of certain identifiable groups in our society [Bremson et al., 1979].

During the 1960s, about the time *feminism* became a household word, a series of federal laws and regulations were adopted to implement the concept of opening and equalizing job opportunities to racial minorities and to women. Despite the fact that most, if not all, of these regulations apply to state courts, two important questions need answers: where and how have they been applied. These issues have been examined in detail by Francis Bremson, and others, under the auspices of the National Center for State Courts, in their article "Equal Opportunity in the State Courts." Suffice it to say that, overall, the record is dismal. The following highlights pinpoint the problems.

STATE COURTS

"State court systems lag far behind other public and private institutions in complying with equal employment opportunity guidelines." Noting that Title VII of the Civil Rights Act of 1964, as amended, covers all state courts employing 15 or more people, the National Center published these findings.

Of the 47 court systems studied, none could show that the percentage of women or minorities employed was equal to the percentage of such groups in the labor force. Only 32% of the states had a written EEO program. Only 18 had a formal EEO officer, and 14 of those devoted less than 20% of their time to EEO-related activities. Only 36% informed their nonjudicial support personnel of their constitutional rights under civil rights legislation, and 14% felt it was not a relevant issue. A total of 76% indicated that compliance data was either not maintained or unavailable. The courts were criticized for their "woefully inadequate personnel records," and "ineptness of many of their approaches to the EEO challenge."

The National Center's analysis pointed out that application of EEO is often tied to the court's funding status. Because most state courts rely on a combination of state and local financing, personnel systems tend to be extensions of those of the funding agencies. This occurs despite the fact that nonjudicial personnel may be administratively responsible to a chief judge or a court administrator. The key question is one of control: who is the employer—the court or the funding agency. Unless determination of this point is in favor of the courts, their ability to manage their own personnel systems and "themselves to effect major EEO policy changes, will likely be eroded further" (Bremson et al., 1979).

An additional major issue identified by the State Court Report was a lack of judicial commitment to EEO programs. Commenting on that point, a *National Law Journal* article said several observers attributed "this lack of commitment on EEO matters to what they termed inherent cronyism in court personnel appointments" and noted that "most courts lack even the fundamentals of a merit-based personnel system." The news item quoted a state court administrator as saying, "The judges want me to mind my own business with respect to whom they hire" (Burke, 1979).

In the years since these reports there has been little positive to surface concerning advancement of EEO in the state courts. One bright spot is the formation of special State Task Forces on Gender Bias in New Jersey, New York, Rhode Island, and California. The New Jersey Task

Force, in its recommendations, listed six points for judges to examine to ensure equality for men and women in the courts. Recommendation number 2 stated, "Examining your hiring and appointment process," and inquired how often judges "appointed women to positions of administrative or supervisory responsibility" (*New Jersey Law Journal,* 1983).

FEDERAL COURTS

In the Federal Court system, which employs over 14,000 persons, the history of court attempts to meet equal opportunity standards are more positive. Thus the Judicial Conference of the United States endorsed a national policy of a positive program for equal employment opportunity six years before Congress passed the Equal Opportunity Act of 1972.

In subsequent actions, the Conference adopted a Model Affirmative Action Plan and an evaluation process to be used by the Administrative Office of the U.S. Courts as the plans were adopted by the various Circuits and Districts. Since then, the model plan, or a modification, has been adopted by all the Circuit and District Courts and each court files an annual detailed report on its EEO and AA activities (Administrative Office of the U.S. Court, 1985).

On a broader perspective, there are recent signs that the Reagan administration is changing posture with respect to EEO policy by diminishing the role of quotas and goals, as established under the original 1965 Executive order (No. 11246). It required that government contractors establish affirmative action programs, and set hiring goals to implement programs funded by the federal government. It was in this era also that the Law Enforcement Assistance Act (LEAA) became a source of funding to assist the courts in moving toward twentieth-century management techniques. The contracts that provided these funds were entered under bid procedures with a requirement to provide detailed reports on completion. Of particular importance here is the fact that these contractors were also subject to the specific affirmative action mandates of the federal government. While it is not possible to identify the exact impact of Affirmative Action on court-related projects, it is fair to speculate that these principles were not disregarded, particularly in view of the pressures imposed in the private sector. Moreover, as recently as 1981, it looked as if this technique were an accepted viable approach toward achieving equal treatment. At that time, President Reagan issued Executive Order 12336, creating a Task Force on Legal Equity for Women to provide for the "systematic elimination of regulatory and procedural barriers which have unfairly precluded women from receiving equal treatment from Federal activities." While this action was directed primarily at the Executive agencies, it did purport to set the tone of the Reagan administration. In signing the order, President Reagan said, "We are here to reaffirm or affirm again that discrimination of any kind will not be tolerated in the Federal government." He added that the Attorney General was "systematically reviewing laws and regulations with an eye to identifying gender-based discrimination" (Administration of Ronald Reagan, 1981).

Recently, however, the Administration has signaled a change in its stance, at least with regard to the 1965 Executive Order. According to a press item, The Equal Employment Opportunity Commission

> without any vote or public announcement, has abandoned the use of hiring goals and timetables in settlements with private employers accused of race and sex discrimination. [*San Francisco Chronicle,* 1986a]

Further, whether EEO is or can be effective in any arena has recently been questioned, at least in terms of its current authority and the interpretations issued by the courts over its 20-year life (Modjeska, 1985; Jones, 1985).

However, on a more positive path, the Supreme Court upheld in 1987, by a 6-3 vote, a county affirmative action plan that permitted a woman to be promoted over a man who had scored 2 points higher (on a scale of 100) in an interview (*Johnson v. Transportation Agency*).

CONCLUSION

The problems of the woman who wants to be a court manager are substantially the same as those of the woman who seeks a managerial position in business or industry. So too is the current status: More women are entering male-dominated occupations but women are not reaching positions of authority (Brown, 1981).

This despite the fact that any possible hint that women have not achieved top positions because of their managerial capability or style has been completely laid to rest. An extensive study in 1980 compared nearly 2000 male and female managers and found no significant sex-based difference in managerial capabilities between them. This study covered a variety of organizations, including government, and carefully matched and measured five dimensions of managerial achievement.

Commenting on their findings that, in general, women do not differ from men in the management process, the authors cautioned against too much elation on this point, because "all is not necessarily well in today's male-oriented management activities." This view could be transferred to some courts, as well (Donnell and Hall, 1980).

Recent research demonstrates, on the other hand, that women's limited advancement is primarily an outgrowth of a sociological phenomena called "occupational sex-typing." This occurs where a large majority of those in a particular occupation are of one sex and where, concurrently, there is a normative expectation that this is as it should be (Brown, 1981). Court administration is a good example: It is largely occupied by men and carries with it an expectation that this is appropriate (Time, 1986).

Nevertheless, women have made some managerial gains, notably in large corporate structures. One explanation has been the ability of larger organizations to do more internal training of employees (Shaeffer and Avel, 1978). Another explanation rests on stringent enforcement of EEO law and AA programs with respect to larger corporations. In this regard, it has been noted that management's greatest concerns for failure to meet EEO standards are possible imposition of fines, loss of government contracts, and the prospect of adverse publicity. Whatever the motivation, an examination of corporations that have improved their hiring practices suggests it is the result of a clear commitment by top management, holding line managers accountable for attaining EEO goals, and an increase in the influence of the EEO staff (Barnhill-Hayes, 1979).

The courts apparently do not have either the "fears" or the "commitments" of the larger corporations. In the final analysis, the judicial system simply is not being held accountable for meeting either societal norms or legislative directives to achieve occupational equality.

Knowing that the chances of getting to the managerial top are, at present, realistically and statistically stacked against her, what does the ambitious, qualified women do to beat the odds? Most analysts agree: find a mentor—a person who is in a position to fight for a protégé, who helps bypass the hierarchy, and who provides reflected power (Kanter, 1983; Brown, 1981).

This doctrine has been expanded recently to encompass a broad, cross-generational, multilevel spectrum of persons who join in a patron system to assist the protégé. This technique has recently been successfully used by the California Association of Women Lawyers who seek out and back well-qualified female candidates for gubernatorial appointment to judgeships. In doing so, the network is expanded to gain support and reflected power from interested professional groups of women, lawyers, and others with influence. In any event, the value of mentors/patrons/networking is substantiated by U.S. Bureau of Labor Statistics that show 48% of all jobs come through personal contacts

Another avenue for women in court management is to undertake a self-help approach. They could join together, formally, or informally, perhaps by regional groups, to discuss mutual problems and develop ways to solve them. Women judges, for example, now have a national association that encourages networking and provides educational programs that focus both on substantive issues and on "getting ahead" activities.

Numerous programs are presented by the Institute for Court Management for court managers on a variety of topics. Would it be possible to provide a program designed to advance women in management? (Based on the number of women working in court systems, there should be a built-in student body.) A relatively new program conceived by a public utilities company is now in full swing to prepare women "for the real world of physical jobs." Classes are presented that discuss "the ins and outs of working with predominately male crews and by learning from women currently in physical jobs." One graduate said, "In the end, we were not only physically trained, but mentally prepared for our jobs" (*PG&E Progress*, 1986) Perhaps a similar question—are women "mentally" ready to be court managers in a male-dominated court system?—could be addressed by organizations such as the National Center for State Courts or the National Association of Court Managers, given that both are concerned with improving the totality of court administration.

Finally, the literature abounds with reports of women seeking, keeping, and using "power" (Larwood, 1977; Gornick and Moran, 1971; Kennedy, 1984; Trahey, 1978). The woman who is serious about moving to the top in court management could well spend some time researching how women in other management fields climb from the base to the peak of the pyramid.

REFERENCES

Administration of Ronald Reagan (1981) Week Ending Friday, December 25. (Filed with Office of the Federal Register)

Administrative Office of the United States Courts (1985) Annual Report of the Judiciary Equal Opportunity Program for the Twelve Month Period Ended June 30, 1985, Vol. 1.

Annual Report on the Judiciary Equal Opportunity Program for the Twelve Month period ended June 30, 1985, Vol. 1 and 2.

Arnold, Kenneth J. (1983) California Courts and Judges Handbook. San Francisco: Law Book Service.

Barnhill-Hayes (1979) Employer Attitudes Toward Affirmative Action. Milwaukee.

Bremson, Francis L., Mary W. Culhane, John Mayson, and August Milton, Jr. (1979) "Equal employment opportunity in the courts." State Court Journal (Summer): 11-40.

Brown, Linda Keller (1981) The Woman Manager in the United States. Washington, DC: Business and Professional Women's Foundation.

Burke, Edward J. (1979) "Study finds state courts are failing on hiring women and minorities." National Law Journal (May 21).

The Court Administrator (n.d.) National Association of Court Managers.

Donnell, S. M. and J. Hall (1980) "Men and women managers: a significant case of no significant difference." Organizational Dynamics (Spring): 60-77.

Fund for Modern Courts (1985) Success of Women and Minorities in Achieving Judicial Selection: The Selection Process. New York: Author.

Glamour (1986) "1986 women's views study: how far have women gone in the 1980's." (January): 164.

Gornick, Vivian and Barbara K. Moran [eds.] (1971) Woman in Sexist Society, Studies in Power and Powerlessness. New York: Basic Books.

Hepperle, W. L. (1985) Court Administration Survey. (unpublished)

Hepperle, Winifred L. and Janice L. Hendryx (1978) "Women in court administration," in Women in the Courts. Williamsburg, VA: National Center for State Courts.

Jones, James E., Jr. (1985) "Some reflections on Title VII of the Civil Rights Act of 1964 at twenty." Mercer Law Review 36: 813.

Johnson v. Transportation Agency, U.S. Supreme Court, April 1987.

Kanter, Rosabeth Moss (1983) The Change Masters: Innovations for Productivity in the American Corporation. New York: Simon & Schuster.

Kennedy, Marilyn Meats (1984) Powerbase: How to Build It/ How to Keep It. New York: Macmillan.

Kleinman, J. (1979) "Women executives: view from the top." New York Times (March 11): 50.

Larwood, Laurie (1977) Women in Management. Lexington, MA: D. C. Heath.

Mays and Taggart (1985) "Local court administration: findings from a survey of appointed managers." Judicature 69, 1.

Modjeska, Lee (1985) "The Supreme Court and the ideal of equal employment opportunity." Mercer Law Review 36: 795.

New Jersey Law Journal (1983) "Women in the courts, New Jersey Supreme Court Task Force on Women in the Courts—summary report." December 8: 1.

PG&E Progress [California] (1986) (February): 7-8.

San Francisco Chronicle (1986a) "U.S. Equal Employment panel drops race and sex quotas." February 11.

San Francisco Chronicle (1986b) "It's still a man's world" [reporting a California poll conducted by Marvin Field]. February 13: 1.

190WOMEN AS JUDGES, LAWYERS, JURORS

San Francisco Recorder (1986) "Status of minorities voted top priority by ABA delegates." February 13: 1.

Shaeffer, R. G. and H. Avel (1978) Improving Job Opportunities: A Chartbook Focusing on the Progress in Business. New York: Conference Board.

Time (1986) [Review of] Hewlett, Sylvia Ann, A Lesser Life: The Myth of Women's Liberation in America, Morrow. March 31: 6.

Trahey, Jane (1978) Women/Power. New York: Avon.

United States Department of Commerce (1984) Washington, DC: News Bureau of the Census.

United States Department of Labor (July 1985) Women's Bureau Fact Sheet No. 85-7.

8

PRACTICING LAW IN A SEXIST SOCIETY

Lynn Hecht Schafran

To be a woman trial lawyer in the mid-1980s is to be in the midst of a positive transition. Although all is not as it should be for women in our courts, women have made significant advances. The gender bias they still confront has become the focus of serious attention and corrective measures are being taken.

Not every woman litigator has or will encounter the problems recounted in this chapter. But information gathered across the country by bar associations and task forces on gender bias in the courts makes clear that women do not yet find it as easy to become trial attorneys as do their male counterparts and, once in court, are not yet consistently treated with the same dignity and respect or appointed to the same quality of fee generating positions.

These differences in treatment matter. They go far beyond personal irritation and insult to issues of equal opportunity, professional credibility, and whether one's clients receive the full due process of law. Lawyering in a sexist society demands of women not only conventional litigation skills, but an understanding of how gender-biased social standards translate into legal inequities in the courtroom, of strategies for countering these biases, and of participation in the effort to make judges, lawyers, and court personnel aware of these biases and their consequences and eliminate them.

ACCEPTANCE INTO THE PROFESSION

The influx of women into the legal profession is a recent phenomenon. Women law students were few until the combination of classes that had to be filled during the Vietnam war and Title IX of the Education Amendments of 1572 barring sex discrimination in schools receiving federal funds produced a sharp increase in women's enrollment. Between 1970 and 1986, the number and percentage of women law students rose from 7,031 (9%) to 47,920 (40%) (American Bar Association, 1985) and the number and percentage of women lawyers rose from 11,000 (4%) to 106,000 (17%) (Bureau of Labor Statistics, 1986: 29, table 22). The numbers, however, do not tell us about women lawyers' acceptance into the profession.

Since the United States Supreme Court denied a woman a license to practice law on the ground that God and nature intended her for the "domestic sphere" rather than "the occupations of civil life,"[1] 113 years have passed, but the attitudes that shaped that decision are not yet history. The tenacious power of the stereotype of woman as primarily wife and mother was attested to in a recent speech by Judge Dolores K. Sloviter of the United States Circuit Court of Appeals for the Third Circuit. In 1979, the American Bar Association representative evaluating her for this judgeship asked how she would care for her husband and child because, she was told, "that was expected to be a woman's role" and that "every lawyer and every judge believed women were less productive in the law than men." In Judge Sloviter's words (1984: 19-20), "Until we are willing to take firm steps to excise and exorcise those demons, women as a group will not be able to proceed to their rightfully equal place in the legal profession."

The persistence of the beliefs described by Judge Sloviter was evident in the responses to the 1983 New Jersey Supreme Court Task Force on Women in the Courts' attorneys survey. Women's reports of judges' discriminatory questions about family responsibilities were echoed by a man who wrote that he was not "attuned" to gender bias until his wife graduated from law school in 1982, sought a clerkship, and was asked by two appellate judges: "(1) Did she have my permission to do this job? (2) Would she be able to handle the job while being a wife and stepmother? (3) Did she plan to have children?"

At the January 1986 Florida Judicial Nominating Commission Institute, an industrial psychologist whose firm interviews thousands of people each year instructed the commissions to ask about judicial applicants' managerial abilities and stated, "And if it's a female—I don't want to be sexist—but if it's a female—to what extent can she balance the demands of home, child, shopping."[3]

A consequence of society's identification of women with the "domestic sphere" is that the one area of law in which women are expected to practice is family law, dealing with matrimonial issues and juveniles. An American Bar Association study revealed that in 1983, 13% of women attorneys specialized in family law compared to 5% of men (Winter, 1983: 1386).

GETTING INTO COURT

In her comprehensive study, *Women in the Law*, Cynthia Epstein (1981) chronicled the difficulty women have had in getting out of the law firm library and into court. This problem, too, is not yet a thing of the past. A 1981 study recorded the number of women attorneys appearing before a particular San Francisco federal judge over a four-month period. Women made 12.7% of the total of 401 appearances recorded, but when government attorneys were excluded, women attorneys' appearances dropped to 9.6%. Women attorneys were present in 13.1% of civil matters and 10.8% of criminal cases. These figures dropped to 10.8% in civil matters and 0% for criminal matters (no women were criminal defense attorneys) when government attorneys were excluded. The author observed that although women were only 7.5% of the legal profession in 1981, the fact that they were 15%-20% of the associates at large law firms, the firms that represent the largest number of federal court litigants, suggested that women should have been appearing in federal court in greater numbers (Bryant, 1983).

Although women are often legal aid criminal defense attorneys, the complete absence of women criminal defense attorneys in this federal court study is not surprising. Criminal defense attorneys in these courts are usually former U.S. attorneys and assistant district attorneys, positions that, until recently, were closed to women. In a 1983 speech, Judge Patricia Wald of the United States Circuit Court of Appeals for the District of Columbia described the continuing difficulties women lawyers face in rising in the criminal justice system. "Traditionally the criminal courtroom has been the macho arena of the law. Anecdotes abound: one of my women prosecutor friends was told on applying for criminal trial work by an old U.S. Attorney 'pro'—'When you're fighting a war against crime, you don't send a girl into the front lines' " (Wald, 1983: 2). A respondent to the 1985 New York Task Force on

Women in the Courts' attorneys survey who is now an Assistant District Attorney in an upstate county echoed the comments of many participants in the task force's regional meetings when she described the "extreme" difficulty women had in obtaining such positions until the last three or four years. She reported having learned from the men in her office of decisions made "not to hire women because of a belief that they 'would not get along with the cops' or they would spoil the 'camaraderie' of the all male office" and noted the effect this had on women's future careers. "I have *never* seen or heard of a woman defense attorney trying a felony case" (New York Task Force, 1986: 240).

A positive note at the New York Task Force's public hearings, which demonstrated the difference that a woman at the top who is committed to bringing other women along can make, was the testimony of Brooklyn District Attorney Elizabeth Holtzman, one of the few women DAs in the country. She reported that when she took office in 1982, no women held executive positions in the Brooklyn DA's office. By November 1984, five of eleven bureau chiefs and six of eighteen deputy chiefs were women (New York Task Force, 1986: 216).

On the civil side, the earlier cited American Bar Association study revealed that in 1983, 65% of male attorneys had no female colleagues at work (Winter, 1983: 1384).[4] Also in 1983, the Association of Trial Lawyers of America membership was only 6% female and the American College of Trial Lawyers, an invitational organization, had four women members making up one-tenth of 1% of the group. When New Jersey attorney Blanche Vilade was concluding her clerkship with the Chair of the New Jersey Supreme Court Task Force on Women in the Courts, Judge Marilyn Loftus, in 1984, she found in her interviews with law firms that not only was she asked about family responsibilities but that when she asked how quickly she would be allowed to do trial work she was sometimes told that the firm had no women in its litigation department. Judge Loftus reports that one consequence of the Task Force's work that brought to public attention pervasive gender bias against women lawyers and litigants in the New Jersey courts is that New Jersey law firms have begun sending women associates into her court to try cases, not just seek adjournments and make motions.

WOMEN LAWYERS IN COURT

Because of women's long exclusion from the legal profession and litigation in particular, the vast majority of today's lawyers and judges are men (white) who went through law school, years of practice, and years on the bench with no women peers. Their culturally ingrained expectation is that lawyer-equals-male. When they find themselves in a situation where lawyer-equals-female, some react with conscious or unconscious unease and even hostility.

The stories of overt hostility on the part of judges are legion and come from every state. The examples cited by Brooklyn District Attorney Elizabeth Holtzman in her testimony before the New York Task Force on Women in the Courts give the flavor.

- On a very hot summer day after a male defense counsel was given permission to remove his jacket, an assistant district attorney in my office asked the male judge in open court if she too could remove her jacket. The judge replied "Don't remove your jacket unless you intend to remove all of your clothes."

- During a plea conference another male judge told a buxom Brooklyn prosecutor "My clerk and I have a bet on whether you have to wear weights on your ankles to keep you from tipping over."

- A woman prosecutor in my office who disagreed strongly with a male judge over a legal point was told "I will put you over my knee and spank you" (New York Task Force, 1986: 216).

Less shocking than sexist gibes but no less discriminatory are the many other ways women attorneys are overtly denigrated in courtrooms and chambers. One of the most common complaints of women attorneys of all ages is being asked if they are attorneys when men are not asked, the implicit assumption being, again, that lawyer-equals-male.[5] Obviously it is offensive to an attorney to be presumed to be a litigant or support staff and told not to sit in a courtroom area reserved for counsel, not to approach the bench, or not to enter the judge's chambers for a conference. But this insult is particularly disturbing when it occurs in front of a client. The attorney's status as a professional is undermined and clients wonder whether they will be well represented and get a fair hearing.

Comments on clothing and appearance that are perhaps intended as compliments, but do not belong in the formal courtroom setting, are commonplace. A federal district court judge once asked Nebraska litigator Lindsey Lerman to stand for the sole purpose of complimenting her on her suit. How does a lawyer establish her credibility when she has just been defined by the judge as a fashion plate?

Demeaning forms of address is another frequently cited problem. The judge addresses and refers to male attorneys as Counselor or Mr. X.

Female attorneys are "honey," "young lady," 'girls," or "Susie." Clients notice these differences in address and they are highly revealing of judges' respect, or lack of it, for counsel. Florida attorney Elizabeth du Fresne, describing her beginnings as a public defender, says that when she was "honey" to the judge while her opponent was "Mr.," she knew that her client, who was already worried about having a woman lawyer, was sure he was not going to get justice in that courtroom.

A woman now a California Municipal Court Judge once became so irate with a judge who repeatedly addressed her adversary as "Mr." while addressing her as "young lady" that she responded to a question from the judge with "I will stipulate to that, old man." The judge was speechless for a moment, then said, "Do you know I could hold you in contempt for that?" The lawyer replied, "Your honor, I'm not the one who raised the issues of age and sex, you did." This is an anecdote to dine out on, but few of us could think of this perfect rejoinder on the spot, and few of us would have the courage, or perhaps the foolhardiness, to say it aloud if we did. Indeed, the woman in this incident says of herself, "I won my point but I lost my case."

One of the most difficult aspects of the discriminatory behavior women litigators encounter is that whatever her personal irritation, humiliation, or anger, the attorney cannot respond for herself. She must weigh her response in terms of whether it will prejudice her client.

As damaging as overt expressions of gender bias are, the unconscious, nonverbal expressions of this bias are even more insidious. Some judges who are not comfortable with women attorneys sit straight and pay attention when men counsel speak but slump, shuffle papers, and look at the clock when it's the women's turn, having nothing to do with the merits of her presentation or her style. Others delay responding only to women, a sign of inattentiveness, or talk to male attorneys in a straightforward voice but use a consistently long-suffering or angry tone with a female attorney, no matter what she is saying, implying that only a fool would raise that objection or make that argument.

Body language and tone of voice that reveal discomfort, disinterest, or hostility to a woman lawyer speak volumes to juries and clients. Communications researchers report that nonverbal messages carry four times the weight of verbal messages (Sadker et al., 1983). A judge does not need to say aloud "Women lawyers make me so tired," as once happened to an Oregon public defender, to communicate that message. Certainly women lawyers rise above such comments and behavior and are highly successful, but why should women have to jump an extra hurdle that men do not face in order to be seen as competent, credible professionals?

At a 1985 Missouri Bar/Judicial Conference program, "Sex in the Courtroom: Does It Make A Difference?," a male judge observed that men lawyers are assumed to be capable until they prove otherwise but women lawyers must prove themselves from the beginning. There is extensive social science research revealing that women as a group are viewed by society as less credible than men.

In the late 1970s, Professor Norma Wikler examined 16,000 teacher evaluation forms filed by students at the University of California, who, after each course, evaluate their instructors on a list of 20 attributes. Both men and women students said that their women teachers were superior in the sense of being better prepared, having mastery of the material, and being more responsive to students. But they gave significantly more weight to the views of their male professors, evaluating them as more credible, more believable, more authoritative, and more persuasive than their female professors. Moreover, male students were much more dramatically prejudiced in *favor* of the male teachers than the women students (Schafran, 1985: 16). A 1984 study at Lafayette College in Pennsylvania yielded similar results (Basow and Silberberg, 1985).

In 1985, a Kent State University professor replicated and extended a 1968 experiment in which 150 male and 150 female subjects were randomly assigned to read an essay with the author's name indicated as either John T. McKay, J.T. McKay, or Joan T. McKay, and asked to rate it on such qualities as persuasiveness, intellectual depth, and author's competence. Although the essays were identical, those believed to have been written by "Joan" consistently received lower ratings from male and female readers than those believed to have been written by "John" or "J. T." (Paludi and Strayer, 1985).

Another study found that in managerial jobs or jobs thought to require male characteristics, good looks are an advantage for men and a disadvantage for women. Attractive men were perceived as having gained success on the basis of their hard work and ability. Attractive women were presumed to have succeeded for reasons other than their skill and/or talent, and to be less capable and credible and have less integrity (Heilman and Stopeck, 1985).

Given women's less credible status, even apparently trivial matters such as inappropriate forms of address and remarks on appearance can have serious consequences in court. As New York State Justice Felice

Shea wrote of a judge publicly admonished by the New York State Commission on Judicial Conduct in 1985 for years of calling women attorneys names such as "kitten," "bitch," and "my favorite JAP," and commenting on their physical attributes and clothing during case conferences, "Respondent's sexist and vulgar comments give the message that women attorneys need not be treated professionally, and the ability of those attorneys to serve their clients is compromised."[6]

MALE ATTORNEYS' BEHAVIOR

Women and men judges and attorneys responding to the New Jersey, New York, and Rhode Island attorneys surveys described in this chapter have consistently reported that male counsel display significantly more discriminatory behavior toward female counsel than do judges and court personnel. A recent National Association of Women Judges' newsletter offered this view from the bench.

OYEZ! OYEZ!

In my courtroom, where it is presumably known that I am somewhat of a "feminist," I have heard and seen the following behavior on the part of male lawyers towards women lawyers, court personnel and witnesses (and sometimes towards the judges):

(1) Calling the judge, women lawyers, court personnel and witnesses "honey", "dear", "sweetie", "darling", "young lady", etc.
(2) Calling women by their first names even if they do not know them.
(3) Making their arguments for them.
(4) Constantly interrupting them.
(5) Calling women 18 and over "girls".
(6) Calling women "Maam" *instead* of judge, Miss, Mrs. or Ms.
(7) Making comments such as "I'm only treating you like my kids" or "You remind me of my wife". (What does this mean—a free hit?)
(8) When the woman attorney is present, coming into the courtroom and asking "Where's the attorney for the other side?"
(9) Getting angrier and angrier in court as it becomes more and more apparent that the woman is very smart or just smart.
(10) Comments on women attorneys' looks and clothes at inappropriate times (e.g., in the middle of a legal argument.)
(11) Anti-women jokes (if you substitute the words "black", "Hispanic" or "Jew" for the woman in these jokes you can determine immediately the discriminatory, if not obscene, character of these jokes).

(12) Patronizing the "little woman".
(13) Propositioning them.
(14) Physically touching them without an invitation of any kind.

Surely, we have an obligation to point out and correct such behavior in our courtrooms. It is very difficult for women lawyers, court personnel and witnesses to do so on their own [Taylor, 1984: 6-7].

Illinois Deputy Attorney General Jill Wine-Banks labels as "sexual trial tactics" these deliberate efforts to undermine women litigators. In 1974, when a woman litigator was a rarity, Wine-Banks was a member of the Watergate prosecution team. In 1976, she wrote an article describing the sexual trial tactics used against her during the Watergate and other trials, and how she decided whether it was to her advantage to object, retaliate, or keep silent. Wine-Bank's 1983 assessment that sexual trial tactics were still flourishing (Schafran, 1983: 38) was born out again at a 1985 "Sex Bias in the Courtroom" program at the Florida Bar Association annual meeting, where a prominent male defense attorney described deliberately using such a tactic against a female adversary in a recent case. The prosecutor was destroying his client on cross-examination and the defense attorney was desperate to stop her. He made a frivolous objection and when the judge overruled it, asked to approach the bench. On the way to the bench, he brushed against the prosecutor, saying, "Okay baby, let's see what you can show the judge." The objection was again overruled, but the prosecutor was rattled and lost the rhythm of her cross-examination. The lawyer stated that it would never occur to him to use a racist remark to distract a minority adversary, but that he had not understood until that panel discussion that what he did to the woman prosecutor was equally reprehensible.

THE PREVALENCE OF
DISCRIMINATORY BEHAVIOR AND
ITS EFFECT ON CASE OUTCOME

A standard response to women lawyers' charges of discriminatory behavior is that it is aberrational, that few judges or lawyers act this way. Regrettably, studies show the incidence of this behavior to be significant.

The New Jersey Supreme Court Task Force on Women in the Courts conducted a statewide attorneys survey in 1983 to which almost 900 women and men attorneys responded. In all, 61% of the women and 25% of the men reported instances in which judges addressed women attorneys by first names or "terms of endearment" (dear, sweetheart, honey) while using men attorneys' surnames or titles. A total of 54% of the women and 28% of the men were aware of judges making comments about women attorneys' personal appearance and dress. Finally, 69% of the women and 40% of the men reported hearing sexist remarks and jokes from judges in courtrooms, in chambers, and at professional gatherings (New Jersey Supreme Court Task Force, 1984: 13-16).

Narrative responses to the survey gave the specifics of offensive incidents in which women attorneys were derided, belittled, and demeaned. One woman wrote about an incident at a crowded calendar call and asked why the judge felt free to say things about women he would not say about other groups in our society.

> In response to a statement by a female attorney that she had "problems" with her case and wanted to be heard at the second call, [the judge] made a pronouncement that "women are the problem." This comment, again, was received by the audience with a great deal of amusement, laughter, clapping, etc.

> What would have happened had this same judge said that Blacks, Jews, Catholics, Orientals or Hispanics were the "problem?" Would that comment have been met with uproarious laughter? Certainly not, but women are still considered a joke [New Jersey Supreme Court Task Force, 1984: 16].

With respect to men attorneys' behavior, 85% of women survey respondents and 45% of men respondents had heard men attorneys use inappropriate forms of address toward women attorneys; 68% of women and 45% of men had heard them make comments about women attorneys' dress or physical attributes; and 86% of women and 68% of men reported male attorneys making hostile remarks and sexist jokes, with a third of the women reporting the incidence of this behavior as "often." The New Jersey study (1984: 13-16) found that court personnel also engage in these same behaviors, to a lesser extent.

Also in 1983, the Committee on Sex Discrimination of the Rhode Island Bar Association surveyed 144 male and female lawyers about discrimination against women attorneys. After describing its findings of "significant" discrimination in employment situations, the Committee wrote:

Of greater concern, however, was the number of reported instances of sex discrimination in the litigative environment. A large number of female respondents (45 percent), and a smaller but significant number of male respondents (17 percent), reported significant instances of sex discrimination on the part of judges, court personnel and opposing counsel, some of it in open court. The instances included unwanted attention, demeaning comments of a sexual nature, studiously ignoring a female attorney, and refusing to negotiate because the opposing counsel was female [Rhode Island Bar Association, 1983: 2].

The New York Task Force on Women in the Courts' 1985 attorneys survey also found substantial discriminatory behavior toward women attorneys on the part of judges, lawyers, and court personnel. For example, with respect to addressing women attorneys by first names or terms of endearment, 49% of the 634 women responding reported this behavior to be engaged in "sometimes" or "often" by judges, 58% reported it "sometimes" or "often" on the part of court personnel, and 74% said "sometimes" or "often" about men attorneys (New York Task Force, 1986: 217). When asked whether judges, counsel, and court employees make sexist remarks or jokes in court or in chambers that demean women, 50% of women said "sometimes" or "often" about judges, 42% said "sometimes" or "often" about court employees, and 67% said "sometimes" or "often" about male attorneys (p. 193).

Does gender-biased behavior toward women attorneys affect case outcome? The Rhode Island report (1983: 2) said of the incidents it described, "In a significant number of these instances the respondent believed that the discriminatory conduct had a prejudicial effect on the interests of the female attorney's client." When this question was asked in the New Jersey attorneys survey (1984: 16-17), 16% of the women and 3% of the men responding said that it does. Narrative comments reflected many attorneys' belief that even if the ultimate outcome of a case is not affected, the overall litigation process is prejudiced. One woman wrote, "I can't say that a case was ever won or lost because of [this] conduct, but I was so frequently embarrassed that I lost my composure." A New York survey (1986: 208) respondent commented similarly.

> It is very difficult to trace the consequences of being addressed as "dearie" or by other inappropriate terms directly to the outcome of the case. It appears obvious that whatever the outcome of the case, such trivializing discriminatory remarks pose an additional burden upon a woman attorney, requiring her to overcome needless obstacles and irritants not encountered by men.

WOMEN ATTORNEYS'
LITIGATION STYLES

A significant problem for women trial lawyers is finding a litigating style that is both comfortable and effective for the attorney *and* acceptable to her audience. Sociologists call this the professional woman's double bind. The woman who acts in a stereotypically "feminine" manner—soft-spoken, passive, compassionate—is dismissed as lacking the equipment to do the job. The woman who is forceful, aggressive, and cross-examines like a tiger is put down as a bitch. Behavior that is expected and lauded in a male trial attorney is denigrated in a woman. New Haven trial lawyer Janet Arterton was dubbed a "schoolmarm" at a trial lawyers' seminar because of her stern, authoritarian courtroom manner. She explained that she had thought it necessary to suppress smiles and compassion in order "to avoid the emotional woman stereotype" (Sorenson, 1983: 1416). A perceptive male respondent to the New Jersey attorneys survey (1984: 19) wrote:

> A woman attorney must walk the fine line between being feminine and being assertive. She is held to a different standard than a man. If she is too feminine she is accused of trying to use it to her advantage and is therefore resented, but if she is equally assertive to her male counterpart, she is accused of being too aggressive. To their credit, most of the women attorneys with whom I have had dealings have been able to walk that fine line, but it is usually with much more pressure than is experienced by a man.

FEE GENERATING APPOINTMENTS

An issue raised by women criminal and civil litigators across the country is lack of access to desirable fee generating appointments. In a recent panel discussion on women in the courts for the Michigan Bar Journal, Detroit attorney Carol Chiamps observed that in the 1970s, women received the paternity and misdemeanor appointments while men got the receiverships and felonies, and that not all that much had changed. In 1984, "few women regularly (or even not-so-regularly) receive appointments such as receiverships or condemnation cases which normally pay very well." She stated that there are a number of Detroit women attorneys with the requisite experience and theorized that the judges do not appoint women because they "subconsciously believe that women do not understand business and cannot control male subordinates" (*Michigan Bar Journal*, 1984: 462).

At the New York Task Force on Women in the Courts' public hearings (1986: 23), Irene Sullivan, President of the Women's Bar Association of the State of New York, testified:

> An almost overwhelming impression exists that women attorneys are not favored with the same number or the same quality of assignments as their male counterparts. In some locations women attorneys have been regularly assigned to women clients and male attorneys to male clients. This impression extends to appointments to receiverships and foreclosures, as guardian *ad litem* and as assigned counsel in criminal cases. The perception is that the most complex, interesting and lucrative cases are assigned to male attorneys and the leftover cases go to the women. This is not simply a bread-and-butter issue. For many women these cases provide the only means available to develop the skills and experience necessary to advance in the profession.

The investigation of the Rhode Island Supreme Court Committee on the Treatment of Women in the Courts into court appointments for fiscal 1984 revealed that of the 209 attorneys who submitted vouchers for defense of indigents, 88% were men and 12% were women. Because women were approximately 14% of the Rhode Island Bar, these figures suggested that they were not underrepresented in appointments, but breaking the data down by court revealed a different picture. In Family Court, women were 15% of guardians *ad litem* and 12% of attorneys submitting vouchers for other types of appointments. But women were only 7% of those submitting vouchers in District Court, 2% of those submitting vouchers in Superior Court, and 0% of those submitting vouchers in Supreme Court (Findley, 1985: 14-15).

It appears that with respect to fee generating appointments as in other areas of the law, the attitude toward women is still: keep them in the "domestic sphere."

HOW WOMEN LITIGATORS ARE
COUNTERING GENDER BIAS

Women litigators individually, in their organizations, and working with women judges and concerned men are using a number of strategies to counter the gender bias they encounter in the courts. Some women talk directly to the offending judge after trial to explain the meaning and consequences of the behavior. Florida attorney Elizabeth du Fresne says that her heart used to be in her mouth when she went into chambers to ask a judge to stop calling her "honey," but she knew that if she did not do it, nothing would ever change. Audrey Holzer Rubin of Chicago and Nancy Stearns of New York have used the tactic of sending a posttrial letter to a judge explaining why it mattered that he repeatedly referred to them as "girl."

At least one woman has gone directly to a judicial conduct commission. During a 1981, argument a Brooklyn judge asked attorney Martha Copelman several personal questions including how long she had been practicing, called her "little girl," and apologized when she objected and asked to be addressed as counselor. Then, to quote the New York State Commission on Judicial Conduct decision, "As the argument on the requested adjournment was concluded respondent told Ms. Copelman: 'I will tell you what, little girl, you lose.' Respondent's voice was raised and he conveyed the impression of insulting and demeaning Ms. Copelman" (*New York Law Journal*, 1983). In 1983, the Commission publicly censured the judge, the strongest sanction short of removal.

This judge gave as his defense that calling the lawyer "little girl" was analogous to calling her "sweetheart" or "darling." Similarly, the judge cited earlier who was admonished by the Commission for calling women attorneys names such as "kitten" and commenting on their bodies and clothes explained that he was merely trying to inject camaraderie into case conferences and thought of his remarks as "affable pleasantries and compliments." These judges' defenses illustrate how little understood is the impact of these belittling and inappropriate forms of address and comments.

Dealing with judges on gender-bias issues as an individual, and particularly bringing a formal complaint, is difficult. This is especially so in a small community where one regularly appears before the same judges and cannot risk angering them. Thus women's bar associations in many states, working with the National Judicial Education Program to Promote Equality for Women and Men in the Courts, have presented programs on sexism in the courts for themselves and their state bar associations at which the bias encountered by women litigators and strategies for dealing with it are discussed.

Women lawyers are also joining with women judges in asking their chief justices to follow the example of New Jersey, New York, and Rhode Island and create task forces to investigate gender bias in their individual court systems. These task forces address not only how women lawyers are treated in the courts, but the treatment of women litigants and witnesses and gender bias in the application of substantive law (Schafran, 1987).

CONCLUSION

Some women lawyers are reluctant or unwilling to talk about the gender bias they encounter in the courts, or say they simply see no problem. Although there may indeed be some who have never encountered bias, for most women these reactions stem from fear that publicizing the problem will discourage clients, from an inability to admit the reality even to themselves because they have spent so many years trying to be one of the boys, and from having become so inured to gender bias that they must be reminded that there is a name for what they have been coping with and ignoring. Moreover, women are acutely aware that while a man who objects to the way he is treated is seen as standing up for himself, a woman who objects is often stereotyped as whining or worse. But women lawyers must come forward because the issue is not simply whether they are personally insulted, but whether their clients are receiving the full due process of the law.

Requests to investigate gender bias in the courts often elicit the response that if we just let time pass, retirement and death will take care of the problem; older male judges and lawyers cannot be expected to change. There are two fallacies in this response. First, time is not the panacea for this problem. Gender bias is so deeply rooted in every generation that it cannot be eradicated without discussion and education. Second, the idea that older judges and lawyers cannot change ignores the way law is practiced. When the new Bankruptcy Code took effect in 1978, there was no exception to allow those who practiced under the old code for at least 20 years to continue using it. And woe betide lawyers who do not keep up with the latest decisions in their specialties, because the law is changing even as you read this. The law demands adaptability to change from all its practitioners. There is no reason that it should stop at eliminating gender bias against women lawyers and litigants in our courts.

NOTES

1. "Man is, or should be, woman's protector and defender. The natural and proper timidity and delicacy which belongs to the female sex evidently unfits it for many of the

occupations of civil life. The constitution of the family organization, which is found in the divine ordinance, as well as in the nature of things, indicates the domestic sphere as that which properly belongs to the domain and function of women. . . . The paramount destiny and mission of women are to fulfill the noble and benign offices of wife and mother. This is the law of the Creator" (*Bradwell v. Illinois*, 86 U.S. [16 Wall.] 130 [1873], Justice Bradley concurring).

2. At the 1984 New Jersey Judicial College, the Task Force presented a course that included a segment on how to conduct a nondiscriminatory judicial clerkship interview (New Jersey Supreme Court Task Force, 1984).

3. This incident and all incidents and oral statements recounted in this chapter and not otherwise cited took place or were made in the author's presence and are taken from her notes.

4. In 1986, ABA President William Palsgraf stated, "Our law firms, corporations and indeed bar associations have miles to go before they sleep comfortable in the knowledge that the profession has finally achieved true equality of opportunity for women" (Palsgraf, 1986: 11-12).

5. The New York Task Force on Women in the Courts' attorneys survey asked if women are asked whether they are attorneys when men are not asked. Among 634 women responding to this question, two-thirds of those under 35, one-half of those 36-50, and one-third of those over 51 reported it happening "sometimes" or "often" (New York Task Force 1986: 220).

6. Justice Shea had sought the more serious sanction of censure (*New York Law Journal*, 1985: 1).

7. For information about establishing and operating a task force see Lynn Hecht Schafran and Norma Wikler, *Operating a Gender Bias Task Force: A Manual for Action*, obtainable from the Women Judges' Fund for Justice, 1225 Fifteenth Street, N. W., Washington, D.C. 20005; (202) 462-4243.

REFERENCES

American Bar Association, Section of Legal Education and Admissions to the Bar (1987) The Review of Legal Education in United States, Fall of 1986.

Basow, Susan A. and Nancy T. Silberberg (1985) "Student evaluations of college professors: are males prejudiced against women professors?" Presented at the Eastern Psychological Association, Boston, March.

Bureau of Labor Statistics (1987) Employment and Earnings. Washington, DC: Government Printing Office.

Bryant, Barbara (1983) "Sex and race in federal court: a courtroom survey." Golden Gate University Law Review 13: 717-730.

Epstein, Cynthia (1981) Women in the Law. New York: Basic Books.

Findley, Sally (1985) Final Report on the Objective Evidence of Gender Bias in the Courts (Prepared for the Rhode Island Supreme Court Committee on the Treatment of Women in the Courts, Providence).

Heilman, Madeline and Melanie Stopeck (1985) "Attractiveness and corporate success: different causal attributions for males and female." Journal of Applied Psychology 70: 379-388.

Michigan Bar Journal (1984) "Michigan women in the law since 1871." Michigan Bar Journal 6: 477-506.

New Jersey Supreme Court Task Force on Women in the Courts (1984) Report of the First Year. Trenton: Administrative Office of the Courts. Published in Women's Rights Law Reporter (1986) 9: 129.

New York Law Journal (1983) "In the Matter of Jordan." March 2.

New York Law Journal (1985) "In the Matter of Warren M. Doolittle." July 24.

New York Task Force on Women in the Courts (1986) Report of the New York Task Force on Women in the Courts. New York: Unified Court System. Published in Fordham Urban Law Journal (1987) 15: 1.

Palsgraf, William (1986) Speech to the National Cathedral School, Washington, D.C., January 27.

Paludi, Michelle and Lisa Strayer (1985) "What's in an author's name? Differential evaluations of performance as a function of author's name." Sex Roles 12: 353-361.

Rhode Island Bar Association Committee on Sex Discrimination (1983) Report of the Committee on Sex Discrimination to the Executive Committee.

Sadker, Myra, David Sadker, and Joyce Kaser (1983) The Communications Gender Gap. Washington, DC: Mid-Atlantic Center for Sex Equity, American University, School of Education.

Schafran, Lynn Hecht (1983) "Women as litigators: abilities vs. assumptions." Trial 19: 36-45, 100-101.

Schafran, Lynn Hecht (1985) "Eve, Mary Superwoman: how stereotypes about women influence judges." Judges' Journal 24: 12-17, 48-53.

Schafran, Lynn Hecht (1987) "Documenting gender bias in the courts: the task force approach." Judicature 70: 280-290.

Sloviter, Dolores (1984) "Women in the law." Speech to the National Association for Law Placement, Inc., Minneapolis, April 30.

Sorenson, Laurel (1983) "A woman's unwritten code for success." American Bar Association Journal 69: 1414-1419.

Taylor, Margaret (1984) District 2 Report. New York: National Association of Women Judges.

Wald, Patricia (1983) "Women in criminal justice." Speech to the American Bar Association Criminal Justice Panel, Atlanta, August 2.

Wine-Banks, Jill (1976) "How one woman tamed the Watergate tigers." Redbook (April): 86.

Winter, Bill (1983) "Survey: women lawyers work harder, are paid less, but they're happy." American Bar Association Journal 69: 1384-1388.

9

WOMEN JURORS:
SEXISM IN JURY SELECTION

Anne Rankin Mahoney

Though a woman, she is a citizen and a juror.
(Belli, *Modern Trials*, 1982)

"Why would a woman *want* to serve on a jury?" asked a man after listening to the history of women's struggles to be treated fairly in jury selection.

Why indeed? One certainly wouldn't do it for the pay, which can be as low as $2.00 a day and rarely goes above $20.00. It brings little status or recognition, sometimes is boring, and can be highly disruptive to family and personal life. Yet women have fought for equal treatment in jury selection and participation just as they have fought for the right to vote and hold public office.

Jury service is one of the few ways in which citizens can participate directly in the governmental process. It provides an opportunity for an individual to absorb the values of the American legal system and become involved as a citizen responsible for the welfare and just treatment of other citizens. The denial or restriction of this opportunity to participate is a denial of the full experience of citizenship.

It is also a denial of a litigant's right to be tried by a jury that represents a cross-section of the community. An impartial jury helps legitimize society's perceptions of the jury as the collective conscience of the community. If one or more of the groups that make up the community are underrepresented, the jury can become dominated by the conscious or unconscious prejudices of the groups who are represented and the jury fails in its legitimizing functions (McCauley and Heubel, 1981: 127-128).

Stereotypic assumptions about women and their behavior played an important role in the exclusion of women from jury pools and continue even today to influence the questioning and perception of women during the jury selection process. "Sexism is part and parcel of the American jury system," noted Soler in 1976 (p. 35). "It is voir dire that can—and should—isolate, confront and 'minimize' sex based discrimination in order for half our population to be considered equal before the law" (1976: 36). To the extent that stereotypes influence the ultimate selection of women for juries, they limit both the woman's right to participate in the judicial process and the plaintiff's and defendant's right to a representative jury.

This chapter focuses primarily upon the use of stereotypic—or generalized—views of women during the jury selection or voir dire examination. The purposes of this chapter are three: (1) to provide a brief history of American women's struggle for the right to jury service, (2) to examine several stereotypes about women jurors that were common in the mid-1970s to see if they continue to dominate the literature on jury selection today, and (3) to discuss whether stereotypes about women continue to limit the equal participation of women on juries.

HISTORY OF THE RIGHT TO
JURY SERVICE

Exclusion of women from juries dates back to English common law, under which women were denied the right to jury service (Kanowitz, 1969: 259). This general prohibition was relaxed in the Wyoming Territory in March 1870 when a Grand Jury impaneled for the regular term of court of the First Judicial District of Wyoming included several women. For the first time in criminal court history, a courtroom heard the words, "Ladies and Gentlemen of the Jury" (Wortman, 1985: 208).

Justice John H. Howe assured the women that there was no impropriety of women serving as jurors and that he would see that they received the fullest protection of his court. "You shall not be driven by the sneers, jeers, and insults of a laughing crowd from the temple of justice, as your sisters have from some of the medical colleges of the land. The strong hand of the law shall protect you" (Wortman, 1985:

208). Women served during three terms of court, but were excluded again after Justice Howe was replaced by a new judge opposed to women's suffrage (Wortman, 1985: 209).

In 1879, the United States Supreme Court gave support to the common law exclusion of women from juries by declaring in *Strauder v. West Virginia* (Virginia, 100, U.S. 303 [1879] that a state could constitutionally "confine" jury duty to males. Women could not sit on juries in any state until 1898 when Utah granted that right. Of the sixteen states that gave women the right to vote before the nineteenth amendment, only five (Idaho, Kansas, Michigan, Nevada, and Utah) ruled that the right to vote also entitled women to serve on juries (Lemons, 1973: 69).

RIGHT TO VOTE DID NOT BRING THE
RIGHT TO JURY SERVICE

With the passage of the Nineteenth Amendment, women assumed that along with the right to vote they had also won the right to serve on juries and be tried by juries that included women. They were wrong. Legislators and judges argued that women belonged in the home, that they were too emotional and sensitive to be exposed to the unpleasant events occurring in courtrooms, and that they were intellectually incapable of following complex legal arguments (Lemons, 1973: 69).

Controversy arose over whether the word "men," as it appeared in state constitutions and statutes, stating that juries and officeholders must be men, was used as a generic term or as a specific exclusion of women. States with almost identical statutes came to opposite conclusions, but most ruled against women. Women organized drives to change the statutes or constitutions, but progress was slow. The fight for the right to serve on juries in Connecticut, for example, lasted until 1937, although the Connecticut League of Women Voters attempted to introduce the change into the legislature every session from 1921 to 1937 (Lemons, 1973: 71).

Although the 1957 Civil Rights Act gave women the right to sit on all federal juries (Hole and Levine, 1971: 59-60), courts continued to restrict the right of women to serve on juries at the state level. In 1961, the United States Supreme Court avoided a reexamination of the validity of the *Strauder* dictum in its consideration of *Hoyt v. Florida* (369 U.S.57 [1961]). In Hoyt, the court upheld the constitutionality of a Florida statute that, while it made women eligible to serve on juries, did not require them to serve unless they "registered with the clerk of the court (their) desire to be placed on the jury list" (Kanowitz, 1969: 29). The court found no suspicion of denial of equal protection when only 10 out of 10,000 jurors were women. It simply concluded: "Woman is still regarded as the center of home and family life" (*Hoyt v. Florida*, 1961). As of August 1, 1962, only 21 states permitted women to serve on juries on the same basis as men.[1]

THE WOMEN'S EXEMPTION

In 15 states, women were granted exemptions on the basis of sex alone. Litigation about the "women's exemption" continued in state courts for several years, resulting in conflicting opinions.[2]

In 1975, the woman's exemption was finally successfully challenged in the United States Supreme Court decision in *Taylor v. Louisiana* (419 U.S. 522 [1975]). It held that women cannot be categorically excluded from jury service because of sex alone. Taylor argued, and the court found, that such exemptions result in juries that do not represent a cross-section of the community and thus violate the Sixth Amendment guarantee of a fair jury trial (p. 531).

Taylor was an important step in the struggle for representative juries. Before the decision, clerks in states with automatic women's exclusions often did not even include women in jury calls because they assumed they would take their exemption. In Erie County, New York, in 1974, for example, women made up 53% of the population but only 16.7% of persons available for jury duty (Levine and Schweber-Koren, 1976: 43, 49). In Montgomery, Alabama, in 1972, 54% of the population was female, but only 16% of the jurors (VanDyke, 1977: 366). In three counties in Georgia, women made up at least 53% of the population in 1973 and 1974, but only 16% to 49% of the trial court jurors (VanDyke, 1977: 368).

Women who might have wanted to serve on juries were never given the chance because administrators assumed that they would not want to—a stereotypic assumption regarding what women would do that limited what they could do.

THE RIGHTS OF WOMEN DURING VOIR DIRE

With the end of automatic exemptions and other gender-based excuses, women have fairly conclusively won the right to be included in jury pools on the same basis as men. But the right to jury service includes two separate steps. The first is the right to be included in the wheel; the second is the opportunity actually to sit on a specific jury. The inclusion of women in jury pools is a prerequisite for their inclusion on juries, but it is not a guarantee. Groups who have won the right to be called for jury service see that right melt away at the second stage of jury selection—voir dire.

Wisconsin v. Patri (No. 78-187 - CR [Wis. Ct. App. Dec. 19, 1980]) illustrates this problem. Mrs. Patri, accused of manslaughter of her husband, alleged on appeal after conviction that her right to have a fair cross-section of the community on her jury was violated by the prosecutor's exercise of peremptory challenges exclusively against women. The Wisconsin appellate court denied Mrs. Patri's claim, holding that the Wisconsin constitution did not prohibit prosecutors from exercising peremptory challenges to remove members of a particular group from jury service (McCoin, 1985: 1228).

During voir dire, a prospective juror for a designated trial is questioned by the judge and attorneys to determine the juror's potential for impartiality and fairness. During this selection process, many lawyers and judges continue to respond to women primarily in terms of their gender. They evaluate their potential as jurors in general and for particular trials in terms of the characteristics they attribute to all or most women.

Bobb v. Municipal Court (143 Cal. App. 3d 849, 192 Cal. Rptr. 270 [1983]), a recent case involving women's rights to serve on juries on the same basis as men, shifted the struggle for equal treatment from the jury pool stage to the jury selection stage. Carolyn Bobb, an attorney called for jury duty, refused to answer voir dire questions about marital status and spouse's occupation that were asked only of women. She explained respectfully to the judge that she would be glad to answer the questions if they were asked of both men and women; if they were relevant to women, they were relevant to men (Riddle, 1985: 775).

When she refused to answer the questions a second time, after being instructed to do so by the judge, she was held in contempt of court and taken into custody. She spent 15 minutes in a holding cell and then was released on her own recognizance on the condition that she return later that day for sentencing. After she was denied a continuance of her case to give her time to find an attorney and research her case, Ms. Bobb was sentenced to one day in jail with credit for time served (Riddle, 1985: 776, n. 38; McCoin, 1985: 58).

The superior court denied Ms. Bobb's petition for certiorari and her contempt judgment was affirmed. She then took her case to the First District Court of Appeal, which reversed the contempt judgment in a split decision, in which Justice Miller found that posing the challenged questions only to the female members of the venire violated the equal protection provisions of the California Constitution (Riddle, 1985: 776).

Although ultimately a victory for the equal treatment of women in jury selection, the case shows how entrenched stereotypes about women remain in the 1980s and the depth of the resistance to breaking them down. The questioning not only took place in 1983, but even respectful resistance to it led to the full range of legal sanctions (charging, custody, conviction, and sentencing), all of which were upheld by a superior court. Even the eventual reversal in the Court of Appeals was by a split decision. Presiding Judge Kline concurred with the decision but refused to see the case as one involving the rights of women. He argued that Justice Miller "reached the right result for the wrong reason. The most significant issue raised by this case relates more to the proper treatment of jurors than the rights of women" (*Bobb v. Municipal Court*, 1983). Associate Justice Rouse, who dissented, saw Bobb's behavior as a serious disregard for authority:

> I cannot accept appellant's assertion that her refusal to answer such innocuous questions is a matter of constitutional dimensions.... I have asked similar questions of prospective jurors on many occasions.... The presiding officer's authority was challenged—the gauntlet hurled in his face—how must he respond? [*Bobb v. Municipal Ct*, 1983: 280].

Women in jury venires have traditionally been asked the questions Bobb was asked: "Are you married?" "What does your husband do?" In the jury selection process, lawyers look for evidence of bias or an inability to be objective or impartial, and decisions about the acceptability of women jurors in the past have often been made on the basis of the status or occupation of their husbands. "Excuse the housewife whose husband might be an undesirable juror," cautions Owen (1973: 98).

WHAT LAWYERS LOOK
FOR IN VOIR DIRE

Lawyers see jury selection as an extremely important part of the trial and some argue that the case has been won or lost by the time the jury is sworn in.

In general, lawyers are looking for jurors who will be sympathetic to their case, their client, their arguments, and their style. They want someone who will act as an advocate for them in the jury room, someone willing to stand up for their position against all the other jurors, if necessary. Attorneys evaluate jurors for a specific case in terms of

(1) how they will respond to parties, witnesses, and attorneys in the case;
(2) how they will react to the offense and legal case;
(3) whether they tend to be conviction prone or acquittal prone in a criminal case;
(4) whether they will support high or low damage awards in a civil case; and
(5) how they will participate in jury deliberations.

Lawyers can remove prospective jurors during voir dire either for cause or through peremptory challenges. The latter occur often because they require no stated reason for dismissal. This low visibility makes discriminatory or stereotypic treatment of women difficult to identify.

When a lawyer makes a decision about who will sit on a jury, he or she is making a decision about a person's behavior usually based on limited information. Relatively simple questioning and observation can ascertain age, sex, ethnic background, race, occupation, and social status. Stereotypic descriptions of the behavior of jurors with these characteristics have been the mainstay of jury selection practices for many years.

The folklore of jury selection has stressed gender in particular as an important and easily identifiable characteristic, and trial practice books and articles have been readily giving advice about women that has gone essentially unchallenged until recently when women began to study and practice law.

STEREOTYPES ABOUT WOMEN JURORS:
1970s VERSUS 1980s

A comparison between statements about women in trial practice books and research on the actual behavior of women jurors in the 1970s showed that women were described in stereotypic terms even though the stereotypes were not well supported by research (Mahoney, 1978). A similar review of advice and research on women jurors in the mid-1980s shows that the old stereotypes persist, but that they are giving way to more open and nonsexist attitudes. The amount of research on women jurors remains small, but there is some indication that it is beginning to be taken into account by lawyers and jury selection experts. This section includes a brief review of the Mahoney findings on women jurors in the 1970s and a summary of current research and writing on women jurors in the 1980s.

WOMEN AS JUDGES OF WOMEN—A CHANGING VIEW

Perhaps the most frequent message in the jury selection literature in the 1970s, and the one with greatest potential impact upon women litigants, was that women jurors should be avoided by the lawyer whose client was a woman. "Where the client is a woman," wrote one author in 1970, "avoid other women upon the jury so far as is possible. There is some truth to the ancient adage: 'Woman is man's best friend and her own worst enemy' " (Schweitzer, 1970: 162).

Thus lawyers undid at the voir dire stage what the women's movement worked so hard from 1919 to 1975 to achieve—the opportunity for women to be tried before a jury that includes female members. The adages about woman's dislike for woman persisted in the 1970s in spite of available research that suggested that both women and men tended to support defendants and plaintiffs of their own sex (Nagel and Weitzman, 1971: 194-196; Stephan, 1974: 305-312: Rose and Press, 1955: 247).

What is the message now in the 1980s? Beliefs about women being natural enemies die hard and can still be seen in the literature, but there is a growing tendency to put aside this stereotype of women and to utilize research about men's and women's behavior. On one hand, Belli continues to caution lawyers about women's dislike of women.

> If a plaintiff is a woman and has those qualities which other women envy—good looks, a handsome husband, wealth, social position—then women jurors would be unwise. Woman's inhumanity to womankind is unequalled. They are the severest judges of their own sex [1982: 446].

Blinder, in his book *Psychiatry in the Everyday Practice of Law* reiterates this theme. "All other things being equal, men are disposed favorably, and women unfavorably, to the words of an attractive woman" (1982: 456). He carries it even further in recommending women jurors for rape cases. "A coupling of the innate attraction between the sexes with this initial, instinctual distrust between many women makes them surprisingly good defense jurors in rape trials" (1982: 457).

The 1982 handbook of basic trial advocacy put out by the Association of Trial Lawyers of America Education Fund stresses the inadvisability of using older female jurors when the plaintiff is an attractive young woman (Norton, 1982: 307), and Kelner highlights the problem of female juror jealousy in a 1983 issue of *Trial* (1983: 48). Given the evidence that women jurors are not harder on women than men, the continued emphasis on this theme in current trial practice literature is surprising. Not all authors continue to utilize traditional stereotypes, however. Some reflect the transition from stereotypic to more open attitudes toward women by citing the stereotypes, then adding caveats about their validity. Wagner mentions women's envy of younger or attractive women, but shows his sensitivity to changing times, "Many people believe that female envy is a thing of the past, particularly in cosmopolitan areas. Judge for yourself—You know your locale best" (1985, s1.04[a]).

Herbert and Barrett go even further:

> For the most part, these notions are simply without foundation. The jury research which has been done on such topics prompts different conclusions. Attempts to generalize, classify or relate good or bad jurors to such isolated factors as sex or body composition seem misplaced to say the least [1981: 405]. Women, despite what many trial attorneys suggest, are not *natural* enemies of other women, in court or anywhere else. Women often are the best judges of other women [1981: 421-422].

Smith and Malandro caution lawyers that their prejudice may color their own judgment:

> We must realize that we are viewing jurors through our own rose-colored glasses of prejudice. Our belief system, stereotypes, and trade associations play a role in the evaluation process [1985: 556].

In the 1970s, there was little discussion about the woman juror's response to female attorneys because there were so few. In the 1980s, women attorneys are more common, but studies on jurors' perceptions of them and of their reactions to women jurors are scarce. Are women attorneys more likely to retain or select women jurors? Are women jurors more receptive to female attorneys? Ginger (1984: 163) suggests that a woman juror

> may hold a woman lawyer to a higher standard than she would hold a man. The female juror may be alienated by a woman's hard driving cross examination of a woman witness, even if she would not be alienated by exactly the same tactics used by a man. She may think women lawyers should be "better than" men or should practice in a more genteel or ladylike way [Ginger, 1984: 163].

A poll by the Minnesota Women Lawyers in 1980 questioned 100 jurors who heard 60 jury cases (40 criminal and 20 civil) tried by women in Hennepin County. The study concluded that sexual stereotypes are still widespread and may interfere with the ability of women lawyers to represent clients in jury trials. Many of those polled said they would hire women lawyers only in family or juvenile cases. A number characterized women as appearing inexperienced, unsure of themselves, and less convincing than males (Ginger, 1984: 163-164).

Interestingly, one study of the effects of sex of defense attorney, sex of juror, and age and attractiveness of the victim on mock trial decision making in a rape case showed a high acquittal rate for cases in which the defense attorney was female (acquittal rate of 71% for female attorneys and 49% for male attorneys) (Villemur and Hyde, 1983: 883).

Review of trial practice material in the 1980s shows fewer references to women's dislike of women, but the themes still appear frequently. There is still not much research on the response of female jurors to women participants in court cases, but the evidence that is accumulating does not support the "women enemy of women" theme.

DOMINANCE OF THE WOMAN JUROR'S MOTHER-WIFE ROLE

The mother-wife role was believed in the 1970s to be predominant for women jurors. There were frequent references to characteristics of women jurors that closely correspond to the traditional view of female emotionality and nurturing—women were unpredictable, tenderhearted, and quick to react to pain and suffering. These "feminine" characteristics were believed to make them generally acquittal prone, good jurors for children or plaintiffs in civil cases, and conviction prone in rape cases, except when the rape victim's respectability was in question. Women were also seen as being more sensitive than men to the deportment and dress of lawyers and other participants in the courtroom.

Lawyers were warned, however, about women's behavior in regard to damage awards. As housewives, they were believed to be unused to handling or thinking about large sums of money and thus were prone to support low awards in civil cases (Busch, 1959: 832). Evidence to support most of these stereotypes was lacking. Studies about women's tendency to acquit were often based on simulated jury studies using college students rather than on actual jurors, and results were mixed at best. So were results on the research on women's tendency to favor plaintiffs. There was some support in the 1970s for the tendency of women to favor children. There was little for their greater likelihood to convict in rape cases. Contrary to expectations, men, not women, were more likely to be influenced by the victim's respectability and reputation.

By the mid-1980s, a different image of women was emerging and research results about the behavior of jurors were more widely disseminated.

Research now entering the literature suggests that women are not more likely than men to acquit (Villemur and Hyde, 1983: 883; Moran and Comfort, 1982: 1052). On the contrary, some research suggests they are more likely to convict (Simon, 1980: 43; Mills and Bohannon, 1980: 27). In a study sponsored by *Trial Diplomacy Journal*, questionnaires were completed by 323 jurors after their trials. The study found that women convicted slightly more than men (60% compared to 53%) although the difference was not statistically significant. Women with degrees were significantly more likely to convict than acquit (Sannito and Arnolds, 1982: 10-11).

A study of randomly selected jurors from criminal jury panels in Baltimore City, which held race constant, found that the greater tendency of women to convict held up only for black women, who were more likely to vote initially for conviction than black men or white men or women. Between white men and women there was no significant difference (Mills and Bohannon, 1980: 29).

There are still references in the literature to the woman's compassion for the plaintiff, although Tanford notes that women are good jurors for defendants in civil cases because "to married women with children, the only real pain is child birth, i.e. the labor pain" (1983: 244).

If they do continue to promote stereotypes, the new trial practice books are more likely than older ones to differentiate between different kinds of women. *The Art of Advocacy: Jury Selection* (Wagner, 1985) distinguishes between "housewives in the suburbs" who are "conservative on damages and not particularly sympathetic" and "working women," whose tendencies can be expected to be shaped by the professions in which they are engaged. Wagner warns lawyers especially about "women's liberationist women who may feel antagonism toward male plaintiffs or male lawyers." Such jurors "may appear strident, self assertive, or hostile. If a female demands to be addressed as Ms. and not Miss, you probably should take heed" (Wagner, 1985: 1.04[a]).

There is little recent research on the size of damage awards women recommend, but the changing roles of women would suggest that any predictions about women's behavior based on the housewife model would be of questionable value. As Ginger notes:

> Until the development of the civil rights and women's movements, and of strong ethnic organizations, trial lawyers operated on the basis of a set of long-term assumptions about the kinds of people who would be called for jury duty, and how best to question them. The statutory, decisional, and administrative changes in jury composition flowing from the movements of the 1960s and 1970s have wiped out the validity of most of these assumptions for two reasons: many people are being called for jury duty who were not called in the past and many traditional jurors have undergone experiences that have led them to hold some nontraditional views [1984: 838, Vol. 2].

THE WOMAN JUROR AS DECISION MAKER

Lawyers are concerned about how jurors will behave in the jury room and are eager to identify potential leaders and possible jury foremen. Research in the 1950s and 1960s showed that women had lower status than men in jury deliberations, participated less, and were less likely to be elected foreman (Strodtbeck and Man, 1956; Strodtbeck et al., 1957: Hawkins, 1957; Simon, 1967: 113). Unfortunately, little research on the behavior of women in jury rooms has been done since then and these studies continue to be cited even though the changing role of women in work and family could be expected to spill over into jury room behavior.

More recent research suggests, however, that women continue to be less active and less persuasive in jury deliberations. Sannito and Arnolds found that of 62 forepersons they studied, 30% were females and 70% were males (1982: 12).

Constantini, Mallery, and Yapundich (1983: 124) note that a jury's deliberative process tends to affect men and women differently, with women being more deferential to men, less influential in affecting verdicts, and more likely to change their predeliberation opinions as to a defendant's guilt.

Mills and Bohannon (1980: 28) found that 65% of the foremen were men and 35% were women, percentages similar to those found by other researchers. What is interesting here, however, is that the method of selection in the research court dictated that the individual whose name was first called was the foreperson. With a roughly equal number of men and women, there should have been a roughly equal number of male and female foremen. Judges and attorneys could affect the process of selection by excusing the first listed juror and calling for a second. In this same study, researchers asked jurors about their influence on other jurors and found that fewer females than males felt responsible for changing the decisions of other jurors (26% compared to 43%).

Some trial practice books discount the possibility that women will play leadership roles simply by their use of the masculine pronoun. Belli uses *he* and *him* throughout his trial practice book, but seems particularly heavy-handed in a discussion of the foreman.

> The lead juror may well become the foreman of the jury. As foreman, he may have great weight. He may insist upon further ballots, he may suggest a break for lunch, he may call for exhibits, he may decide when to vote [1982: 432].

After such socialization, how could a lawyer even think of the foreman as *she*?

GENERAL TRENDS IN
GENDER AND JURY SELECTION

A review of trial practice books and jury selection articles shows some general trends. One, the jury selection literature is beginning to take note of the lack of empirical support for jury selection folklore based on demographic and social characteristics. As Simon notes in her review of this evidence, "These beliefs (about the demographic and social characteristics on how jurors will vote in specific trials) have so little basis in fact" (p. 41). The assumptions about the effect of background factors is particularly problematic in regard to women because as Ginger notes:

> Lawyers selecting juries must seriously consider the recent dramatic changes involving millions of women in this country and the men in their lives. The shifts in women's occupations, income, and lifestyle have had a direct effect on women's views on many issues that may be relevant in a jury trial [1984: 839, Vol. 2].

Two, as women study and practice law, they discover and question assumptions about gender that previously went unchallenged. Older textbooks were all written by men. Increasingly, materials for practitioners are being written by women and in general are much less sexist and more sensitive to the avoidance of a variety of traditional stereotypes. Ginger's book, *Jury Selection in Civil and Criminal Trials*, published by Lawpress Corporation, is a model. Its treatment of issues of discrimination on the basis of sex or race is sensitive, scholarly, and thorough.

Likewise, it was a female attorney, Bobb, who extended the rights of women in voir dire in the Bobb case. Women are slowly making a difference in the courts and the practice of law. As more women challenge unfounded assumptions about women in courts, classrooms, and legal literature, we can expect to see trial practice books and journals revised accordingly.

A third observation from this review is that women are still not participating in juries equally. What evidence is available suggests that, in the 1980s as in the 1970s, women are participating less in juries than men and being less influential.

The purpose of widening jury pools and limiting discriminatory challenges in voir dire is to allow truly representative juries. But if those juries continue to be dominated by a small number of traditional elites, victories at earlier stages are lost.

The next steps are research on the participation of women in juries, concentrated efforts by courts and lawyers to provide opportunities for women to exercise leadership in juries, and emphasis in educational and occupational settings on the importance of women's participation and the obligation of women to speak out.

NOTES

1. In three states—Alabama, Mississippi, and South Carolina—women were excluded from jury service entirely; in three other states they could serve only if they registered with the clerk of the court. In other states, women were given exemptions not available to men: women could be exempted because of the nature of the crime or the unavailability of adequate courthouse facilities in three states; they were allowed an exemption on the basis of their sex alone in 15 states; and they, but not men, were granted child care exemptions in 9 states.

2. In 1966, a three-judge Federal District Court declared in *White v. Crook* (251 F. Supp. 401 [N.D. Ala. 1966]) that the Alabama statutory exclusion of women from jury service violated the Fourteenth Amendment's equal protection clause. The court declared, "Jury service is a form of participation in the processes of government, a responsibility and a right that should be shared by all citizens, regardless of sex" (*White v. Crook*, 1969). Yet, in a 1970 decision, a New York trial court rejected the challenge of a female plaintiff to a jury system with automatic exemptions for women. The judge inquired, "What woman would want to expose herself to the peering eyes of women only?" He advised the woman plaintiff that she was in the wrong forum. "Her lament should be addressed to the 'Nineteenth Amendment State of Womanhood' which prefers cleaning and cooking, rearing of children and television soap operas, bridge and canasta, the beauty parlor and

shopping, to becoming embroiled in plaintiff's problems" *De Kosenko vs. Branit* (63 Misc-2d 895, 313 N.Y.2d 827 [Sup.Ct. 1970]).

REFERENCES

Belli, Melvin M., Sr. (1982) Modern Trial. St. Paul: West.

Blinder, Martin. (1982) Psychiatry in the Everyday Practice of Law. New York: Lawyers Co-Operative.

Busch, Francis X. (1959) Law and Tactics in Jury Trials. Indianapolis: Bobbs-Merrill.

Constantini, Edmund, Michael Mallery, and Diane M. Yapundich (1983) "Gender and jury partiality: are women more likely to prejudge guilt?" Judicature 67: 124.

DeCrow, Karen (1974) Sexist Justice. New York: Random House.

Ginger, Ann Fagan (1984) Jury Selection in Civil and Criminal Trials, Vol. 1. Lawpress.

Hawkins, Charles (1957) "Interaction and coalition realignments in consensus seeking groups: a study of experimental jury deliberations." Ph.D. dissertation, University of Chicago.

Herbert, David L. and Roger K. Barrett (1981) Attorney's Master Guide to Courtroom Psychology: How to Apply Behavioral Science Techniques for New Trial Success. Englewood Cliffs, NJ: Executive Reports Corporation.

Hole, Judith and Ellen Levine (1971) Rebirth of Feminism. New York: Quadrangle Books.

Kanowitz, Leo (1969) Women and the Law, The Unfinished Revolution. Albuquerque: University of New Mexico Press.

Kelner, Joseph (1983) "Jury selection: the prejudice syndrome." Trial (July): 48-53.

Lemons, J. Stanley (1973) The Woman Citizen: Social Feminism in the 1920's. Urbana: University of Illinois Press.

Levine, Adline G. and Claudine Schweber-Koren (1976) "Jury selection in Erie County: changing a sexist system." Law and Society Review 11: 43.

Macauley, William A. and Edward J. Heubel (1981) "Achieving representative juries: a system that works." Judicature 65, 3: 126-135.

Mahoney, Anne Rankin (1978) "Sexism in voir dire: the use of sex stereotypes in jury selection," pp. ll4-133 Winifred L. Hepperle and Laura Crites (eds.) Women in the Courts. Williamsburg, VA: National Canter for State Courts.

McCoin, Susan L. (1985) "Sex discrimination in the *voir dire* process: the rights of prospective female jurors," Southern California Law Review 58, 5: 1225-1259.

Mills, T. and J. Bohannon (1980) "Juror characteristics: to what extent are they related to jury verdicts?" Judicature 23.

Moran, Gary and John Craig Comfort (1982) "Scientific juror selection: sex as a moderator of the demographic and personality predictors of impaneled felony juror behavior." Journal of Personality and Social Psychology 43, 5: 1052-1063.

Nagel, Stuart S. and Lenore J. Weitzman (1971) "Women as litigants." Hastings Law Journal 23: 192-192.

Norton, John E. [ed.] (1982) The Anatomy of a Personal Injury Lawsuit. Washington, DC: Association of Trial Lawyers of America Education Fund.

Owen, Irvin (1973) Defending Criminal Cases Before Juries: A Common Sense Approach. Englewood Cliffs, NJ: Prentice-Hall.

Riddle, Randy (1985) "Bobb v. Municipal Court: a challenge to sexism in jury selection and voir dire." Golden Gate University Law Review 14: 769-783.

Rose, Arnold and Arthur Press (1955) "Does the punishment fit the crime: a study in social valuation." American Journal of Sociology 61: 247-259.

Rothblatt, Henry B. (1974) "Voir dire." Law Notes for the General Practitioner 1: 10.

Sannito, Thomas and Edward Burke Arnolds (1982) "Jury study results." Trial Diplomacy Journal 5, 1: 119.

Schweitzer, Sydney C. (1970) Cyclopedia of Trial Practice Lawyers. Rochester, NY: Co-operative.

Simon, Rita J. (1967) The Jury—The Defense of Insanity. Boston: Little, Brown.

Simon, Rita J. (1980) The Jury: Its Role in American Society. Lexington, MA: D. C. Heath.

Smith, Lawrence J. and Loretta Malandro (1985) Courtroom Communication Strategies. New York: Kluwer Litigation Library, Kluwer Law Book Publishers.

Soler, Mark (1976) "Voir dire: the art of seating jurors who are free of sex prejudice." Student Lawyer 4, 8: 34-44.

Stephan, Cookie (1974) "Sex prejudice in jury simulation." Journal of Psychology 88: 305-312.

Strodtbeck, Fred L. and Richard Mann (1956) "Sex role differentiation in jury deliberations." Sociometry 19: 311.

Strodtbeck, Fred L. et al. (1957) "Social status in jury deliberations." American Sociological Review 22: 713-719.

Tanford, J. Alexander (1983) The Trial Process: Law, Tactics and Ethics. Charlottesville, VA: Michie.

VanDyke, Jon (1977) Jury Selection Procedures: Our Uncertain Commitment to Representative Panels. Cambridge, MA: Ballinger.

Villemur, Nora K. and Janet Shirley Hyde (1983) "Effects of sex of defense attorney, sex of juror, and age and attractiveness of the victim on mock juror decision making in a rape case." Sex Roles 9, 8: 879-889.

Wagner, Ward, Jr. (1985) Art of Advocacy: Jury Selection. New York: Matthew Bender.

Wortman, Marlene Stein [ed.] (1985) Women in American Law, Vol. 1. New York: Holmes and Meier.

IV

OVERCOMING GENDER BIAS
IN THE COURTS

This last section addresses the most important question—"can judges be educated?" The previous three sections have documented the nature and extent of gender bias in Supreme Court decisions, in treatment of female victims, offenders, and litigants, and in access and employment opportunities for women as decision makers in the court. There remains little doubt that the judicial world continues to see women through the male lens that distorts the reality of women's lives, judges them through traditional male values, and denies them full access to the male club. Legislation has been passed to alter that but interpretation of that legislation is often subject to the male perspective.

How can change be promoted and, in fact, solidified, in this once exclusively male domain? Social change theory identifies the following three separate levels within society that must incorporate change before it becomes part of the fabric of society: the social structure (stable characteristics of the society such as institutions, the family, educational systems, and so on); the technology of society (including skills, machinery, tools, and so on); and the culture of society (values, ideologies, and attitudes). According to this theory, change may be initiated at any one of the three levels but must be incorporated by all before it is institutionalized.

Much change has taken place in the social structure. Women are well represented as students in the universities and the law schools. They are now active members of the work force at all levels. And the roles of women in the family are changing as a consequence of the above. They are no longer expected to confine their activities and interests to the domestic sphere. Courts, as part of that social structure, have experienced significant change regarding women, seeing them in greater numbers and more expanded roles than ever before.

The second level, the technology of society, has also experienced change with more women acquiring the skills necessary to apply for and perform competently in a wide variety of jobs, including judges, lawyers, and administrators.

The final level, cultural change, which includes attitudes, ideologies, and belief systems, is frequently the most difficult to achieve. And this is the level addressed by this section. Schafran's chapter gave evidence of the entrenched nature of attitudes regarding women. Social science research continues to find evidence, in males and females of all ages, of bias against women's credibility, competency, and abilities. Thus those concerned with providing justice and equal opportunity for women in the courts cannot comfortably assume that attitudinal change will be achieved with younger generations. Such change requires an active rather than passive approach.

Dr. Wikler describes the development, progress, and results to date of the National Judicial Education Program to Promote Equality for Women and Men in the Courts (NJEP). It is encouraging how the issue of gender bias in the courts has become one of increasing interest and concern. The 1986 Conference of Chief Justices addressed the issue, state task forces across the country are documenting the nature and extent of gender bias in their courts, and education on the issue has become a regular feature of judicial training programs. While this, alone, is not the panacea, such training can make great strides in expanding judicial awareness regarding the extent to which they continue to be influenced by outmoded beliefs regarding the role and nature of women.

10

EDUCATING JUDGES ABOUT GENDER BIAS IN THE COURTS

Norma J. Wikler

The American legal and judicial systems reflect the same kind of gender bias that permeates the rest of society. Despite the fact that the courts proceed upon the premise of equal treatment before the law, women are treated differently and unequally from men both in and by the courts. Although men are sometimes disadvantaged by gender bias, there is overwhelming evidence that women as a group are affected much more severely by gender-based myths, biases, and stereotypes embedded in the law itself and in the hearts and minds of some of those who serve as judges.

The task for those who seek the goal of equal justice is to find an effective strategy for eliminating gender bias from the courts. During the past 15 years, the women's rights movement has pursued, with uneven success, a variety of means to that end: legislative reform, litigation, enhanced legal representation for women, and an increase in the number of women lawyers and judges.

A more direct strategy is to attempt to change the attitudes and assumptions of the (largely male) judges themselves. Though the judges must take existing legislation as they find it and cannot themselves compensate for poor legal representation, the discretion accorded them in judicial fact-finding and decision making is a key variable in determining the fairness of legal outcomes. The problem, of course, has been how to reach this select group. Though judges, like other citizens, are affected by mass social movements, including the women's movement, the diffusion of new ideas in the general culture is not an efficient means of educating the judiciary about the changing roles of men and women and the pernicious impact of sexism in the courts.

Since 1980, however, the National Judicial Education Program to Promote Equality for Women and Men in the Courts (hereinafter referred to as the National Judicial Education Program or NJEP) has been underway to educate state court judges directly on gender bias and its effects on the administration of justice. This endeavor, undertaken originally by the author with the sponsorship of the National Organization of Women's Legal Defense and Education Fund (NOW LDEF) in cooperation with the National Association of Women Judges, has succeeded in placing the subject of gender bias in the curriculum of judicial education programs in many states across the country.[1] Despite warnings that judges would be unwilling to learn about sexism, unfriendly to social science methods and arguments, and unlikely to change their outlook, the project has produced concrete and significant results. My purpose here is to provide an account of the project's strategies and progress, and to attempt to analyze the special problems and opportunities that present themselves to those who might consider judicial education as a means for effecting social change.

THE NATIONAL JUDICIAL EDUCATION PROGRAM

Sylvia Roberts, a pioneer Title VII litigator, first conceived of a national judicial education program on gender bias. She made the proposal in 1970 to the newly formed NOW Legal Defense and Education Fund, for which she was serving as counsel. The Fund's leadership, like Roberts herself, was dedicated to challenging sex discrimination and to securing equal rights for women and men. Those who were lawyers had seen firsthand how judges' stereotypes and biases guided their judicial behavior and undermined even the most progressive and enlightened legal reforms.

NOW LDEF's first effort to launch such a program, in 1977, found no support among potential funders. Some refused to believe that the judiciary was biased. Others doubted that an avowedly feminist organization could gain access to judges. Without funding, the idea was put on the shelf, but NOW LDEF's interest continued. The organization made a concerted effort to bring media attention to bear on sexist statements made by judges, typically in cases of sexual assault, and additional data were collected in a court-watching project.

Three more years passed before NOW LDEF was able to get the program underway. The media campaign had succeeded in bringing public attention to the problem, and the women's movement had gained in strength and stature. The key event, however, was the formation in 1979 of the National Association of Women Judges and its decision to cosponsor the judicial education program with NOW LDEF. The women judges were not outsiders demanding change within the judiciary, but colleagues and peers. What might otherwise have been perceived as a set of demands of a special interest group was translated by the women judges into insistence on the core norms and values of the judiciary itself: fairness, objectivity, and impartiality.

With their judicial imprimatur, the project was poised to develop and organize. My background as a sociologist interested in the professions and in women's rights prompted NOW LDEF to recruit me to design the Program and serve as its director, a post for which I took a two-year leave from my professorial duties at the University of California, Santa Cruz. With my small staff I created an Advisory Board of prominent male and female judges, legal and judicial educators, attorneys, and social scientists and obtained the endorsement of the National Judicial College, the American Academy of Judicial Education, the National Center for State Courts, and other centers of judicial education. The Advisory Board and the support of these prestigious organizations lent credence to the necessity of educating judges about gender bias and conferred legitimacy on the NJEP as the appropriate vehicle through which this could be accomplished.

The NJEP's general aim is to achieve equality for women and men in the courts. However, the NJEP's primary purpose was and remains to develop and introduce into established judicial education programs for state judges curricular materials that examine the effects of gender on the interpretation and application of substantive law and on courtroom interaction. The Program's first goal was to introduce at least one session on the subject into a judges' school. This was accomplished in August 1980, as a male judge and I presented a two-hour seminar to the National Judicial College. Our session discussed recent research on differential sentencing of male and female adult criminal offenders, the economic consequences of divorce for women and men, and the effects of gender on the courtroom experience. This event proved to be an important learning experience for the Program's staff. The response of the "students"—generally negative—clearly demonstrated that gender bias is a sensitive, even explosive, subject for judges. A special pedagogic approach was needed, and those leading discussions would have to be alert for and adept in dealing with the inevitable denial and occasional intense hostility.

During the next several months, the staff worked with consultants— lawyers, social scientists, and judges—to develop a four-hour pilot course, "Judicial Discretion: Does Sex Make a Difference?"[2] It was first presented to California judges in January 1981, with a male and a female judge as primary instructors. A law professor and a sociologist, both experts in family law, taught part of the course, and two other judges served as discussion group leaders.

The purpose of the three-part course was to examine the impact of sex stereotypes, myths, and biases on judicial decision making in different areas of the law and on courtroom interaction. The first segment of the course used rape as an illustration of the role of sex stereotypes and attitudes toward women in laws and in judicial decisions. The second examined the impact of judges' attitudes toward changing women's roles on women lawyers, litigants, witnesses, court personnel, and judges. The final and largest part dealt with the differential economic and social impact of divorce on women and men. Using statistical data from governmental agencies and recent legal and social science research, the course documented how the trend toward shorter duration of support awards, and the lack of enforcement, have combined with job discrimination against women and with inflation to create gross inequities between spouses after divorce.

This time around, the reception was well-received. The additional time in preparation of materials and in training of instructors, and the valuable experience of the earlier, less successful session at the National Judicial College, produced a course that the judges found useful and important. At their insistence, the third segment was made a mandatory session in a subsequent program for family law judges, and the course was endorsed by the Director of the California Center for Judicial Education and Research. The National Judicial Education Program was off and running.

FURTHER EDUCATIONAL ACTIVITY

Following the course in California, "Judicial Discretion: Does Sex Make a Difference?" was adapted for use in other states, and new courses were created as well. Whenever possible, the NJEP assisted legal and judicial groups in developing their own courses by providing materials, speakers, and/or curriculum design. The Directors (the author and Lynn Hecht Schafran, Esq., who succeeded to the director-ship of the Program in late 1981) further stimulated awareness of gender bias in the courts by extensive public speaking and by writing for professional journals. Through its function as a national clearinghouse for materials on gender bias in the courts, the NJEP reached beyond legal and judicial circles to serve also community groups, women's rights activists, and academics.

In spite of the fact that the Program's offerings gained increasing acceptance, progress was uneven. Especially in the early years, doors opened only after careful strategic planning and much negotiation and persuasion. There were periodic setbacks: approaches rebuffed, invita-tions rescinded, sessions that did not go well. Success came most easily when key persons in the organizations we hoped to approach became interested in our work and prodded their groups to extend an invitation to us. As might be anticipated, the workshops held at meetings of the National Association of Women Judges were particularly effective in this regard. Members who valued the workshop experience returned to their home states to stir interest among female and male judges in our work, who then pressed judicial educators to include gender bias in their curricula and to invite the NJEP to participate.

The most significant outgrowth of the National Judicial Education Program has been the creation by several state supreme courts of task forces to investigate gender bias and to recommend reforms. The first task force was established by Robert N. Wilentz, chief justice of the Supreme Court of New Jersey, in October 1982. Its mandate was to "investigate the extent to which gender bias exists in the New Jersey judicial system and to develop educational programs to eliminate any such bias" (New Jersey Supreme Court Task Force on Women in the Courts, 1984).

The group of 31 male and female trial and appellate judges, lawyers, and legal educators, which is chaired by Judge Marilyn Loftus, conducted a broad survey of New Jersey's attorneys and has collected other data as well. Its report on the treatment of women in the courtroom and on the effects of gender on decision making—in the areas of damages, domestic violence, juvenile justice, sentencing, and matrimonial law—was presented to the New Jersey judiciary at the 1983 Judicial College. The task force has continued its work since then, issuing a lengthy report of its findings in 1984, and conducting subsequent inquiries into the status of women in the personnel system and equity in property distribution and support awards.

The New Jersey Task Force's work was nationally publicized, a fact that made it easier for women judges in other states to press for similar efforts. The highest courts in New York and Rhode Island established their own task forces in 1984, and as of this writing several more states have task forces in place or under serious consideration.

The National Judicial Education Program has worked closely with each of these task forces. The current and former directors serve as members and advisors, providing expertise on gender bias, written materials, and advice on research methods. In turn, the task forces have significantly amplified the project's work. The data collection process itself, involving regional meetings with and surveys of attorneys, public hearings, and courtwatching, has brought the problem of gender bias to the attention of the legal and judicial communities and to the public. The data from the various states have become an important supplement to the National Judicial Education Program's materials, because many judges tend to discount data drawn from national studies that do not report on conditions in their particular jurisdictions. Moreover, the task force survey reports are full of specific data about individual cases, and these are often more impressive to judges than the findings of social science reports that involve aggregate data, generalities, and are based in part on theory. Finally, the task forces have further legitimated the problem of gender bias as one worthy of judicial investigation and action, transforming the issue from a problem "for women" to a problem "of the judiciary."

CURRENT EFFORTS

Today the multiple efforts of NJEP, the state task forces, and the National Gender Bias Task Force (created in 1985 by the National Association of Women Judges) continue the work of educating the judiciary on gender bias. During the first six years of its existence, the National Judicial Education Program has given courses, talks, workshops, and other presentations in more than 20 states, reaching several thousand judges and nearly as many attorneys.

Though as recently as six years ago gender bias in the courts was an issue discussed rarely by judges and judicial educators, it now seems poised to become a part of the normal curriculum for judicial education and has been taken to heart by important elements of the judiciary itself as a topic of investigation and reform. As important as this development is, it may have equal significance as a case study of a particular strategy for social reform, that of attempting to transform the "hearts and minds" of the nation's judges. The strategy was successful for the NJEP, in part, because it was based on a deeper understanding of the structure of judicial attitudes and behavior and of the sources of both resistance and motivation among various elements in the judiciary. In the following section, I attempt an analysis of these issues drawn from the National Judicial Education Program's experiences in judicial education.

SOURCES AND FORMS OF
JUDICIAL GENDER BIAS

American men—and women—generally have learned rigidly defined sex roles. A set of assumptions, stereotypes, and judgments underlies and supports this social casting, and these are carried into social institutions that reflect and reinforce them. Like most adults, judges learned as children that women are as a group inferior to men in important respects and deserve to be subservient.

For most judges on the bench today, legal training reinforced rather than challenged this cultural inheritance. Historically, American law tended to group women with children and idiots, lacking the qualities needed for ownership of property and the vote. Until recently, the inflexible sex-role stereotyping of the law was an important factor in maintaining sex discrimination in society generally. Few current judges ever took a course in law school designed to correct these biases and stereotypes. During their legal education and throughout their careers, most lawyers had contact only with women who held subservient positions. Law journals contained almost no writing on gender bias, and, as noted above, the topic was absent from judicial education curricula until this decade. Because of the small number of women in the judiciary even now, many judges are denied the experience of shared work among peers of both sexes, a corrective force that has traditionally led men and women to examine critically their sex stereotypes and beliefs.

Moreover, judges are structurally insulated from social and political pressures for reform. Legislators become aware of social inequities and new social problems through the pressure of organized constituencies, but judges are not to be lobbied. Although the public secures important benefits from this arrangement, it has the disadvantage of providing one less potential corrective to a judge's preconceived beliefs, assumptions, and misinformation, whether on gender-related issues or other matters.

The gender bias that results from this takes several forms, and it is critically important to identify and differentiate these. Otherwise, it remains unclear just what it is that judges should seek to change.

The basic form of gender bias is the assumption that women conform to a single profile or small range of profiles, regardless of individual differences. Schafran identifies three stereotypes of women that are reflected in judicial decisions: "Mary," chaste, domestic, and unsuited to positions of authority; "Eve," the eternal temptress; and now "Superwoman," who, despite years of unpaid domestic labor in the home, can leap into the work force upon divorce, fully equipped to earn a good living and care for her children with no help from others (Schafran, 1985: 14).

The legal implications of accepting these profiles is obvious. "Eve" makes an unsympathetic rape victim; "Mary" may lose a suit filed to protest employment discrimination and may lose child custody if she works outside the home; and "Superwoman"'s support awards in divorce are likely to cover only a fraction of her economic needs (Schafran, 1985). Of course, men are sometimes the losers when these stereotypes govern judicial decision making, especially in custody challenges.

A second important element of judicial gender bias is the pervasive tendency to regard men as more credible than women. This tendency is not confined to judges; for example, college students were found to be much more willing to accept the contents of a lecture when delivered by a male than the same material presented by a female (Wikler, 1976). In the courtroom, credibility may be the greatest asset an individual possesses, whether one appears in the role of lawyer, witness, litigant, complainant, or defendant, and, as a result, this form of bias can be devastating in its effect. That such bias is unconscious on the judge's part may add to rather than subtract from its impact. Similarly, judges may be entirely unaware of the extent to which credibility can be undermined by the seemingly unimportant practice of calling female attorneys by the first name, or using terms of endearment (e.g., "honey"). Unless the real issues at stake can be presented to judges in a convincing manner, objections to these practices will seem to reflect nothing more than thin skin.

A third source of bias consists simply in the ignorance and misinformation of many judges about the economic and social realities of most women. The judge's decisions on property settlement and support awards in divorce cases may depend crucially on the judge's personal estimates of the facts in these matters. Yet little in a judge's education or life experience may have taught him or her what a divorced woman's employment or remarriage prospects really are, and judges may have only the vaguest notions of the real cost of raising a child. When judges consistently underestimate the problems faced by divorcing women and overestimate their likelihood of success in staying afloat, the judge's decisions may be fairly characterized as biased against women. Once again, the fact that this bias is in one sense unconscious, and indicates no particular malice against women, in no way lessens the urgency of reform through judicial education.

Male identification with males is a fourth element of gender bias, though it is difficult to demonstrate. A male judge's tendency to see things the way a male attorney does, or to consider it axiomatic that a divorcing male must have the means to "start a new life," may spring from early socialization. We learn to think of ourselves as male or female before we learn to identify ourselves as white or black, and the process of learning to peel off our layers of bias may proceed in accord with the order in which they were laid down. The authors of one major study of reported judicial opinions in sex discrimination cases found that judges have, as a group, made more progress in freeing themselves from racial bias than from gender bias (Johnson and Knapp, 1971: 692). They also concluded that "for the present generation of judges it may be easier to assume the imagined mental state of a black male, of whatever station in life, than it is successfully to imagine that one is a *female* (even a white, middle-class one)" (Johnson and Knapp, 1971: 744).

Finally, some of the gender bias in judges' decisions may represent a backlash against feminism. Feminism is perceived by significant numbers of Americans, inevitably including some judges, as a threat to traditional social institutions. Women who may or may not be feminists may be made to live with divorce settlements that reflect a particular judge's unsympathetic response to feminist demands for equal treatment. The judge may feel that women are best protected under traditional arrangements, and be disinclined to offer the law's protection to women whom he sees as insisting on different roles.

Courses for judges, then, must be designed to correct for these and similar sources and forms of gender bias. Specific evidence of these forms of bias and their damaging effects on women and men can provide the impetus for judges to adopt practices more closely in keeping with the legal ideal of equal treatment.

FACTORS IN THE EFFECTIVENESS OF
JUDICIAL EDUCATION ON GENDER BIAS

Gaining access to judicial education centers was, as noted above, the first major obstacle for the National Education Program. Once this was achieved, the challenge was to get the judges' attention and to persuade them to take the issues and our materials seriously. This was uncharted terrain. Despite the voluminous literature that exists on sex-role socialization in children, there was almost no analytic work on the reeducation of adults. What literature on attitude change existed in journals of social psychology offered limited help, because nearly all of it was conducted under controlled experimental conditions with little relevance to the context of judicial education. Although some management consultants had offered counsel to corporations concerning affirmative action plans, judges are much more autonomous than those who report to a corporation's top management, and the consultants' strategies could not be adopted.

SOME PROBLEMS

Educating judges about gender bias, particularly their own, is not like acquainting them with new features of the tax code. Gender bias is inevitably a sensitive, sometimes explosive, issue. The accusation of bias suggests a failure to live up to the cardinal judicial virtue of impartiality. And it strikes close to home, to relations with women that male judges maintain in their private lives.

Certain features of current judicial education make the reformer's work especially difficult. Many judicial educators adhere to the belief that "only judges can teach judges." They argue that nonjudges, especially social scientists, may not understand the specific roles and duties of judges, and may not be adept at adapting their knowledge for judges' use. They also lack the credibility of a fellow judge. But special problems present themselves when only judges teach each other. Since *Brown v. Board of Education* (347 U.S. 483 [1954]), a chief vehicle for combatting judicial bias has been social science data (Haney, 1982). Judges, not trained in the field, may lack familiarity with the methods and findings of social science, and hence be unsuitable instructors.

Regardless of the professional identity of the instructor, many judges do not take to social science. Judges are said by their educators to favor "nuts and bolts" learning that imparts discrete skills and information rather than general understanding of large cultural issues. The judges deal with individual cases, not aggregates, and often feel that aggregate data have no appreciable bearing on the cases that will come before them. This resistance supports their own images of themselves as free of the kinds of bias documented in the social science reports, which they believe reflect only what happens "elsewhere."

Even if individual judges are receptive to social science data, presentations in judicial education programs are, in certain respects, seen as suspect. From their courtroom experience, judges know that social science data can be manipulated to support almost any case. The adversarial clash of opposing counsel in the courtroom permits each side to challenge the distortions of the other, allowing the truth to emerge. Because judicial education does not employ an adversarial approach in teaching, the "necessary" corrective to the use of social science data will have been removed, as far as some judges are concerned. Especially with a subject like gender bias, the judges may suspect that the data are being manipulated by the presenters—especially if they are women, an impression that they know they cannot test for themselves because they are not trained to evaluate the validity of social science research.

SOME SOLUTIONS

(1) Concrete information. The National Judicial Education Program's courses were designed to be similar in format and "feel" to the other courses the judges were taking. We incorporated material that was technical, specific, and directly related to judicial activity. The judges' responses to our presentation of actual and hypothetical cases were analyzed to bring out the gender-based attitudes they embodied. When possible, we used data from the state in which the course was given.

For example, the segment on rape in the NJEP's pilot course (presented in California) scrutinized current and precedent jury instructions to determine the portrayal of rape victims and the accompanying attitudes toward women. In small groups, judges reflected on their own responses to a series of hypothetical cases devised to highlight ambiguities in current California evidentiary procedures regarding admission of evidence of prior sexual contact in rape cases. The discussion leaders, themselves judges, clarified ambiguous sections in the criminal code and guided group members in exploring how biased attitudes toward rape victims might have influenced their decision making in the hypothetical cases. The groups then discussed what the correct decision under law would have been.

The segment on support awards and enforcement was taught by two judges and two other experts in family law, and examined step-by-step the ways in which a hypothetical family's postdivorce experience was determined by the decisions made by judges in setting levels and duration of support awards. This permitted us to introduce, with the help of elaborate visual aids, detailed information about such issues as the cost of child care in the state, employment opportunities for women of varying ages and levels of experience, and patterns of postdivorce standards of living for divorced men and women in California and in the nation. In the course of these presentations, common myths and misconceptions among the judges were challenged.

(2) Suggesting reforms. The National Judicial Education Program's courses relied on several design elements to increase their effectiveness in brinqing about change. The emphasis was not only on what judges might have done wrong, but what would be right. And frequent mention was made of areas in which the judiciary has already made progress, citing examples of good decisions worthy of emulation. Further, judges were encouraged not only to correct their own behavior, but to intervene in the case of gender-biased behavior (such as inappropriate forms of address) on the part of counsel or personnel in their own court. This "affirmative role" was stressed heavily, for judges who make an effort to stop the sexist behavior of others are more likely to be aware of their own practices.

(3) "Legitimating" the material. Judicial resistance both to the subject and to social science was overcome in part by strategic selection of instructors. As mentioned above, judges had greater credibility than nonjudges, and male judges generally more than female ones. Credibility also was proportional to status in the judicial hierarchy and to the degree of respect from peers.

The instructors smoothed the introduction of social science research by raising frankly the issues of its validity and its relevance to the judicial enterprise. Similarly, instructors who were judges took time to introduce instructors who were not and to explain their presence by reference to their specific areas of expertise. These "endorsements" were helpful in deflecting unreflective criticism and dismissal.

(4) Creating a personal stake in ending gender bias. With crowded curricula and weighty concerns in other areas, a central task was to convince the judges that gender bias was an issue worthy of personal interest.

The tendency for males to identify with other males was used to advantage in this regard. We found that male judges were very attentive when other male judges told of their own past blindness to gender bias and subsequent rethinking of the issues. Males also became absorbed in the travails of male victims of gender bias, such as the protagonist of the film *Kramer vs. Kramer*, who loses a custody fight because of a judge's bias against fathers.

An especially potent technique for securing the personal involvement of male judges in ending gender bias was emphasizing the effects of bias on the judges' own daughters. The fact that half the judges' married daughters will, if present trends continue, themselves go through divorce, gave the judges a very personal reason to be concerned about the fairness of settlements. The same was true of judges who were asked to contemplate the treatment received in courtrooms by those of their daughters who were training to be lawyers.

RESPONSES

The response of the judges to the National Judicial Education Program's courses was, of course, a chief concern for it determined the effect the courses would have on courtroom procedure and decision making. There was also a short-term concern: if the judges indicated on their course evaluation forms or by other comments that they did not like the presentations, they would not be repeated, nor would they be adopted elsewhere.

The structure of the judicial education system made this short-term issue especially important. Judicial educators are evaluated by the judges they serve, and they have a personal stake in keeping their clients satisfied. While some judicial educators were receptive to our programs from the outset, others offered much resistance. Even when pressure from judges forced the issue onto the agenda, the courses were at times inexplicably scheduled at odd hours. On occasion, there was something akin to sabotage; course materials would be "lost," and course evaluations tampered with. Beyond any personal distaste for the subject or for the National Judicial Education Program on the part of the educators, this resistance reflected a response to the potential for upsetting some judges.

As it turned out, the judges' reactions were varied. A few insisted on denying the existence of the problem of gender bias in any form. These also rejected any responsibility to examine the issue. The courses left them unchanged. A larger group was resistant to the material but could be sensitized to the issues under optimal conditions of judicial education. They tended to be more open to suggestions on proper courtroom conduct than to reflection on bias in the application and interpretation of the law. A third group maintained some wariness over the course's designs, but their abiding commitment to the norms of fairness and objectivity allowed them to be reached provided that they could be shown specifically how gender bias translates into decision making, fact-finding, and communication. Their basic attitudes may not have altered, but their conduct and judgments could be made more impartial. Finally, there was a small, but critically important, group of judges, both male and female, who were deeply concerned about gender bias and were willing to take an active role. Some of these judges had become familiar with the issues through service on task forces, or by prior legal practice with female attorneys. They formed a pool of internal professional "change agents" from whom instructors and allies could be drawn.

The National Judicial Education Program staff had to learn that the immediate reaction of the judges was not the important one. A judge encountering an example of gender bias in his courtroom may just then recall and absorb a point that had been made months before in the course. Even heated, hostile arguments served a purpose. Some judges told us that through these exchanges they became aware of the depth of bias on the part of some of their colleagues and thus were impressed by the reality of the problem the courses attempted to deal with.

The response of women judges deserves special mention. Most women judges have been staunch supporters of the National Judicial Education Program, but others have denied the existence of any problem. To this observer, some women seemed to voice this attitude in an unconscious attempt to be perceived (by others and perhaps by themselves) as closely identified with male peers. Other women acknowledged the problem, but felt that, as women, they did not need education on the subject. In general, women judges spoke more often about the gender bias they had experienced in legal and judicial contexts when there were more than one or two women in a group of judges. Such personal testimony proved very effective in causing male peers to admit to the seriousness of the problem.

CHANGING THE "NORMATIVE ENVIRONMENT"

Judicial practice and judicial education both take place in a climate of attitude and expectation that can be called a "normative environment"—which can either support or oppose gender bias. If sexist jokes and remarks demeaning to women are tolerated (or even encouraged) in such settings as the courts, judicial education programs, and professional gatherings, the task of reducing gender bias on the part of individual judges through judicial education is much more difficult. Contrarily, if judges expect that such behavior will be negatively viewed or even sanctioned, this task is facilitated.

The environment at some of the judicial education sessions I attended in state and national programs was surprisingly rife with sexist references and "humor." These practices were defended even by leading educators; one said that "if it takes a few dirty jokes to keep the judges happy, we will keep the dirty jokes." This is a symptom of a normative environment in courtrooms that permits women to be referred to as "girls" and in which (as the New Jersey task force discovered) a county bar association could have as an annual tradition a clambake and a strip show. Informal reports of women judges indicate that these practices dwindle in states with task forces or in which the National Judicial Education Program has been active.

The authority of the highest judges is invaluable in securing changes in the normative environment. After the New Jersey Task Force's presentation of its findings at the 1983 Judicial College, Chief Justice Robert Wilentz told the New Jersey judiciary:

> There is no room for gender bias in our system. There's no room for the funny joke and the not-so-funny joke, there's no room for conscious, inadvertent, sophisticated, clumsy, or any other kind of gender bias, and certainly no room for gender bias that affects substantive rights.
>
> There is no room because it hurts and it insults. It hurts female lawyers psychologically and economically, litigants psychologically and economically, and witnesses, jurors, and law clerks, and judges who are women. It will not be tolerated in any form whatsoever [*New York Times*, 1983].

Later Wilentz sent a memorandum to all New Jersey judges directing them to read the task force's 1984 report carefully and to follow its recommendations. He also showed a videotape on gender bias, prepared by the task force, to all the state's assignment judges, suggesting that they show it to judges and court personnel in their counties. New Jersey's top court administrator took a similarly supportive role.

Finally, the normative environment can be changed by the presence in greater numbers of women in positions of authority and leadership, and by active intervention by nonbiased women and men on occasions when bias is shown by others. This modeling in the courtroom, in chambers, and in professional gatherings may have an even more powerful effect than didactic presentations in the classroom.

How can these changes be made permanent? This question has been very much on the minds of the staff of the National Judicial Education Project. There is a danger that gender bias will survive for a few years as the currently fashionable topic of conscience, to be jettisoned in favor of new reformist enthusiasms.

The task, then, is to institutionalize the effort to eradicate gender bias. This requires judicial education in the subject to continue as long as it is needed, and for this material to be incorporated into other courses, such as those on matrimonial law and criminal evidence.

Similar institutionalization must occur away from the classroom. The courts must establish grievance systems for complaints, shaping the normative environment with real sanctions. New York's Commission on Judicial Conduct, for example, recently disciplined two judges for offensive behavior toward women, one for inappropriate comments in a rape case and the other for numerous sexist remarks to female attorneys.[3]

Finally, gender bias can be fought on a continuing basis by increased public visibility and accountability for the judiciary. Bar association polls, court-watchers, media access to the courtroom, and public attention to the judicial selection process can help. The elective recall of a Wisconsin judge who justified probation for a young rapist by referring to "normal" responses to sexual allure was an effective notice to judges elsewhere.

THE EDUCATIONAL APPROACH:
PROMISE AND LIMITATIONS

As the earlier narrative suggests, the National Judicial Education Program believes that it has succeeded in many of its initial aims.

Favorable responses by judges who have taken the courses, favorable course evaluations, and requests from judicial educators and judges for speakers and materials are signs of appreciation and support. Reports of lessening bias in states in which we have been active indicate that the attention we helped to focus on the problem is having a beneficial effect. There is also increasing acceptance of the National Judicial Education Program in the judicial mainstream. Lynn Hecht Schafran, Esq., the current director, distributed the Program's materials on economic consequences of divorce to all family law judges in New York State through the state's Office of Court Administration, and the present author spoke to that state's family law judges not as a representative of the National Judicial Education Program but on behalf of the National Council of Juvenile and Family Court Judges.

These data are, of course, unsystematic, and the actual impact of the National Judicial Education Program on the general conduct of the law has not been measured. Indisputably, the Program has achieved one important goal, that of making gender bias a subject that judges and judicial educators think and care about. When the program began, there was but one comprehensive article on the subject in the mainstream legal literature; today there are dozens, many solicited by leading legal journals. Whereas there had been no systematic discussion of gender bias in any judicial education program as late as 1980, today it is included in state programs across the country, and in national programs as well. It appeared, for the first time, on the agenda of the 1986 Conference of Chief Justices, attended by the ranking judges from each state. The many state task forces will be joined by others, which can now avail themselves of advice in a manual on the establishment of such groups, which was written by the past and present directors of the National Judicial Education Program and published by the National Association of Women Judges' Foundation for Women Judges (Schafran and Wikler, 1986).

Still, it must be kept in mind that the education of judges is but one route to reform and is not itself sufficient. Women must have access to courts in the first place, and they must have good legal representation. While some extrajudicial forces support the work of the National Judicial Education Program—a good example is the budget-minded effort of states to improve enforcement of child support orders—others work against it. The feminist movement has by no means fully attained its goal of eradicating gender bias in society generally, and the residual forms of this injustice continue to support bias in the courtroom. The general regression and backsliding in this area occurring in recent years in the legislative and executive branches of government could eventually occur in the judiciary as well.

Even if education on gender bias becomes a regular feature of judicial education courses, and grievance procedures and other institutional reforms help to lessen the impact of bias on judicial decision making, much work remains. New issues continually arise, necessitating new campaigns and new educational efforts. On this side of the horizon, for example, are such issues as new reproductive technology, the role of mediators in divorce, and the new enthusiasm for joint custody. In any case, many current problems have been left for the future. The special difficulties of poor and minority women need specific attention. Necessary, too, are continuing reappraisals of past efforts at reform. Some of these, such as no-fault divorce, have not had the benefits that were expected.

The audience for projects such as the NJEP should be expanded. The Program deals almost exclusively with the state judiciary, but the federal bench stands in need of education as well. More attorneys, too, should be reached, both as aides in educating judges and in their own right. Attorneys for divorcing women, for example, cannot make an effective case in settlements unless they are aware of, and can demonstrate, the economic realities of postdivorce women.

Nevertheless, the National Judicial Education Program demonstrated that a tiny staff—there were never more than two or three professionals, and often only one—with relatively little funding can find a way to reach and even convince the nation's judges on an issue of social justice. Though judicial education is by no means the most important route to social change, it has proved to be an essential one in the efforts to eliminate gender bias in the courts.

NOTES

1. Judges participate in judicial education programs of various kinds. Most states provide some in-state educational programs (with emphasis on orientation programs for new judges and specialty courses) that judges attend on a mandatory or voluntary basis. Other states send their judges to national programs such as the National Judicial College and the American Academy of Judicial Education.

2. "Judicial Discretion: Does Sex Make a Difference?" has been published as a model text based on the transcript of the instructors presentations and the participants' responses. It also includes supplementary readings, copies of visual aids, and bibliographies. Materials can be purchased from the NJEP, 99 Hudson Street, 12th Floor, New York, NY 1003.

3. The New York State Commission on Judicial Conduct censured County Court Judge John Fromer for responding to a reporter's request for information about a rape case, with the opinion that "maybe they ended up enjoying themselves" (Matter of John J. Fromer, Unreported Determination [N.Y. Comm'n October 25, 1985]) reported in *The Judicial Conduct Reporter* (1985: 1).

In 1985, Nassau County Supreme Court Justice William Dolittle was admonished by the New York Commission on Judicial Conduct for his sexist remarks to female attorneys over the years (*New York Law Journal*, 1985: 1).

REFERENCES

Haney, C. (1982) "Data and decisions: judicial reform and the use of social science," pp. 43-59 in P. Dubois (ed.) The Analysis of Judicial Reform. Lexington, MA: D. C. Heath.

Johnston, J. 0., Jr. and C. L. Knapp (1971) "Sex discrimination by law: a study in judicial perspective." New York University Law Review 46: 675-747.

New Jersey Supreme Court Task Force on Women in the Courts (1984) New Jersey Supreme Court Task Force on Women: Report of the First Year. [The first and second reports of the New Jersey Task Force on Women in the Courts may be obtained from Melanie Griffin, Esq., Administrative Office of the Courts, CN 037, Trenton, NJ 06825. The first report is published in Women's Rights Law Reporter, 9, 129 (1986).]

New York Times (1983) "Panel in New Jersey finds bias against women in state court." November 22: Al, col. 1.

Schafran, L. H. (1985) "How stereotypes about women influence judges." Judges Journal 24: 12-27, 49-53.

Schafran, L. H. and N. J. Wikler (1986) Establishing and Operating a Gender Bias Task Force: A Manual for Action. Washington, DC: Foundation for Women Judges. [This manual may be ordered for $35.00 from the Women Judges' Fund for Justice, 1225 Fifteenth Street, NW, Washington, DC, 20005.]

Schafran, L. H. (1987) "Documenting gender bias in the courts: the task force approach." Judicature, 70, 280-290.

Unified Court System Office of Court Administration (1986, March) Report of the New York Task Force on Women in the Courts. [The Report of the New York Task Force on Women in the Courts may be obtained from the Public Information Office, Office of Court Administration, 270 Broadway, New York, NY 10007, and is published with commentary in Fordham Urban Law Review, 15 (1987).]

Wikler, N. J. (1976) "Sexism in the classroom." Presented at the American Sociological Association meetings, New York.

Wikler, N. J. (1980) "On the judicial agenda for the 80's: equal treatment for women and men in the courts." Judicature 64: 202-209.

V

CONCLUSION

The preceding articles have analyzed the role and treatment of women within the court and several themes arise:

(1) The intent of legislation designed to improve the lives of women has been frequently subverted consciously, or unconsciously, by dominance of the male perspective.

(2) Substantial resistance still remains to full acceptance of female judges, lawyers, administrators, and jurors by the dominant male group.

(3) Decisions regarding women seem too often to be based on an appearance of equality of opportunity for women that belies a reality of unequal life experience and unequal opportunity.

In short, the authors have painted a picture in which the role and treatment of women within the court continues to be actively influenced by gender considerations that generally operate to the disadvantage of females; and that this is due largely to the fact that those gender considerations rise from the perspective of the opposite sex, males. The socialization and life experience of men in our society is sufficiently different from women that it is understandable how the masculine perception of women's reality falls short.

While it was clear from the articles that the women's movement has made significant progress in promoting legislation designed to improve the lives of women, this legislation has frequently worked to their disadvantage or had minimal positive impact on their treatment by and within the courts.

Some examples: protective order legislation, such as that designed to protect women from abusive husbands, when viewed through the male lens is often seen as a law forcing a man out of "his" home. Judicial refusal to sign or enforce court protective orders leaves women even more vulnerable to abusive husbands who now see their behavior as outside the rule of law.

No-fault divorce legislation was heralded as a substantial victory for equal rights for women, but, as Weitzman discovered, the implementation ignored the reality of women's lives, plunging many of them into poverty.

In divorce settlements, judges have shown themselves to be insensitive to the dismal employment opportunities available to middle-aged homemakers without a work history, to the costs of raising a child, and to the impact on children and displaced homemakers forced to move from their communities and support groups so that their homes can be sold. Judges have also failed to recognize the wife's contribution to her husband's career success.

Significant progress has been made in revising rape laws to remove the blame from the victim. Even so, women are still judged in court by their moral character, and by such "issues" as whether they use birth control pills, go alone to bars, keep late hours, or wear a bra. The effect of revised "consent" requirements has also been diluted by a male's perspective of both female seductiveness and her ability to use physical force to thwart an attack. This view does not incorporate the female socialization experience attitude that is oriented to verbal negotiation and avoidance of physical confrontation.

EEO laws designed to assure equal employment opportunities for women have been largely ignored by state and local court systems. Lack of judicial commitment to EEO is due often to cronyism that finds males in the power structure appointing and hiring those like themselves—other males. The result, for women aspiring to be judges and court administrators, is that they will be stuck at mid-level of the hierarchy or, if appointed to a high-level position, will find their influence diluted by the effects of tokenism.

Thus while substantial progress has been made in passing legislation intended to reduce the effects of gender bias on the treatment of women as victims, litigants, and employees, the implementation of that legislation often has not achieved its intent. What should have been socially significant and effective legislation has taken on the tone of the male perspective, a view that lacks an understanding of female reality. The result is that women are falling into the large gap that exists between the "appearance" of equality and the reality of their lives.

Why have the growing numbers of women lawyers, judges, and court managers not diluted the strength of the male perspective. To some extent, perhaps, they have, but not in proportion to their numbers, for several reasons.

Women in the highest, most influential, positions are often tokens and thus subject to being victims of a token psychology. Those in token positions, including women, tend to distance themselves from the needs of their historic associations in order to be accepted by the coveted elite. Wikler writes of her experience in training judges. While a lone woman judge would deny existence of gender bias in the court, as the number of women judges in the training session increased, the likelihood that they would openly offer examples of sexism grew. Hewlett, in her book *A Lesser Life*, found token female executives unwilling to pay the potential costs of being identified with a research panel addressing the economic and child care problems of women. One such executive told her, "It has taken me 15 years to get a hard-nosed reputation, and I just daren't risk it. If I were to get involved in these messy women's issues it could do a lot of harm to me in my company" (Hewlett, 1986: 370).

In particular, some female judges, especially at the local level, may also face a dilemma in bringing the perspective of their female experience to deciding cases involving women. Some may have been appointed to the bench in part because of their "objectivity," that is, their ability to set aside concern with the needs of women and assume the male worldview. Consequently, it is difficult for women in a field dominated by men not to go out of their way to avoid the appearance of weakness, emotional sensitivity, or lenience toward other women. By doing so, some women judges may, in fact, assume a less flexible view toward women in their court than do their male colleagues.

Women lawyers now exceed token numbers in the profession and, as a substantial percentage, could be expected to have an impact on the traditional role and treatment of women in the courts. Their energy to do so, however, may be displaced by the draining experience of dealing with demeaning and sexist attitudes and behavior of male judges and colleagues.

What about male judges who are currently in a position to influence implementation of important legislation affecting women, as well as the treatment of women in the court environment? A few have taken the lead in their state court system in calling for task forces to examine and confront gender bias in the courts. Others have responded openly to training sessions conducted by the NJEP. But at this time, these appear to be in the minority.

It can be argued that men have less to lose in acknowledging and addressing the needs and realities of women's lives. Unlike their female peers, they are not "outsiders" called on to prove their commitment to the status quo in order to be accepted by the majority group. They are the majority group. While many of them may not find it possible to set aside their identification with the needs and values of men, others may be sufficiently invested in the principles of equality that they are open to confronting issues addressed in this book. However, at this juncture, their dedication and strength are not a reliable reed.

Nevertheless, several reasons for optimism remain at the end of this litany of obstacles. First is the campaign begun by the National Judicial Education Program to Promote Equality for Women and Men in the Courts (NJEP). After a difficult beginning, NJEP has now gained both acceptance and momentum. Its techniques in addressing the issues of gender bias have been refined, and the message is being heard. It is critical that this educational effort continue because progress simply will not occur with the mere passing of generations.

A second source of optimism is the activism of the National Association of Women Judges and various state and local women's bar associations that are providing a climate for openly addressing the role and treatment of women in the court.

Finally, under the influence of both NJEP and the National Association of Women Judges, states have begun examining and documenting the nature and extent of gender bias in the courts. The first and most influential such effort was the New Jersey Supreme Court Task Force on Women in the Courts. Other states are following suit.

As a result of the research of these task forces as well as research discussed throughout the book, we have a better understanding than ever before of the extent of gender bias in the courts and its effects in the implementation of laws designed to provide equal rights and opportunities for women.

The next stage is to act on that information by targeting specific issues. This can be done both through individual efforts, such as confronting incidents of gender bias when they are seen, and by a collective coalescing of efforts of women in the legal and judicial system. Using their growing numbers and commensurate clout with policymakers as well as the media, this united approach can serve as a catalyst to focus attention on the concerns addressed in this book.

For example, at the instigation of the California Women Lawyers (CWL), the California Judges Association in 1986 adopted a black letter Canon making it "inappropriate for a judge to hold membership in any organization, excluding religious organizations, that practices invidious discrimination on the basis of race, sex, religion or national origin" (Canon 2C, CA Code of Judicial Conduct). This language is stronger than the comparable section of the ABA Code of Judicial Conduct on which it is based.

Soon after a policy was adopted by the California Franchise Tax Board disallowing business expense for individual memberships in clubs which do discriminate. Commenting on this issue, Pamela Jester, President of California Women Lawyers, said, "The CWL resolution will not necessarily end the discriminatory membership policies of various organizations but it will focus public attention to the impact of discriminatory clubs on those of us who are excluded" (*San Francisco Recorder*, 1986b). What this suggests is a narrowing of focus, of aiming at specific discriminations rather than shot gunning at a large, but unknown, expanse of possible or potential violations.

In this vein, the American Bar Association House of Delegates voted to establish a new primary goal for the association—the promotion of "full and equal participation in the profession by minorities and women" (*San Francisco Recorder*, 1986a). Certainly this is a specific approach to achieving a specific goal.

Almost ten years ago, most of the issues reviewed in this volume were discussed in an earlier book, *Women in the Courts* (Hepperle and Crites, 1978). At that time, we aspired to chart a course of guidelines for future actions toward female equality in the courts. On reflection, it is fair to conclude that the recommendations were viable, realistic, and practical. Yet many, if not most of them, were not achieved. What obstacles stood in the way then, what should we anticipate now?

First, perhaps, should be the open acknowledgment that legislation pushed through to benefit, or, more accurately, to equalize, the status of women has been thwarted by poor drafting, by actions of design and inadvertence, and by social resistance to the ultimate goals.

Consider the bulwark of women's rights, Title VII of the Civil Rights Act of 1964, the Equal Opportunity Act. In a retrospective analysis, two decades after its enactment, Law Professor Lee Modjeska said:

> The EEOC lacks direction, funds, organization, and power. Its influence is virtually minimal, its lawsuits narrow and few. Cast in the role of a private plaintiff, its mission is inherently undercut. The EEOC's problems are compounded by the ambivalence of the statutory scheme. With no adjudicatory authority or administrative sanctions in reserve, the EEOC is rendered rather impotent in the conciliation and settlement process. The EEOC's difficulties are undoubtedly also caused by individual and societal resistance to the fundamental changes inherent in the policies of Title VII. Again, however, the inadequacy of the enforcement mechanism limits the extent to which the EEOC can overcome this resistance, especially in the case of systemic discrimination [Modjeska, 1985: 809].

Thus women's reliance on EEO was misplaced. Modjeska explains that because the EEOC does not have rule-making authority, "little deference has been accorded by the courts to informal EEOC guidelines."

Second, we should remember that even "sweeping" legislation must be written in terms to encompass many situations. Its actual judicial implementation is the result of various individual cases each concerned with different aspects or issues of the law. How the judge who decides each point turns on his or her interpretation of the intent of the policymakers, the persuasion of the attorneys arguing the case, and personal inherent perceptions. Close critical points often flip-flop from the decision at the trial court level though the intermediate court of appeal to final decision by the state or U.S. Supreme Court. Given this system, it would seem obvious that there should be constant surveillance of critical court decisions at both the trial and appellate levels. Prompt analysis of the immediate and long-range implications of such decisions should then be incorporated into policy aims of special interest groups. Refutation, support or modification should be pursued, before the point is "engraved in stone."

Finally, concerned women should critically examine their strategies vis-à-vis their asserted policy goals. Identification of priorities, political timing, and astute use of resources are considerations that should not be left to chance. Lessons can be learned from other issue-oriented action efforts.

Mechanisms for change, such as women's, citizens, and issue-specific organizations are now in place. It remains for these and other supportive groups to mobilize, establish goals, and develop a plan of action. In short, it is time to rethink, regroup, and move forward.

REFERENCES

Hepperle, W. and L. Crites [ed.] (1978) Women in the Courts. Williamsburg, VA: National Center for State Courts.

Hewlett, Sylvia Ann (1986) A Lesser Life: The Myth of Women's Liberation in America. New York: William Morrow.

Modjeska, Lee (1985) "The Supreme Court and the ideal of equal employment opportunity." Mercer Law Review 36: 795.

San Francisco Recorder (1986) March 7.

San Francisco Recorder (1986) February 10.

ABOUT THE CONTRIBUTORS

MEDA CHESNEY-LIND, a criminologist, is a researcher with the Youth Development and Research Center at the University of Hawaii. She also teaches in the university's Women's Studies Program. She has published numerous articles on female juvenile offenders, beginning with the seminal work, "Judicial Enforcement of the Female Sex Role," *Issues in Criminology*. Other articles include "Juvenile Justice Legislation and Gender Discrimination" with Hancock in *Juvenile Delinquency in Australia;* "Women and Crime: A Review of the Literature on the Female Offender" in *Signs: Journal of Women in Culture and Society;* "Women Under Lock and Key: A View from the Inside" in *The Prison Journal.* She received her B.A. in sociology from Whitman College and her M.A. and Ph.D. in sociology from the University of Hawaii.

BEVERLY BLAIR COOK is Professor of Political Science at the University of Wisconsin-Milwaukee. Some of her court-related publications include *The Judicial Process in California;* "Judicial Roles and Redistricting in Kansas," *Kansas Law Review;* "The Socialization of New Federal Judges," *Washington University Law Quarterly;* "Sentencing Behavior of Federal Judges," *Cincinnati Law Review;* "Women Judges: The End of Tokenism," *Women in the Courts;* "Political Culture and Selection of Women Judges to Trial Courts" in *Women in Local Politics;* "Will Women Judges Make a Difference to Women's Legal Rights" in *Women, Power and Political Systems.* She received her B.A. from Wellesley College, her M.A. from the University of Wisconsin-Madison, and her Ph.D. from Claremont Graduate School.

LAURA L. CRITES is director of The Family Violence Program, a court-funded counseling program for victims and perpetrators of spouse abuse. She is also a lecturer in criminal justice with Chaminade University in Honolulu. For seven years, she was on the overseas faculty of the University of Maryland in Germany teaching courses in criminology and women's studies. She was founder and co-director of a spouse abuse program for the American military community in Kaiserslautern, West Germany, and has served as a private and group therapist for battered women. She has published several books and articles on women's issues, including *The Female Offender; Women and the Courts,* edited with Winifred Hepperle; and "A Judicial Guide to Understanding Spouse Abuse" (*The Judges Journal*). She has an M.S. in the administration of justice from American University and an M.A. in counseling psychology from Ball State University.

WINIFRED L. HEPPERLE is a consultant in court planning and administration. Previously, she was Director of the Office of Court Services, Alameda County, California. She has also served as Associate Director, National Center for State Courts, and Public Information Attorney for the California Supreme Court. Her publications include *Women in the Courts,* edited with Laura Crites; *The U.S. Legal System;* and "Women Victims in the Criminal Justice System" in *The Changing Roles of Women in the Criminal Justice System.* She holds a J.D. from Hastings College of Law, University of California, an M.P.A., Judicial Administration, University of Southern California, and a Certificate in International Legal Studies from McGeorge School of Law, University of the Pacific. She also has taught at the McGeorge School of Law, Salzburg Institute on International Studies (1978-1987).

ANNE RANKIN MAHONEY is Associate Professor of Sociology and Director of the Center for Studies of Law and Deviance in the Department of Sociology at the University of Denver. Her recent publications include "Jury Trials for Juveniles: Right or Ritual," *Justice Quarterly;* "Jury Selection Practices and the Ideal of Equal Justice" in *The Journal of Applied Behavioral Science;* "Female Delinquents in a Suburban Court," with Carol Fenster, in *Judge, Lawyer, Victim, Thief: Women in the Criminal Justice System;* and "The Effect of Prior Record Upon the Sentencing of Male-Female Codefendants" with Carol Fenster in *The Justice System Journal.* She has just completed a book on the political and economic context of juvenile justice. She received her M.A. from Northwestern University and her Ph.D. from Columbia University, where she was a Russell Sage Fellow in Law and Sociology.

DEBORAH RHODE is Professor of Law at Stanford Law School, and Director, Institute for Research on Women and Gender, at Stanford University. She has published numerous books and articles including the forthcoming *Feminist Theory and Legal Thought* (Harvard University Press); *The Legal Profession: Responsibility and Regulation* with Geoffrey Hazard; "Feminist Perspectives on Legal Ideology" in *What is Feminism 1986;* "Equal Rights in Retrospect," *Journal of Law and*

Inequality; "The ERA and the 19th Amendment" in *Encyclopedia of the American Constitution* (forthcoming). She received her B.A. and J.D. from Yale University and clerked for Chief Justice Thurgood Marshall.

LYNN HECHT SCHAFRAN is an attorney and Director of the National Judicial Education Program to Promote Equality for Women and Men in the Courts. She is a member of the New Jersey Supreme Court Task Force on Women in the Courts and advisor to similar task forces in New York, Rhode Island, and Arizona, Special Counsel to the New York City Commission on the Status of Women, and Chair of the Committee on Sex and Law of the Association of the Bar of the City of New York. She is the author of several articles relating to gender bias in the courts including "How Stereotypes About Women Influence Judges," *The Judges Journal,* and "Women as Litigators: Abilities vs. Assumptions," *Trial.* She received her B.A. from Smith College and her J.D. from Columbia University School of Law.

CASSIE C. SPENCER is a private therapist providing therapy to victims of sexual assault and incest and is an associate with Nicholson, Spencer and Associates, a training firm specializing in child and sexual abuse and neglect. She has provided training to attorneys, judges, police, social workers, and foster parents throughout the western region. She is co-author of "Incest Intake Assessment and Treatment Planning for Child Protective Services" in the forthcoming *Handbook on Sexual Assault of Children.* She has a M.S.W., L.S.W., and M.P.A. from the University of Denver.

LENORE J. WEITZMAN is an Associate Professor of Sociology at Harvard University. She is the author of three books and numerous law review articles. Her most recent book, *The Divorce Revolution: The Unexpected Social and Economic Consequences for Women and Children in America* (Free Press, 1985), won the 1986 Book Award given by the American Sociological Association. Her book has also been honored by symposia at the national meetings of the American Bar Association, the American Sociological Association, and in the American Bar Foundation *Research Journal.* She has served on the faculty of the National Judicial College and the National Council of Juvenile and Family Court Judges. She received her Ph.D. from Columbia University, and she was a visiting fellow at Oxford University, a member of the Institute for Advanced Study in Princeton and a Guggenheim Fellow.

NORMA J. WIKLER is Associate Professor of sociology at the University of California Santa Cruz. She was founding director of the National Judicial Education Program to Promote Equality for Women and Men in the Courts and currently serves as an advisor to the New Jersey and New York task forces on gender bias in the courts. She is also a senior advisor to the National Foundation for Women Judges. She is co-author of *Up Against the Clock: Career Women Speak On the Choice to Have Children,* and has written or co-authored numerous articles including "Economic Consequences of Child Support" with Carol Bruch in the *Juvenile and Family Court Journal,* and "On the Judicial Agenda for the 80's: Equal Treatment for Women and Men in the Courts," *Judicature.* She has an M.A. and Ph.D. in sociology from University of California, Berkeley.